Walk Through Your Shadows

Walk Through Your Shadows

a novel by
Oscar Valdes

Copyright © 2017 by Oscar Valdes

All rights reserved. No part of this publication may be reproduced, distributed or transmitted in any form or by any means, including photocopying, recording, digital scanning or other electronic or mechanical methods, without the prior written permission of the publisher, except in the case of brief quotations embodied in critical reviews and certain other noncommercial uses permitted by copyright law.

This book is a production of Editorial Madruga,
P.O. Box 78, Pasadena, CA 91102

You may visit the author online at oscarvaldes.net.

Library of Congress Control Number: 2017918791

Published 2017
Printed in the United States of America
Print ISBN: 978-0-9793558-5-1
E ISBN: 978-0-9793558-6-8

Cover and interior design by Ann Valdes

*For Teresa, Ray
and
my daughter*

1

*J*anice Blanco-Wilson left early Saturday morning, before dawn, for the drive up to the Los Angeles County State Prison in Lancaster, California. She drove west on the 10, hooked on to the 210 to skirt the bustle of LA, then onto the 14 which turned around and pointed her east, straight onto the Antelope valley beyond.

It would be the first time she visited her son since his transfer.

She climbed through the mountain pass – up over three thousand feet – past the jutting, slanting formations of the Vasquez Rocks around Agua Dulce canyon, before the terrain opened up with its gently sloping hills, winding country roads and picturesque ranch houses.

Moving at a steady clip in her late model car she thought of Joey, of her life, of the turns of fate that had her driving to that destination. It had been a trying time for the family. She opened the window and a whoosh of cool air caressed her face. She breathed in the freshness.

Joey, 23, her eldest, had been locked up for the past 3 years. She had started visiting him the moment he was arrested and taken to County jail in Los Angeles. But then, after his conviction, he had been transferred up north to start serving his sentence and the distance had made the visiting harder. Janice went anyway, and she did it because she thought he needed her.

Nearing the Crown Valley Road off ramp, by Acton, she thought of pulling over for a cup of coffee. Was there something else she needed to think about before she saw him? Maybe, but she did not want to delay her arrival.

An LA based radio station had been streaming in pop songs but just as she approached Palmdale, reception broke off and a talk show host with a British accent crept in speaking of the Old Testament. What had she done wrong? What had estranged her from her Joey?

She had already begun her descent into the valley when she found herself overtaking a large bus with darkly tinted windows. The lettering on the side read, *County of Los Angeles Sheriff's Department.* Was it in a bus like that that her Joey had been sent up north? Same bus? Same driver? The thought of him shackled to his seat made her gasp. Why had things gone so wrong?

A horn blared behind her. A hard charging pickup truck was stepping on her tail. She sped up.

A long forgotten memory slipped into focus. At age 14 or 15, as she stood in the back of a crowded church for Sunday Mass, a portly priest with a collection plate and a scattering of coins and bills appeared in front of her. Janice had only a couple of bucks left in her small purse, meant for a coffee and doughnut. The priest stared at her. Janice stared back. The priest tapped the bottom of the plate in stern prompt. Janice clutched her purse. The standoff... and the priest moved on. Now she smiled at the remembrance. Forty years. She had pluck all right, but sometimes it had not served her well.

At 7:57 am, Janice pulled into the driveway to the prison. The ride up had taken her 2 hours and ten. A few vehicles were already queued up before the gatehouse where a guard was checking for IDs. Driver's license in hand, Janice inched forward for her turn.

"Good morning," said the guard, "Visiting?"

"Yes. My son, Joey Wilson."

"Been here before?"

"No."

The guard checked the driver's license against his list, then handed it back. "Make sure you park in the Visitors Area."

Janice thanked him and drove on.

Several visitors, mostly women and children, were walking toward the administration building as she entered the parking lot. A light, early November chill had set in and they wore their winter wraps.

Inside the administration building, conversation ran lively while two toddlers chased after each other and a young mom bounced her bawling child on her knee. Janice took in the scene and thought of all she shared with the strangers in the room. A warm feeling of kinship rose in her.

She took a seat in the front row next to a young, plump woman of ample bosom. Janice eyed her discreetly. The woman wore a pearly white shiny outfit with a large bow on her head. She seemed overdressed, her lips lathered in red gloss. Janice was curious.

"Is this your first time?"

The woman turned and stared back, "First time what?" The tone was gruff.

"First time visiting?"

The woman's eyes softened. "My fiancé is here. I come to visit every week."

"Oh. You must live close by?"

"I live in San Diego."

What was that, a four-hour drive, one way, every week? Janice felt shamed by the show of devotion.

"We're getting married today," added the bride, smiling proudly.

"Congratulations," said Janice with a look of surprise.

"Thank you."

"Good morning to you," interrupted an officer as he strode up to the front of the room. "I'm sergeant Loomis and welcome to the CDCR." A corpulent man in a crisp green uniform, he wore on his sleeves the three golden chevrons that befitted his rank. A scattering of voices returned the greeting. "We're going to start calling your names. Please follow the officers so they can ask you a few questions and check your personal items before you go in to visit your party. It is standard prison procedure. You will be asked to go through a metal detector. We'll try to do this as quickly as possible so you can enjoy your visit and do so safely. Thank you for your cooperation."

A woman officer handed the sergeant a list. He called out the first name. "Brenda Denham."

"That's me!" cried out the lady next to Janice as she sprang to her feet, filled with joy.

"Good luck."

She probably didn't hear Janice in her excitement for she darted across to the counter and began to take off her shoes and put her belongings in a wooden box.

"Chavela Smith" called the sergeant again.

"Here!" replied the visitor.

Janice's turn wouldn't come up till nearly 30 minutes later. She passed through the checkpoint and filed out with the rest, turning right to amble up the road to the visiting area.

Two high chain link fences topped by coiled barbed wire ran alongside the road. There was a gap between them with the outer fence marked High Voltage. If you touched it you fried. After a stretch, the visitors made a left turn into a squat, dun colored building. A spacious room was filled with tables and chairs and a line of vending machines stood along the inner wall.

Some visitors were seated with the prisoner they had come to see. Janice found an empty table and sat down. Through a side door at the front, the guards were escorting in other inmates. She hadn't seen her son in over a month. She closed her eyes for a moment to ask in silence that all be well and her Joey be allowed to join her this day. A scheduled visit could be interrupted at any time, even at the last minute, no matter how far you had traveled. She had seen it happen. When she opened her eyes again she fixed her sight on the door through which Joey was to come in.

A moment later there he was. She stood up to wave at him and Joey spotted her. He was happy to see her and gave her a big smile. They embraced and she took his face in her hands. She was thrilled. "You look so handsome!"

"I'm glad to see you," he said, still holding her in his arms. She felt so small in his embrace. Broad shouldered and muscular, Joey stood 5 ft. 10. He was dressed in the standard issue: blue denim, brown ankle boots, a bright orange jacket and a black beanie for a hat.

"Sit, tell me all about it."

"How's everything?"

"We miss you so much."

"I miss you, too."

"You're eating well?"

"Everything they serve." He chuckled.

"You're young and strong. The food must be good." She rested her hand on his shoulder.

"I don't know about that. Is dad all right?"

"Yes. You know he did his best to get you down here."

"You told me that."

"I'll be able to keep visiting you often." And drawing in closer, so as not to be overheard, she whispered, "He has a friend here, too." She was anxious that he see the significance of it but Joey was unmoved. He was relying on his own wits to keep his head above water and was determined to continue to do so.

Janice caressed his hands. "Are you staying out of trouble?"

"Of course."

"Are you sure?"

"Really. I wouldn't lie to you."

Janice pulled herself up in her chair. "Isn't that something? You not having had a single incident in the three years you've been locked up, when people with the crime you were charged…"

"Mom… please."

She paused.

"Goes to show you did a good job with me," he continued, looking at her with a half smile. There was no need to worry her. Whatever happened inside those walls was his to mind, and the heaviness he felt every day the burden he had to carry.

Janice wanted to soothe him, to reassure him that all would be well. "What you had was a mishap. It could've happened to anyone."

He didn't want her to feel sad for him. When others felt sorry for him it drained his strength. And he needed every ounce of it to put up with prison life.

He felt Janice's eyes on him. "How are you, mom?"

"I'm fine… always thinking of you, you know that."

He nodded. "I feel it."

"Really?" She didn't believe him but she smiled anyway.

"How's dad?"

"The same. He loves you, it's just that he's so old fashioned."

"Didn't send me a note, did he?"

Joey searched her expression but Janice went mum. A wisp of regret shone in her eyes. His father's silence was always hurtful and there it was again.

"He could've at least scribbled something," said Joey.

"He's been so busy at work…" she began and caught herself in midsentence. She was making excuses for his father again. She lowered her eyes and bowed her head slightly.

"What about Margaret?" asked Joey.

"She's fine, thinking of going into law." She felt relieved that the conversation might be heading for safer ground but then she saw him looking off.

"What's the matter?"

His little sister Margaret heading for law school, building a life of her own. Why had their paths been so different? Would she even want to associate with him in the future, if he had a future? He, a felon, she, a lawyer? They were only two years apart but had never been especially close. Still he missed her. "Didn't send me a note, either, did she?"

"No, but she thinks about you, Joey, she really does."

Did she? She owed him nothing. But why should she? He was the brother who had not been there for her, the brother who was always getting in trouble. And maybe it was better that way, to break off all ties, to cut himself loose from all of them. Wouldn't that lighten the shame he felt?

He closed his eyes.

The walls around him, the guards with clubs and spray cans, the gunners on the towers holding rifles ready to shoot you, all of it made him feel expendable, worthless. But he was guilty and this was punishment, wasn't it? He had not seen it coming but long before the doors had been slammed on him he had been a prisoner of his muddled brain, as in a perverse labyrinth that falsely promised a way out.

And yet, the confinement had hardened his resolve. The struggle to stay alive had lit something in him. Merely a glimmer but it mattered. He had sensed it when, up in Salinas, the blades had torn into his flesh, when the fists had crushed him, when the blood had splattered all over and he had felt his life hanging by a gasp. Something in him snapped and demanded that he roar back, something deep in him screamed that the battle was worth it, that he was worth it, and no matter how flawed a human being he had been, he deserved to live… and he had made up his mind not to give up… father or no father, sister or no sister, mother or no… and he stopped.

He turned to Janice and there she was, smiling at him, like she had been reading his every thought. And he felt glad that she had come. His mom, his patient and loving mother, who still thought he was innocent. And he put his arm around her and drew her close and kissed her on the forehead. "I love you, mom."

She curled up to him feeling a sense of release and affirmation. Whatever her mistakes she would not be running off, like her husband had, but she would be showing up to face them instead.

She ran her fingers through his hair and saw his mood lighten.

"You know that when I go on parole," said Joey, "I'll have to wear that ghastly monitor and register for the rest of my life. When I go for a job my employer will do a check and he'll find out. No matter what I do, I won't be able to shake it." But there was a glint in his eyes and his words carried a sense of defiance. Ahead of him may lay a mountain to climb when he got out but he was up for the challenge.

Janice nodded. They had talked about this before. "You're not the only one. And you know I'll always be there."

He pressed her close to him, squeezing her hard. "I'm glad you came to see me." He caressed her head slowly, the look distant. "Just tell dad what I said before. He has nothing to worry about. No one will know I'm his son. And no matter what, I love him."

2

*U*pon his arrival from Salinas in late September, Joey was assigned to his present quarters in Bravo yard. He and four other inmates had walked in to building three, sacks in hand, at one in the afternoon. The officer on duty had asked if they had had lunch and then got them a lunch pack each. Joey was assigned to cell 128 and told that his cellmate would be one LB Legrand, who happened to be on kitchen duty at that moment.

Joey stepped into the cell and found a room that was tidy and warm, with a faint scent of incense in the air, "To keep the devil away," Legrand would later say. The impression was that the dweller had been there a very long time and yet, the top bunk, which would be Joey's, was clean and empty, except for the bedding and the rolled up mattress.

Joey glanced about. On a shelf, against the wall, several books stood side by side next to a small TV. He didn't recognize the authors. A reader, thought Joey. That was a good sign. Just above the shelf, taped to the wall, a few photos featured a white middle-aged couple smiling happily. Joey grimaced. He didn't want to go back to sharing a cell with a white or Hispanic man. He had his reasons and that had been the arrangement with staff during the latter part of his stay in Salinas, after his third incident on the yard. That the staff had slipped on this matter annoyed him but he would deal with it later when he could talk to the sergeant.

Joey had felt tired from the trip down and leaned on the frame of the bunk. What would his cellmate be like? The cell space was so small that you were always in each other's face. No hiding was possible. Forced intimacy. It grated the nerves and it was all bad if you ended up with the wrong person. He knew well.

From next door, a radio started to blast. Joey thought the volume had been deliberately turned up but no, he shouldn't think that way, he shouldn't be jumping to conclusions, he had just got in. He took a deep breath. Seconds later, from the same side, a toilet flushed: two, three, four, five times in a row. Here we go again, thought Joey, closing his eyes in exasperation. But he was too fatigued from the trip to bother. He made his bed, unpacked his sack, took off his boots, climbed up on his bunk and fell asleep.

It was nearly 7 pm when Legrand came back to the unit. At the first sound of the cell door cranking open Joey sat up in his bunk and, to his surprise and relief, saw that Legrand was black.

"Good evening," said he, an imposing figure with a cleanly shaved head. Joey swung his legs to the side and dropped to the floor. All muscle, long armed and 7 inches taller than Joey, he extended his open hand, "Name is Legrand, but you can call me LB."

"Nice to meet you," said Joey as they shook hands, "Name is Wilson, but you can call me Joey. Just in from Salinas."

"Welcome home. Make yourself comfortable." There was a kind tone to Legrand's deep voice that had the effect of putting people at ease, but to Joey's ever vigilant mind a stranger was a stranger and trust came very, very slowly.

"Thank you," answered Joey courteously.

"How long were you there?"

"One year."

"How was it?"

Joey averted Legrand's probing gaze. "All right."

"I was there in '97," said Legrand. "A riot broke out and they sent me up north for a while. Never made it back."

Riots were a frequent reason why inmates got shuffled from one prison to another and Joey had been in a couple already.

"You're welcome to watch TV when I'm not here," offered Legrand.

"Thank you."

"My rule is live and let live, so you won't get any trouble from me, I don't care what you've done. You've been around, so you know what's it like to live in a tight space. I do snore, though… loudly, too, but there's nothing I can do about that. If it keeps you up you can ask for a cell change. They usually grant it. That's how come I've been single cell for a while."

"I think I'll be all right with that," replied Joey.

"You're welcome to read my books, too. You'll know which one I'm reading because I put a marker in it. Just don't dog-ear the pages."

"Okay. Thanks."

"You're welcome. You look like you might be Hispanic…"

"Half and half."

"You run with Hispanics or whites?"

"I don't run with anybody."

"Independent, that's cool. So you're all right celling with a black man?"

"I'm all right with that."

"Okay, then, let's make it work."

Legrand extended his hand again and they shook once more. Then he turned his back on Joey and crossed to the sink so he could wash his face.

Bravo yard housed inmates of what was called general population. There were four buildings to each yard, each following a 270 degrees configuration, two tiers of concentric cells facing a spacious day room below and a control room or tower above it, from where the opening and closing of all cell doors was operated. Below the control room ran a short passage way connecting the day room to the yard itself. It wasn't round but someone had called it the rotunda and the name had stuck, maybe because sounds reverberated in it. On either side of the rotunda, also opening onto the yard, an auxiliary entrance stood with its heavy, teal colored, steel door. Altogether, there were 100 cells per building, designed for housing two inmates each although some men, for a variety of reasons, had a cell to themselves.

The cell itself was a narrow space, 11 feet deep, five feet wide, with two stacked steel bunks down its length, a toilet and a washbasin by the door. At the opposite end of the cell door stood a short steel plank jutting out from the wall, serving as a desk, and above it a narrow, vertical slit of a window covered with thick, transparent, sturdy plastic. Facing the bunks, a three-foot-long shelf ran alongside the wall.

Lying down on his bed, Joey reviewed in his mind the protocol for harmonious cell living. Don't be nosey, stay out of each other's hair, don't linger on the potty, clean up after yourself, make sure you shower every time your turn came up, offer to share what you got from canteen, talk about neutral subjects, respect each other's differences and always be polite. In other words, all the things that if you had practiced before, you would not have landed in prison. And then there were his own rules: if he found a weapon in the cell or any kind of drugs, he was out of there. He had a date to get out of prison and he wasn't going to let any dimwit drag him down the sewer, no matter how big or intimidating he might be. He had been incarcerated three years plus, two in county fighting his case and one in Salinas, and he had had his share of characters to contend with. The Legrand fellow seemed all right but only time would tell. As far as the snoring was concerned, if you were a decent type, he would adjust. He wasn't going to take it personal.

At 8 pm nurse Turner began her rounds to dispense meds. Tall and stout, with a no-nonsense attitude, she addressed everyone as mister, no matter how long she had known him, and so seldom did she crack a smile that the inmates took bets on when she would do so next. They would try jokes and make bets, hoping for that smile, but she would not give it up.

Tonight it was officer Rivers' turn to escort her as she went door to door, carrying the plastic basket with the small envelopes that stored the inmates' medications.

Seeing her advance in his direction, Legrand filled his cup with water and stood by the door.

"Mr C., here's your meds," said Ms Turner as she came up to the window of cell 127. Paytrell C. lay under the covers, his head not visible.

"Paytrell!" cried out officer Rivers as she rapped on his door. "You want your meds?"
Paytrell stuck out a hand and waved no. Ms Turner looked at Rivers, "That's the fourth time in a row he refuses."

They moved on to 128. "Good evening Ms Turner," said Legrand in a merry tone.

"Good evening, Mr Legrand." Rivers unlocked the port hole on the cell door, pulled down the rectangular steel cover, Legrand put out his hand and Ms Turner tapped out the tablets from the envelope.

"Thank you." Legrand took the pills and swallowed them with a sip of water.

"Your roommate has medications also," Ms Turner announced.

Legrand turned around toward Joey who was lying on his bunk. Joey raised himself on his elbow, "I don't want it," and lay back down.

The officer locked up the porthole and Ms Turner moved on to the next cell.

Legrand sat down on his bunk and picked up the book he had been reading.

From a cell in the vicinity, on the upper tier, an inmate called out to a fellow prisoner, "Ey, Bazooka, how do you spell Hyena?" And Bazooka spelled it out for him: "H as in helpless. Y as in yo-yo. E as in enema. N as in nasty. A as in avoid."

"You love that man, don't you?" said the inmate.

"Sure do," returned Bazooka.

A moment later, from cell 107 in section A, another inmate began to sing Lift Every Voice and Sing, a rendering he delivered every so often in the evening, and for which the entire unit stopped to listen. "Lift every voice and sing, till earth and heaven ring, ring with the harmonies of liberty…" He sang all the way through, "… shadowed beneath thy hand, may we forever stand, true to our God, true to our native land." Silence followed.

"That was nice," said Joey.

"We have some talented people around here."

"What's his name?" asked Joey.

"Butterfly."

"Butterfly? Does he flit?"

"In his mind, but he weighs 400 pounds."

"I don't think I've seen him."

"He doesn't come out of his cell. Good man." Legrand paused briefly, then asked, "If it's not being too nosey, why are they giving you meds?"

Legrand was being too nosey and knew it, but Joey was in an agreeable mood.

"I was depressed when I first came in. I'm all right, now."

Legrand returned to his book.

"How 'bout you, you on anything?" asked Joey.

"A mood stabilizer."

"Has it helped?"

"I wish I'd had it when I was out there."

From cell 221 in the upper tier, a loud, angry and raspy voice rang out, "I'm a Vietnam vet, you hear me? I know how to defend myself. I know what you want. You're just in for the financial support. I'm no fool." There seemed to be no one specific he was addressing but his tone was so vehement that it was clearly intended for someone he was quarreling with, whether real or imagined. He ranted on for a few minutes, intermittently banging or kicking his cell door, before he tired out. Then, the calmer sounds of other inmates' voices began to rise: lively chats between neighbors, music from radios and CD players, patter from TV sets. The 'hood was coming alive.

3

Most mornings Joey had the cell to himself since Legrand was frequently on Kitchen duty. Still, he got up right after Legrand left and went through his exercise routine. Thirty minutes every day, sometimes twice a day.

A light drizzle had been falling all night and Joey stood by the window looking out into the fields beyond. In the distance, up on the sides of the hills, he could see family homes. He thought about his own family, the things that could have been done differently, and it always came to him that so much could have been avoided if everybody had paused a moment to reflect on what they were doing. If everybody had been willing to think a little.

He raised his hand and held it up against the window covering. The sturdy plastic was aging and soon the view through would be blurred. He had to be careful he reminded himself daily. The environment he lived in was like quicksand, it swallowed you easily if you didn't pay attention. But what would he be doing if he were out there that very moment? He let his thoughts wander as he gazed out. He would be going to work, or maybe school, stopping at a coffee shop to have a pastry and a cup of joe, flirting with a gal. The simple things. How he had taken them from granted and how they mattered so much to him now. Three years and still another five to go, unless something happened and he caught another case, which was not uncommon at all. Life passing him by -escaping him - and the perennial question, would he have the intelligence to learn enough to turn things around?

"Wilson, get ready to see the doctor... 128, get ready to see the doctor." The call had boomed out the PA system as the cell door cracked open simultaneously. Joey waved back at the officer in the tower. He grabbed his orange jacket and stepped out into the day room. Just as he did he saw two small birds daintily skipping about near the steel tables. He smiled. The rotunda was open and the birds had flown in.

Officer Bealey, a tall man in his late forties stood at the podium, a counter with a phone planted in the center of the day room. He was looking at a list as Joey began to approach him, ID in hand. Just then, a voice thundered out, imperiously, from the upper tier, "Joey Wilson!". Joey stopped on his tracks. He looked up trying to locate the source but all he could see was a lone, backlit figure standing by the door of cell 240.

"That's me, what's up?" replied Joey, almost lightheartedly, thinking for an instant that someone friendly had landed in there. But when the voice came back again it was burning and accusing, "You're the child molester from Salinas."

A chill went through Joey. Stunned, he could not muster the words for a reply. He felt exposed, ripped of identity. He wasn't a man, not even a flawed one at that, but a child molester. And the memories of the assaults he had survived - the two knifings - all rushed in. Joey's jaw tightened, his teeth clenched, his hands balled up into mighty fists and drawing himself up boomed back, "Fuck you!"

"That won't help you, sucker. This is Leroy. If you say you're not a 'chester' you'd better have some papers."

A chorus of voices erupted instantly, ringing out in vigorous unison, "Papers! Papers! Was is it a caper? Are you a faker? Are you a taker? You'll meet your maker!" A loud drumming of cell doors began.

Officer Bealey, with grim expression but speaking calmly, almost soothingly, checked Joey's ID. "You know where to go?"

"No."

"Walk across the yard: an officer will be waiting for you at the gate to take you to the doctor." He gave back the ID and nodded for him to go on. As Joey crossed to the rotunda to exit the building, the roar of the banging cell doors seemed only to get louder.

In the mental health building Joey was put in a holding tank where he was to remain until it was his turn to be seen. There were four other inmates with him, all black. He glanced at their faces but didn't recognize any of them. But news traveled fast. There was no getting away from it. And now that everyone would know he had to be extra careful. He glanced at them again. Two were younger than him, one about his age and the other possibly in his forties. He never had had a problem with a black inmate but you never knew. Better to be ready. He had hoped that the transfer to Lancaster would give him some relief from all the fighting that he had been involved in but now it was clear that it was too much to expect.

Having been convicted of child molestation singled him out as a target. Never mind the details. Once you got the 'R' jacket you were stuck with it. Forever. He was lucky that he was strong and could fight but he also knew that, sooner or later, he would find his match. Would it be this guy Leroy that had called him out?

Joey stared down at his new pair of brown boots. He sat leaning forward, deep in thought, his hands gripping the edge of the bench. This was part of prison life, he reminded himself, and it was unlikely to change. He had to deal with it. But now that he could think about it, he didn't like that he had got so angry when the Leroy fellow had exposed him. Joey knew better than to react as he did, but he had let the man push his buttons.

The keys clanged at the tank door. The officer in charge was a chubby Latino man with beady eyes, a day-old stubble and a narrow forehead.

"Wilson?"

Joey stood up. The officer opened the door and signaled for him to walk down the hallway.

"Office 15, Dr Jeffries, on your right."

"What's this about?" asked Joey.

"Psych. Keep your hands behind your back."

Joey started to stroll down the hallway. Brightly lit with fluorescent lights, his sneakers squeaked against the shiny linoleum floor. Toward the end an inmate porter quietly swung his mop right to left and back as he wiped the floor. As Joey approached office 15 the two men exchanged glances. Then Joey turned into the doctor's office.

A slender woman sat at a desk as she navigated on the computer. She glanced up at him and with a wave of her hand asked him to sit across.

"Doctor Jeffries," she said, now looking him in the eye and taking the measure of him. She was wearing a brown suede jacket with a purple scarf round her neck and her blonde hair fell gently to her shoulders. She folded her hands on a notebook she had in front.

"How are you today?"

"I'm fine. What's this all about?"

"I am a psychologist. I will be your clinician."

Joey felt a twinge of irritation that he tried to conceal. He lowered his eyes. "I didn't ask to see anybody."

"You have a history of depression and we wanted to monitor."

Joey gave a slow, reluctant nod, then meeting her gaze replied, "Everybody gets depressed when they get sentenced. Everybody does. I've worked through it." He leaned back in his chair. He was ready to leave.

Dr Jeffries thumbed through her notes for a few seconds. "You were depressed enough that you needed medication."

"I'm not taking any now. I took them only for a short while. Actually, I could've done it on my own."

A few strands of her hair had fallen forward on her face. She brushed them back with her left hand. "You had to be hospitalized."

"I'll admit I was a little confused… but that was back then. Look, I don't really need your services. I'm sure there are plenty of people around here that can use your help. I'd like to go now."

Dr Jeffries lay her hands flat on the desk and pulled herself up slightly on her seat. Joey noticed she was not wearing any nail polish.

"As you wish," she said with a frown, which made Joey think he might've been unnecessarily rude.

"May I ask you why you got into this work?"

"Sure," she said, giving a gentle turn to her lips, "I like to help people wrestle free from their demons."

"How do you know I have any?"

"You wouldn't be here, would you?"

"There are innocent people here, too."

"Yes, there are. Are you innocent?"

"It depends on how you look at it."

A wry smile crossed her face. "I can see we have work to do."

Annoyed, he said bluntly, "Have you wrestled with your own?"

"I have."

"And?"

"It takes a lifetime."

He held her eyes for a moment. "I'll let you know if I need your help." And he left the room.

When Joey got back to the cell Legrand was already there. The kitchen supervisor had given him the rest of the day off and he was stretched out in his bunk reading a book. They greeted each other and Joey took off his boots and climbed up on his bed. Paytrell C in cell 127, next door, was now flushing his toilet non-stop. Joey wanted to think over what had transpired in Dr Jeffries' office but the sound of the flushing kept intruding.

"What's he doing?" asked Joey in irritation.

"He's mentally ill. Did you notice he's been putting rags under his door? He's trying to block something out."

Joey slammed his fist on the wall and shouted, "Hey, stop it!" Then to Legrand, "If he keeps flushing he's gonna break it and it'll flood his cell and ours."

The disturbing sound eased for a moment but then started up again.

Joey slammed his fist harder. "Stop it!"

"Let me handle this, I know this guy," said Legrand putting down his book and getting up. "I've had to live with him." He crossed to the door, stood there for a moment and listened to the flushing. Then he climbed up on the sink so he could speak into the vent system between the cells. He could be heard better that way. "Paytrell, what's happening brother?"

Ten, twenty seconds went by.

"Paytrell?" called out Legrand again.

A coarse, wounded voice came back, "They won't leave me alone. I haven't been able to sleep… they were outside my window all night."

Paytrell flushed again.

"What was out there all night?"

"Wild dogs coming to get me. Barking, growling."

"Odd," said Legrand.

"What?"

"I'm right next to you and I didn't hear them. And you know I'm a light sleeper."

"They were right there, man," protested Paytrell, now climbing up onto his sink so he could hear Legrand better.

"You see them?"

"No. It's a trick they play. When I go to the door they vanish."

Legrand mulled it over for a moment. "Bro... a long time ago, something just like that happened to me."

Paytrell was curious. "Dogs, too?"

"Yep. Took a while but it got better."

"How?"

"I had this doc who told me my thoughts were jumbled up and I was giving away my power."

"What?"

Joey sat up in his bunk, ears perked.

"It's something the mind does to protect us," continued Legrand, "too much anger and the mind flips, because you can't hold it anymore... and if you hold on to it, well, it might kill you. So you put the anger in other people... or animals, anything. Your mind does it for you. That gets you relief for a little while, but the catch is you give away your power."

"I'm not giving away nothing," said Paytrell. "LB...?"

"Yeah?"

"You shitting me?"

"When have I ever done that to you?"

"Man, this is really scary."

"I understand."

"So what did you do?" asked Paytrell.

"You're not going to like what I'm going to say."

"Tell me, I want to hear it."

"You sure?"

"Please, I want to know."

"Okay, here it is... I took my medicine."

"Fuck you!"

"See, I told you you weren't going to like it."

"I can't take this shit. It feels like they're running my life!"

"Bro, I can only tell you my story. You may be different, but that's what happened to me, and I was going through the same stuff."

Paytrell was desperate for relief. He stood down from the sink and paced the floor. He looked at the toilet and thought of flushing again, not because the sounds of the wild dogs were hounding him just then but simply because the action itself seemed to ease his tension. He knew the medications helped and he had taken them many times, but after a while they slowed down his thinking and he would get angry and throw them away. And that was exactly what got him into a jam this last time, four years ago. After a week or so without the meds, he caught an assault with battery. He had been out only six weeks.

Paytrell leapt up back onto the sink and leaned into the vent again, "You there?"

"I've been here."

"You're saying I'm paranoid?"

"Yep."

Paytrell shook his head. He wanted to believe his friend but… "You sure you didn't hear them last night? They were very loud."

"Not a word. Slept like a baby," said Legrand.

"I've been trying the weed… it helps."

"No kidding? Brother, keep that up and there's going to be more wild dogs barking at your door."

Paytrell loved his weed. Still, "Man… last case I caught I was just walking around, bummed out, thinking the whole world had it in for me, when I saw this guy in a park. He didn't do nothing to me. I just didn't like him. He was sitting there laughing and looking at me. I was sure he was making fun of me… but maybe he wasn't…"

"He was just as troubled as you were," said Legrand.

"You think I was giving him my power?"

"Sounds like it. Why give it away when we don't have much to begin with?"

Paytrell grunted. "Passing it on to the wild dogs… but what am I supposed to use to feel good?"

"The natural thing, my man… love, work, friendship."

"Not a lot of loving in this hell hole, is there?"

"Brotherly love, man, it's in us."

And Paytrell smiled to himself. "I haven't told you, but I've got myself a fine lady waiting for me. She has a car and everything. She writes, tells me to hurry back. She used to be homeless, too, but she got her act together."

"Good for her."

"Not giving her power away, that's for sure. That's what these gang members around here want you to do, give your power to them."

"You're thinking, Paytrell. Do any drugs or don't take your meds and you're giving up your freedom."

"I like that... don't give up your freedom... I'm going to remember it. Don't escape your freedom."

"That's a keeper, brother. Don't escape your freedom."

Paytrell laughed.

"Good to hear you laugh," said Legrand.

"Yeah. Can't remember last time I did."

"Brother, if I had been able to laugh at my problems, I wouldn't have come to prison," remarked Legrand.

There was something to that, thought Paytrell, but he could not think just then of how the hell the laughing was going to keep the damn wild dogs away come night. But he trusted Legrand enough and right then and there made the decision to give the medications another try. He was short to the house – maybe eight more months if he stayed out of trouble. "Will you keep talking to me, LB?"

"What are neighbors for?"

"Thanks, man."

Legrand stepped down from the sink and returned to his bunk. "The docs patch him up and he does well for a while, but then the family doesn't write or he does drugs and he's back again tripping," he said to Joey.

Joey thought that Legrand had made up at least half of what he'd told Paytrell but if it worked, so be it. Anyway, he had liked the way his cellmate had extended himself for his fellow prisoner. "That's pretty cool what you did."

"Thank you."

Joey lay back on his bunk for a moment and thought of how important the visits with his mother had been. "Do you get visits, LB?"

Legrand looked off for a moment, a melancholy veil descending on his face. "Now and then," he replied, but he was lying. His mother, Simone, had come to see him every month for the two and a half years she had lived after he came to prison. But after that there had been no more visits. Not even from his girl, the one he had got pregnant just before he had committed his crime. She had left town right after his incarceration and did not leave an address behind. She had moved to Cleveland, Ohio, his mother Simone had told him, because she had relatives up there and wanted to enroll in college and start a new life.

4

*E*arly next morning, with the slanting rays of the sun brightening up the day, the air still nippy, birds chirping and pigeons cooing, the inmates from Bravo Three filed out slowly into the yard. Having stripped down for a double line of officers inside the building who had checked them for weapons or drugs, they exited in their shorts and tee shirts, hurriedly dressing up again as they did, and stepping onto the cool, dewy grass in the center of the yard. It was their time to stretch the body and mind, to lollygag, walk the perimeter with a friend, catch up with an old buddy, enjoy the freedom to roam that their cramped cells forbid.

From the sidelines, a cluster of officers kept a watchful eye on their movements while a gunner up in the yard tower, rifle at the ready, scanned the scene. Some inmates came out to settle a score.

Poncho Sterling stood just outside block three, right by the wall near the auxiliary entrance, along with a group of fellow guards. He was tall and slender with a slight stoop, which he tried always to rectify, frequently pulling back his shoulders or impulsively dropping to the ground to do fifteen or twenty pushups. There was an easy manner about him, though, and it went down well with the inmates. If a difficult situation arose he could assert his authority, and he would do so by talking and persuading, often taking some ribbing from his fellow guards who told him that he should go over to the mental health camp instead, which he laughed off while replying, "You should be paying attention to what I do, I'm the guard of the future. I'm an educator. That's what these guys need." He could back up his talk, too. In eight years as a guard he had never had to scuffle with an inmate.

"What's the trick, Pancho?" asked Officer Tanpuro, a note of mocking in his words. Tanpuro was an old hand in the prison system but new to Lancaster where he'd transferred from Folsom State Prison. "I hear you've never slammed down one of these shitheads?"

"That's because I never call them shitheads," said Poncho coolly, averting Tanpuro's gaze. "And it's not Pancho, it's Poncho."

Tanpuro glanced at the other officers expecting they would fall in with him but they did not. Leaning against the wall of the building, one foot up on bended knee, he tugged at the neckline of his green crew neck sweater. He had put on one layer too many.

From the moment he had arrived in Lancaster, two weeks prior, Tanpuro had been assigned to Brave Three, but he was having trouble blending in. He was part of the old guard and proud of it, the old guard where a guard was a cop, first and foremost. What the hell was that bull about being an educator, anyway? Didn't they have a department for that? He glanced again at the officers next to him: they were all very young. Was this the future? He dismissed the thought. But he knew that prison was changing and you had to be blind not to see it. Still, you couldn't throw the old out the window just like that. Inmates were there to be punished not coddled. Give them a good kick in the pants so they could snap out of it. That's what society was paying men like him to do and by god he was going to give those suckers what they had coming.

And there were some people in mental health who shared his belief.

A game of soccer had started up on the far side of the field with a group of Hispanic men. On the near side, some blacks and a lone Chinese were setting up for a game of touch football.

"That shithead, Wilson, he's a child molester, you know that, right?" said Tanpuro. "Soon as I heard about it, I called a friend of mine up in Salinas. Sure enough, a troublemaker, always getting into fights. Asking for it. That's why he got transferred."

"He hasn't given us any bad action," replied Coronado, the senior officer on the shift.
"A man is entitled to a new beginning."

"Mark my words," continued Tanpuro, "he's trouble."

Out on the field, Legrand and Joey were strolling along the periphery engaged in animated conversation. They were out near the far end where the soccer game was being played. It was a noisy affair - sweaty and gutsy - young men jostling and bumping in their struggle to gain control of the ball. One fellow got hold of it in midfield and quickly began a furious charge toward the goal line. To the rousing calls of the spectators he drove on, passing to one and then back, dashingly elegant in his moves. Two defenders surged forward to block him but he swiftly evaded them, pushed on and drove, drove, drove till he kicked it hard toward the net, a cannon of a shot, just inside the goal post and barely out of reach of the lunging goalie. "Goaaaaaal!!" rang out the loud cry.

Joey and Legrand turned round to see what the fuss was about. That's when they noticed the two men, Leroy and his sidekick, Hyena, striding in their direction.

Legrand gazed at them. They weren't changing course, which might mean trouble. He turned to Joey, "Got a problem with any of these guys coming our way?"

Joey didn't recognize the men. "Not sure."

"The one in front is Leroy, guy who called you out in the day room the other day," observed Legrand.

"How'd you know?" asked Joey.

"Just do."

So now Legrand knew he was a child molester, thought Joey.

As the approaching men drew closer, Leroy signaled to Hyena to hang back and let him come forward by himself. All the while staring at Joey, Leroy walked right up to him before stopping. A strapping Hispanic man, 28, with a thick neck, large hands and a beanie pulled down to his eyebrows, Leroy demanded impertinently, "Joey Wilson?"

"That's me," said Joey, stepping up boldly to meet the challenge.

"I'm Leroy. Need to see your papers."

At the other end of the field, Poncho Sterling's alert eye had spotted the brewing confrontation and was walking briskly toward them. But he had a way to go.

Joey was shorter than Leroy by a couple of inches but gave up nothing in strength.

The men locked eyes and dropped their arms.

Poncho Sterling was now jogging to the scene and other officers were right behind.

"You hear what I said?" pressed Leroy.

"What business is it to you?"

And Leroy swung at Joey. It was a quick right hand that tagged Joey just above the left eye. Joey took the lick and fired off a bruising right hook that caught Leroy smack on the left cheek and took him off his feet. Hyena sprang forward to assist his comrade. Legrand blocked his path and Hyena stalled. And it was over.

The alarm went off and the piercing sound signaled to all inmates on the field to drop to the ground.

Leroy lay flat on his back, still in a daze, blood oozing out of a small cut on his left cheek, when Poncho Sterling arrived. Joey had stepped away.

"Disagreement between gentlemen, no doubt," said Poncho. No one replied. "Okay, hands in back," he commanded. The rest of the officers were now arriving on the scene, Tanpuro trailing a distance behind, huffing and puffing.

"Have to find another way of settling our differences, don't we?" said Poncho, as he leaned over and extended a helping hand to Leroy who was beginning to come to. "C'mon, man, it's over." But Leroy ignored him and pulled himself up on his own.

Two of the officers handcuffed the feuding men and instructed them to head back, across the field, to the Program Office.

"Let's get Leroy over to Medical," said officer Coronado, "He'll need some stitching."   He radioed a message in and the alarm was turned off. The remainder of the men in the yard stayed on the ground and watched the cuffed men file past.

Usually, in the evening, Bravo Three had day room after chow but today, because of the fight in the yard, the inmates were kept in their cells. And so the food carts trundled in from the kitchen and the officers served it up in plastic trays and took it up to the cell doors. Everyone ate without incident and, after a while, the usual after dinner hubbub followed. The warring parties had been brought back from the Program Office – having signed a marriage chrono - code for agreeing not to quarrel again - and were now in their respective cells.

The swelling over Joey's eye had spread and almost closed it. Nurse Turner had given him a cold pack to put over but he was having trouble with it.

"This thing keeps sliding off," he said to Legrand, impatiently, "How am I going to hold it in place when I fall asleep? It's not like I don't need it, I can barely see out of my eye." He was feeling flustered as he lay on his bunk.

"Sleep on it," replied Legrand, "It'll be better tomorrow."

Joey turned on his side.

"Ms Turner said the eye itself was okay."

"Good."

"Who's this Leroy guy anyway?" asked Joey.

"Knucklehead. Likes to bully if he can get away with it."

"Prison brings out the bully in you, doesn't it?" said Joey.

"In some."

Next door, Paytrell flushed the toilet twice in quick succession. Joey and Legrand both held their breaths. But the flushing did not repeat.

"Leroy's part black, right?" said Joey.

"Yes. His first name may come from the French, 'le roi', the king, but his last name is Cadenas, which in Spanish means chains."

"King in chains. Go figure," said Joey.

"He likes to scrap, but you did well. I was surprised." The sight of Joey's performance and the landing of his strong right hand had reminded Legrand of a fight he had had, some twenty years back, with a man with Joey's same last name. "Done a lot of fighting?"

"A couple of times in grade school. It's all happened here in prison. It started down in County, then got worse when I got to Salinas. Didn't know how to fight when I was first arrested. Had to learn fast."

"You have the instincts." The memory of his long ago fight kept returning to Legrand. "Got rough up there for you, in Salinas?"

"Got stabbed twice. In the neck and my side. My counselor recommended I come down, try a change of scenery."

There was no need to explain anything, thought Joey. Since Legrand now knew he was a child molester he could fill in the blanks himself. Things happened to child molesters in prison.

Just then officer Rivers strolled up to the cell door. Standing to the side, to not peer directly through the window, she rapped on the door. "LB?" Legrand recognized the voice and got to his feet.

"What's up Rivers, how are you?"

"Doing well, thanks. Say, Neuman out of cell 149 is paroling tomorrow. He's single cell. You want to move there for a while? It wouldn't be permanent."

The offer came as a surprise and Legrand hesitated for a moment. Neuman, the former bond trader turned drug addict who had been fired and then made a terrorist threat against his employer, was finally getting out. They had played chess on occasion. "You think Neuman will make it as a rabbi?"

"He's been studying for it," replied Rivers with a smile, "we can only wish him the best."

It flashed through Legrand's mind that sharing a cell with Joey had already led to combat and that more was on the way and yet, something about Joey seemed worth the effort. Then there was the fact that he liked his present cell, so why move. He could be wrong but he decided to go with his gut feeling. "No," he said finally to Rivers. "I'm good. Thank you, though."

"You're welcome."

Legrand turned to the sink and poured some water on his face. He reached for his towel and began to dry off.

"Why didn't you take her up?" asked Joey.

"I'm not sure. I like peace and quiet, though."

"You don't know anything about me."

"Leroy called you a child molester the other day but I haven't heard it from you," said Legrand, beginning to fold his towel carefully.

"I was getting around to it…"

Joey and Legrand had now been roommates for over a week and neither had spoken of what crime he had committed

"They found me guilty of child molestation," said Joey. "Got 10 years for it but only have to do 8 and change. First term. I've got 5 left." His tone was flat. "It's ruined my life."

Had Legrand heard a note of regret or self-contempt in Joey's words? He wasn't sure. "What're you doing about it?"

"What do you mean?" asked Joey, rearranging the cold pack on his swollen eye.

"You have to work on that stuff. It doesn't go away on its own."

"I'll be all right."

Legrand shook his head slowly. He thought of his own offense, the impulsiveness that had stunted his existence, the struggle with his own denial during the first years of his incarceration. He stared out into the empty day room and flicked off the overhead light.

"Thanks," said Joey. "I'll talk to you about it some time." Then, removing the cold pack from his face, said, "LB...?"

Legrand turned to look at Joey. With the light off he could barely discern his features.

"... You look like a mature guy but... do I have to worry about you?"

"I'm cool."

"I appreciate that," said Joey, as he sighed quietly in relief: one less hurdle to overcome.

Legrand remained at the door for a while. When he turned back he saw that Joey had drifted off to sleep and that the cold pack was slipping off and about to fall. He reached over and caught it in time. Legrand held the pack for a moment as he looked at Joey, waiting for him to change positions so he could replace it safely over his eye, but Joey did not stir, so he put it on the shelf. He would check later to see if he could reapply it. He then sat on his bunk and pulled out the book he had under his pillow. It was a book of short stories by Alice Munro. He was fond of reading fiction by women authors, mainly because he still held out hope that one day he would find his daughter, the daughter he had never met, whose name he didn't even know, and reading women authors made him feel close to her, wherever she was.

Sounds of snoring broke his reverie. It was Joey. "Goodness, it's contagious." He waited a few moments, then turned on the light again and began to read a new chapter.

5

Just before 10 pm officers Rivers and Morelos entered the unit. They were the crew for First Watch, the graveyard shift.

From 128, Legrand observed the unit carefully. He did it every night. He would not go to sleep until he knew who would be manning the controls. Strange things happened in the night.

Rivers and Morelos gathered at the foot of the tower as the outgoing officer above lowered their equipment - alarms, pepper spray canisters, flashlights - using a string tied to a makeshift bucket.

The incoming officer was late.

A few minutes went by.

Now a tall lanky man wearing a baseball cap emerged in the tower. He had come up through a separate entrance off the rotunda below. Legrand could only see his outline but that was enough for him. It was Eddie Grisholt. He had been off for a couple of weeks and now was back. A young man, 31, he had been at that post going on three years. He had transferred down from Corcoran four years before and the word was that he had done so under a cloud.

Officer Millie Morelos, a seasoned hand and single mother of two college bound boys, set off to do her rounds. She started with door to door checks looking for anything unusual: a covered window, blood or feces smeared on it, an untreated asthma attack, a man in pain or gasping for his life as another preyed on him, a body unresponsive or, sometimes, hanging from a rope.

She was methodical about her work. She stopped briefly at the cell window and shone her lamp into it so she could see inside. Really see inside. That was her job.

For today's rounds she had started on the lower tier in section A and now was turning the corner to section B.

"I want to go home!" The plaintive cry broke the quiet of the night.

Morelos stopped and perked an ear. It was coming from above. She waited for a moment, then proceeded with the cell checks.

"I want to go home!" the doleful voice resounded again.

From the control room Eddie Grisholt flashed his lamp across and into the second tier, scanning the section. Up against the door on 225 stood the outline of a short, slender man, wearing what looked like a rag on his head. The moment the light set on his door, Johnson gave a slow wave for a reply.

"What's going on?" shouted Grisholt.

Johnson shook his head slowly.

"You'll go home when you'll go home, okay?" barked Grisholt with a don't-bother-me attitude. "Settle down and go to sleep."

"I want to go home," Johnson bellowed out again, only louder this time.

Grisholt had returned to reading his newspaper.

Millie Morelos was about half way down section B doing her checks when she decided to go upstairs and see what was happening. She thought she had recognized the voice but was not sure. Only Johnson stood by his door, quietly rocking from foot to foot, the rag on his head, the face gaunt, the beard scraggly, the eyes distant.

Morelos edged up and stood front to face him.

"I've been having bad dreams, Ms Morelos, very bad." The tone was hollow and pleading. "Can you get me some Heroin?"

Morelos chuckled. "Are you serious?"

"Heroin helps me, Ms Morelos."

"How's it help you?"

"My bad dreams…I can't sleep."

"What're the bad dreams about?"

"Stuff I've done. Stuff I haven't done. It's all mixed up. You don't want to know."

Johnson stopped rocking and bowed his head.

"How long you in for?" asked Morelos.

"Twenty five to life. First strike for having a little crack, second for vehicular manslaughter – I served 8 years for that - and then the robbery. That struck me out."

Hearing the chaotic stories that had ripped apart their lives always gave Morelos pause. She looked down at the ground.

"Twenty five to life," said Johnson again. "It was a residence. The maid was in. She decided not to go out that day. My luck. I thought the place was empty. Prosecutor said I threatened her but I didn't. He made that up. I think he was running for office."

"What did you steal?"

"A hat."

"A hat?"

"It looked fancy. When I heard there was someone in, I started to leave but she saw me going out the window. They caught me a few blocks away. I was wearing the hat. See Ms Morelos, I've been down 13 years and I'm still a junkie. I get scared I might get a chance to get out and I'll blow it."

Johnson raised his hand and placed it against the cell door's window.

Morelos looked at him, then raised her open hand and placed it opposite his. He had seemed adrift, baffled, but now a spark shone in his eye.

"You think I belong in here?"

"I don't know. You think you do?"

He shook his head slowly. "I don't like it."

"What?"

"In my dreams, someone is peeing on me."

"When did you last use?"

Johnson shrugged.

"When are you going to stop the madness?"

A twisted expression seized him and bam!! He slammed his head against the cell door.

Morelos stepped back. "What're you doing?"

Johnson started to calmly roll off the rag he had on his head, then pulled back and wham!! Slammed his head again.

"Stop it!" cried Morelos, "Stop it now!"

From the control booth, Eddie Grisholt flashed his lamp on Johnson while Officer Rivers emerged from the office below, "You all right Morelos?"

She waved them off. "Talk to me, Johnson," she said to him firmly, "Talk to me."

Johnson slowly rubbed his forehead where an ugly bruise was forming. He looked at his fingers.

"You do this one more time and I'm going to put you on suicide watch," said Morelos.

"Don't put me on suicide watch, please. I hate being in those paper clothes."

"Who's your clinician?"

"Ms Granite."

"I'm putting a call to her."

"Ten minutes every three months," said Johnson, "Sometimes five… or one… hello and goodbye. She could be telling me 'fuck you,' for all I know. I just can't figure it out. But she never forgets to ask the main question…"

"What's that?"

"… Are you suicidal?"

Morelos took out a note pad from her back pocket and scribbled in Granite.

"Don't talk much about anything but she sure writes a lot…" said Johnson, "maybe she's just reading my mind. She smiles and checks off all the boxes and does her tidy note so her supervisor is happy and she can keep her job and feed her children. I talk more to you than to her."

Morelos watched him closely. "I'll ask her to come by and look at you."

Johnson stared back.

"I should send you to medical to have that bruise checked out."

"I don't need medical, I need some Heroin."

"Ever thought what could take the place of that junk?"

Johnson shrugged.

"Ever been to rehab?" said Morelos.

"No, but I've been on the list. Several times. It takes so long that I end up doing something stupid, so I go to the hole and when I come out I have to start all over again. One counselor told me I was unconsciously trying to destroy myself. So? Isn't that something we should work on? And he said, 'Just say no.'"

Johnson shook his head. "He gets paid for that."

"How long you've been using?"

"Since Juvenile Hall."

A lifetime of drug use, thought Morelos. It made no sense to her that, addictions being so prevalent in prison, the effort put into rehab was so meager. Not only would proper treatment spare their health, helping to prevent all the associated disease that came with it, but drug use was also a major source of violence in the units.

"I need to get back to my cell checks," she said. "I'll look in on you later. G'night."

Shortly after midnight, the phone rang. Eddie Grisholt had been standing at the window looking out into the yard where two officers were escorting a handcuffed inmate to Bravo Two, the block next door. He crossed to the phone and picked up. "Bravo Three, Grisholt."

"How are you?"

Grisholt smiled as a stream of memories flowed into his mind. He had been expecting the call but it took him a second to reply. "Hey, Buck, how's it going?"

"All right. It's been a while."

"It has."

They hadn't talked in over 4 years.

"Is he still there?" said Buck.

"Oh yeah. Cell 128. I checked the list as soon as I got in but haven't seen him yet. I'm curious, though."

"I pulled some levers to get him to where you are."

"If anyone can do it, you can. And you know me, Buck, I'll do whatever I can to help out."

"Don't."

Grisholt thought he had misunderstood. "I beg your pardon?"

"You commit the crime, you do the time," said Buck flatly.

Grisholt was having trouble fathoming the meaning of Buck's words. Was he joking? "I don't get it, is this your son?"

Buck was silent.

"Buck?"

"My son... yes." The voice had turned cold. "Are you alone?"

"Yes."

"From now on, whenever we talk, I want us to be alone."

"Sure, Buck, whatever you say."

"And don't use my name, just in case someone is close by. I don't want anyone knowing Joey and I are related. You're the only one who knows in there."

Grisholt thought he heard Buck laboring with his breathing.

"When they turn up the heat he's gonna crack and start telling everybody, just to spite me."

"But why would he do that? I mean, unless he's scared and wants some protection..."

"I have almost 30 years in Corrections..." cut in Buck, "a life spent serving the public. I could lose it all."

Grisholt was still confused but hesitant to probe further.

"He's got me over a barrel," continued Buck.

"But what is it you think you'd lose?"

"What kind of question is that?"

"I mean, people commit crimes... what was it, a drug charge?"

"Ever heard of a guard with a child molester for a son?"

"Shit." The thought stunned Grisholt and for a moment he didn't think it was real. He sat down. Somehow, he had never imagined the possibility. It struck him that he had assumed that being a guard granted some kind of magical protection against that eventuality, that going through the academy and being part of law enforcement shielded a family from that type of deviance. "I'm sorry, Buck. What went wrong? I mean… you don't have to tell me."

"I'm not going to."

Buck was calling from his home in Pomona, next to Chino, in which prison he had worked for most of his career, except for two periods when he had been up in Corcoran. It was during the second of those stays that the two men had met, and when Buck Wilson had taken the young Eddie Grisholt, fresh out of the academy, under his wing. There had been good days, too, before things turned sour.

"But if he hasn't said anything, so far – ventured Grisholt - then maybe he's a tough kid, a chip of the old block. Sometimes it takes a while for it to come out." Grisholt just heard Buck's breathing at the other end, "The toughness, I mean."

"I know what you mean."

"What I'm saying is…"

"Horseshit," said Buck bluntly. "What've you been smoking?"

Grisholt thought of saying that he had given it up but it would have come across as a bit of sass and Buck was in no mood for it.

"Since when does tough and child molester go together?" pressed Buck. "He's no good, that's what he is."

"No good?" Grisholt knew he was pushing and it didn't take much.

"A sociopath – said Buck – nothing but trouble from the start. In school, with neighbors, running away, doing drugs, a born schemer and manipulator. It's hard for me to say it but that's what it comes down to. No good. He won't change."

The words were gruff and wounding and the sheer rancor made Grisholt squirm. He recognized that in his own heart and mind his attitude toward the inmates swung wildly: sometimes forgiving, sometimes harsh, even cruel, and while he was still using inmates to punish others that he perceived had disrespected him, he had started to question himself, and because of it, the severity of Buck's judgment stung him.

"It must be hard on you," began again Grisholt, "I remember you sharing with me some of what went on… his mischief… but I didn't know it was this bad."

"It's been a nightmare."

"Makes you think twice about having kids…"

"It's a lottery."

"Hard on your wife, too…"

Buck did not reply and, for a moment, all Grisholt could hear was Buck's breathing. Had he put on more weight? He had always struggled with it.

"I don't know about that," said Buck.

Grisholt and Buck's parting had not been amicable, so he was surprised when told by the yard captain that Buck had called and left a message. He had thought twice about answering but decided to do so because the captain had asked him. But why would Buck contact him, specifically, on a matter as delicate as this? Maybe Buck was not a good judge of character. And it mattered, thought Grisholt, because he still held ill feelings towards his old mentor.

As he sat there, phone in hand, Grisholt still didn't know just what exactly Buck wanted from him. "So… just so I'm clear on this… you don't want me to interfere at all?"

Buck said nothing.

The silence sent a chill up Grisholt's spine.

"I didn't say that... I just want to monitor the situation. I don't know what I'll do if he starts squealing like a sissy. But just remember this, I'm a guard and he's a fucking child molester."

Before Grisholt had time to respond, Morelos and Rivers called up to him from the floor. "Give me a second, Buck." He put down the phone and crossed front to address the officers.

"Everything is quiet down here," said Morelos. "We're going over to the vending machines for a minute. Want anything?"

"I'm good. Take your time." He stepped back to the control panel and pressed the button to release the side door. When he picked up the phone again Buck had hung up

Eddie Grisholt got home at around 7 am, ate a light snack and jumped in bed but lay awake thinking of the conversation with Buck. The whole thing had an ominous feel. Did Buck really not want his son getting any special looking over from his fellow guards, just in case? He had never heard of a similar situation but surely his brothers in arms would understand. True, it would raise some eyebrows and make people wonder about Buck, but stuff happened. And why was his son in general population anyway? Why not in the Sensitive Needs Yard (SNY), where child molesters found a measure of protection?

6

"What happened to you? Why did you come to prison?" Joey dropped down from his bed to sit on the floor opposite Legrand.

It was a Saturday afternoon, the vent in the cell was blowing hot air to keep them warm and Paytrell next door was quiet. It would be an hour before they marched off to dinner.

Legrand had been polishing his boots as he sat on the edge of his bunk. His warm and kind manner intrigued Joey: why was he serving such a long sentence?

"You know if I talk about it, I expect you to tell your story, too," said Legrand. He spoke with a gravelly voice in a rich bass tone.

Joey assented.

Legrand put his boots down and clasped his hands together. "The crime itself was straightforward – he began - I killed two men with brute force. I was working at a factory that made airplane parts in El Segundo and was learning to be a machinist. I was good with my hands and the shop foreman was bringing me along. I took home a paycheck every week and helped my mother who had come down with a bad case of diabetes. I had a girlfriend I was close to and that night, a Friday, we were going to go out and celebrate my 19th birthday. I had worked all day, went home to clean up and then straight to her place. I knocked on her door to let her know I was in; she didn't come out right away but her little pooch, Orpheus, was out in the yard and I got to playing with him. I took my nice shirt off but still had my tee shirt under. So there I was minding my business when a car rounded the corner. A woman was driving and she stopped right in front of the house and just stared at me. Up and down. I looked back and she kept staring. It just so happened that my girl came to the window at that exact moment. The woman in the car took off but my girl stormed out and started yakking, 'Who is she? Where do you know her from? I can't believe you've done this to me!' She wouldn't stop and nothing I said would calm her down. So she tells me to leave. I couldn't believe it. I kept repeating, 'It's my birthday, baby, we're going out, remember? Please sweetheart.' I was begging. But she was hard headed like that. She snatched up her pooch and went inside."

Legrand paused, drifting in the moment he was reliving.

"She didn't come back out?"

"She walked right out of my life." He unclasped his large hands and glanced at them; they were moist. He placed the palms on his thighs and rubbed them dry before clasping them again. A sense of sadness had welled up in him. He looked at Joey. "I knocked on the door, again and again, but she wouldn't answer. Then the anger got the best of me." Legrand dropped his eyes. "It was like the Devil took over. I turned around and headed for a strip joint I knew from before I'd met Chante. It was all downhill from there." He took a deep breath. "I had a couple of drinks and after the show decided to go with one of the girls. They had a little place in back. It didn't mean anything. All the time I'm on top of her I'm thinking of Chante. How could she do that to me? It was crazy. But the anger was stuck in my craw. I didn't realize it until the woman stopped me and said, 'Hey big boy, slow down, you squeezing too hard. Relax. I'm not going nowhere.' So I just rolled off and lay still. She didn't say anything else, just turned on her side and caressed my chest. I was very anxious, couldn't get Chante out of my mind. 'Take it easy,' the woman kept saying, but my head was swimming. I thought, 'What am I doing here?' I knew I had made things worse, violating Chante's trust, but was I going to lose her? I felt a surge of dread, heartache, anger, and I couldn't sort it out. I was filling up with self-loathing and didn't know it. If Chante had been hasty before and rushed to judgment, now surely she'd be able to tell that I had cheated on her. I jumped up from the bed and started to put my clothes on. The woman looked up at me, 'you going to leave me like this, all worked up?' She pulled the sheets off of her and, parting her legs, slid her fingers between her thighs. 'Here, babe, it's calling you,' she said. But I was done. 'You got paid, didn't you? Just let me be.' I fastened my belt and walked out. I went back to the bar and had a couple more drinks. I drank fast. I wanted to forget, to stop the anguish that kept eating at me. I slapped a twenty-dollar bill on the counter and got up to leave. The bartender glanced at me and said, 'One for the road?' I stared back at him as he poured the drink. My thoughts were racing. 'On the house.' 'Sure,' and I gulped it down." Legrand looked off. "Bad choice. It was past midnight when I left. I had a buzz and felt lousy."

"You lived far off?" said Joey.

Legrand shook his head slowly. "About a mile and a half… but I never got home."

Joey felt himself squirm.

"In the next thirty minutes I had committed an act that turned my life upside down. Just like that. I didn't have a drug habit. I had graduated high school. I was a hard worker. I had been stopped a couple of times by the cops but that came with the neighborhood and the color of my skin. There were gangs in my hood, sure, but I kept my distance. My mother had seen to that. She had made all kinds of sacrifices so she could be at home when I got there from school and give me the supervision I needed, but by the time I had finished high school she was worn out. Her kidneys had started to fail. She asked me to go work to help out. I wanted to go to college - no one in the family had gone - but I couldn't ask her to make more sacrifices. So I did what she wanted me to… and I resented it."

Legrand rubbed his face.

"Did you talk to her about it?"

"Yes. She wanted me to be with her, it was that simple. Maybe she knew she would die soon and wanted to enjoy my company. I was all she had. When she first told me I said, sure, but I could do both. I could go to college and be there for her. We could struggle together and I would inspire her to hang on. I pleaded. But she didn't want to hear it."

"Did you talk to any of your teachers?"

"I did. My history teacher. He liked me. He went to see her… then he asked me to be patient, she would change her mind."

Legrand shrugged.

"After my father, she had never had a partner. She wasn't asking for a lifetime, the way she had given to me, but only for a short while. Still, I resented it. Other kids were heading off to college and I was staying back and the anger got bottled up in me. The trouble with Chante just set it off. I didn't know there was so much of it in me until I got close to the two men lying on the ground and I could see their faces… and as I looked at them I thought… these two guys look like nice kids… and they're so young… like me…maybe they're going to college like I should be… what have I done? Are they going to die?" Legrand paused to stare at his hands again. "I don't remember how long I stood there, looking at the two guys, but then I had the sudden urge to run away… and just at that instant I heard a craggy voice behind me, 'Hold it right there, fellow.' I turn around and it's an old man pointing a shotgun straight at me."

Legrand looked anguished.

"Where did he come from?" said Joey.

Legrand shook his head slowly. "I looked at him for a second, then turned around and started walking away. He gave me another warning but I ignored him, I didn't think he'd shoot. He did. He got me in the leg and my butt. It burnt like hell. I started running, limping but running. He chased after me and fired another round. He got me in the back. Still, I kept going. All the while I'm thinking I want to get home, I want to see my mom, and who's going to take care of her with her diabetes and bad kidneys. And I was losing the old man but I still heard him in back, huffing and puffing. 'I'm going to get you again if you don't stop!' But I kept going. And as I ran I began crying, and through my tears I remember saying, 'I'm coming home, mama, I'm coming home, this is not happening, this is a dream, I love you!'"

Legrand's recalling had loosened a storm of grief, and the pain that played out in his eyes and face had transfixed Joey.

"Then I felt someone rush up behind me, to my left… that's all I remember."

"What was it?"

"There were three guys to begin with. I beat up two. The third guy, I'd chased him away but he came back. He'd found a length of pipe, caught up with me and wopped me in back of my head."

Legrand turned quiet, as if emptied of emotion.

When he spoke again he was calm. "I was in a coma for two days. The other two guys were in a coma, also. Same floor. Same hospital. But they didn't wake up. Thirty minutes had changed my life forever."

"Lower tier! Get ready for chow!" the guard bellowed out over the PA system. Legrand's eyes had turned misty, his lips moving ever so slightly, silent words that Joey could not decipher. Legrand covered his face with his hands and rubbed his brow. He then stood up, crossed to the sink and splashed some water on his face.

Legrand's story had drawn Joey to his own and both men sat in reflection.

"Section A, stand by for chow!"

Five minutes later it was their turn.

7

Joey's parents lived in a middle-class suburb of Pomona, about two miles south of the freeway, in an unassuming three-bedroom stucco home with a wattle fence. Tall trees branched over to the other side of the street and formed a canopy that shaded it during the hot summer days. It had been their first and only home.

Janice was a local girl that went to work right after high school, first at a furniture store in the mattress department as a salesperson and model, then moving on to the courthouse where she was assigned to the records section. She made friends, was a good rock and roll dancer, and volunteered at a local nursery. When she was 23 she fell in love with a young lawyer based in Riverside who had come to Pomona on business. Excited with the prospect, she moved out of her parents' and got a place of her own.

They traveled to San Francisco and New York, Miami, the Caribbean, down to Buenos Aires, then to the lowermost point of the continent, so they could see the penguins. And it was a lot of fun but it took her a minute to realize that he had no intention of tying the knot. It was a crushing blow to Janice.

With the help of her friends she got through the heartache, quit the job at the courthouse and went to work as a clerk for a real estate agency in town. She was already 27, had seen all her friends get married and was beginning to feel a bit hopeless when she met Buck Wilson.

It happened at a local dance. She was twirling with a friend she had known for a while but was not a love interest. A local band was playing a Jerry Lee Lewis tune complete with the pianist banging on the keys and even sitting on them and Janice was happily rocking and rolling when she noticed the handsome young fellow on the sidelines who could not take his eyes off her. The piano banging came to a stop, dancers wiped the sweat off their brows, and the soothing strains of a Nat King Cole ballad faded in through the speakers. Her partner slipped his arm around her and pulled her to him but Janice begged off and walked across to Buck. She extended her hand inviting him to dance. He was touched but began to excuse himself mumbling something about not being as swift a dancer as her partner but she would have none of it. She took him by the hand and dragged him out onto the dance floor. He was 29 and had come down from Corcoran to visit some friends over the weekend. Six months later they were married.

It was early morning and Janice was sitting at the dinner table going over the numbers of a real estate transaction when Buck walked in from the kitchen holding a bowl of cereal he was eating from. It was his day off. "Want to go for a walk?"

"I have a client at 10 and have to finish checking these figures," said Janice.

Buck took a seat next to her.

"Joey called me at the office yesterday afternoon," said she. "He said everything was fine. But he always says that. I just think he doesn't want me to worry."

"He's been lucky," said Buck and took another spoonful of cereal.

"But with you telling the principal officers to keep an eye on him, that should be enough, shouldn't it?"

"I can't tell everybody. People like to talk. If the inmates find out, they'll target him."

They had been through this before and Janice couldn't get past the dispassionate tone of Buck's words. "I know that, but so long as you tell the main people, they'll figure out a way to protect him, don't you think?" She was desperate for some token of reassurance.

He stared into what was left of his bowl. The doctor had told him to lose weight but the cereal and veggie business was not cutting it.

Janice waited patiently for a reply.

"There's no guarantee," he said.

"Thank you for doing that," she said, but she couldn't hide her disappointment. She looked down at her paperwork trying to concentrate but could not. She glanced up at him. He seemed distracted. "You okay?"

"Didn't sleep well."

Maybe there was something going on with him and he needed to talk about it. "Anything going on at work?"

"The crime he committed puts him down at the bottom of the barrel," Buck said.

"I know that," she said, the exasperation starting to bleed through, "but you know so many people I'm sure that'll make a difference." Didn't he see she was begging him?

Couldn't he simply acknowledge her worries? "He told me about his new cellmate," continued Janice, "an older man. He said he's good for him, that he doesn't let him get away with anything. You know how Joey sometimes tells stories…"

"Terrific."

The sarcasm rankled Janice but still she tried to ignore it.

Buck got up from the table and crossed to the kitchen.

"He's of French descent, you know," continued Janice as he went by, "Joey says he's like a father to him."

The moment he heard *French descent* Buck remembered a fellow by that description with whom he had had some dealings. A passing thought. "I'm glad he's finally found one." A ripple of scorn ran through his words.

And she snapped. Turning round she shot back, "What's that supposed to mean?"

"He never put much effort into connecting with me, did he?" Buck said.

"Wasn't that your responsibility?"

"I tried, gave it my best. He's just no good."

"Don't say that!" fired back Janice, springing from the table and going to him.

Squaring with her, holding her gaze, he said with muted anger, "I do not like my son, I've told you that and I'm not going to start now."

Janice balled up her fists inadvertently crumpling the paperwork she was holding. She wanted to let her fury fly and rip into him. For the umpteenth time, what was wrong with this man? No matter what their differences, their son was in prison! But she stopped herself. She needed him. She needed his help - for Joey's sake. And she looked down at her hands, opened them and began to slowly smooth out the wrinkled paperwork, even as her hands had started to tremble.

"He needs you now. He just wants you to say you love him… that you forgive him. Why is that so difficult?"

"Because I have a memory, because I remember all the lying and the stealing and the crap, ever since he was 6 years old!"

"Six years old?" she fired back, "And why since he was six years old?"

"You tell me."

"No, you tell me", she raged as she stood tall in front of him.

"How can you forget?" he said, glaring back. "Wasn't that the time you walked out on us?"

They had gone through this so many times and yet there it was for him to beat her up.

"Weren't you gone for 6 weeks?"

"Yes, I was and I would do it again. And I did it for us, so you would come to your senses and stop messing up at the prison. I did it so they would not kick you out. And it worked, didn't it?"

Buck stared back. "You did it because of Joey, not because of me." The tone was disconsolate but jabbing, and it struck Janice hard and she seemed to stagger for an instant.

"Yes, it's true… and I did it because he asked me to."

Buck's eyes narrowed in surprise.

"Six years old and he said that to me, 'Keep us together, mommy.'"

Buck shook his head, uncertainly.

"I was going to take the kids with me, I was going to leave you… yes, walk out on you… but he asked me that we stay together as a family. Six years old and he asked me that."

She regained her calm as she spoke.

"At first I stayed because of him… then things happened between us… and I'm glad they did." And as she said this she let out a little smile, "And except for Joey's problems we've had a good life, haven't we?"

She drew closer, reached up and began to straighten the collar of his shirt. "And you changed, too. I know that it was never the same with Joey and I'm partly to blame for that, but you began to do better at work." She gazed up at him with a loving, gentle expression. "Didn't you?"

And Buck remembered the wrenching pain he had felt when she had walked out, the chilling effect on his behavior, how it had, indeed, become a turning point.

Janice had never told him what she had done behind his back. No, she had kept it as her secret because she had not wanted to wound his pride. But she had gone to see the warden, a Mr. Anderson at the time, to plead with him that he not fire her husband. She had gone to beg him that Buck be given another chance. And Mr. Anderson had done so. And it had been that same Mr. Anderson who then had told her about Buck's fights with the inmates and the tragedy that had occurred

Buck and Janice stood facing each other for a moment, quietly looking into each other's eyes as she ran her hand slowly down his massive chest.

"But if something happens to him… I don't know what I'll do." She said it softly, even tenderly, but Buck read it as a subtle menace.

His face twitched. He had caught a hard edge to her meaning and it frightened and disconcerted him. A pang of anger rose in him. Anger toward Janice jumbled up with the anger he felt for Joey. Anger from wounds he did not know how to heal, from wounds filled with self-blame, for if he had felt that Janice had been possessive with Joey, to the point of excluding him, why hadn't he fought that battle when it had to be fought? If he had resented her fawning over the child, spoiling him constantly, even treating him like a girl, why hadn't he spoken out when he saw it? Why hadn't he roared like he did with the inmates?

"Are you doing your best to keep him safe?" asked Janice, sweetly. Oh, she could be so endearing. And it didn't matter that he towered over her and was nearly three times her weight: she had never been afraid of him.

"I am", answered Buck, as he strained for self-control. "I know you're worried… but he'll be fine. He's strong."

Janice rested her head on his chest and circled his waist with her arms.

He pressed her to him, gently rubbing her shoulders, and a sense of relief begun to come over him as he felt her relax. He let his hands slide slowly down her back to her buttocks. He caressed them softly. He kissed her face, her eyes… but she stopped him.

"I have a client at 10," she whispered amorously.

He wanted to say, "I am it, baby, I'm your client today," but he let it go as she smiled up at him and pecked him on the lips.

Ever since Joey had committed his crime, Buck had got into the habit of taking long walks on his days off, where he would toss about his beliefs of people who molested children. If before prison he had held a vague condemnatory notion of what went into the making of such an offender, prison work had firmed up his view; the offender had to be pure evil - subhuman. And Joey being of the same ilk… why then… his offense signaled the beginning of a life of evil doing. The thought was oppressive.

But was there more?

Buck did allow himself to wonder, on occasion, if his parenting or lack of it, had had a hand in the shaping of Joey… if his actions… but, no, of course not… surely some errant gene – yet to be discovered - was responsible for it. How else to explain the repeat offender – the ceaseless maiming and torturing of others - but to have been cursed by fate at conception?

Buck walked and the more he did, the more he allowed himself to question his beliefs. Did something happen to child molesters - beyond the womb - to warp them? Did something happen to them when they were children? Oh, the thought of it. Had he, Buck Wilson, done anything to lead his son in that direction?

Buck thought about Janice, too, how sometimes he felt corralled by her, as if his emotional reliance on her had kept him from coming into his own. There was truth to that, he acknowledged reluctantly. He had feared that, without the soothing balm of her presence, his propensity to rage and explode would go unchecked and that he would be at the mercy of the infinite provocations he was subjected to on the job.

He walked four or five miles at a time, sometimes more, turning things over in his head, with no one there to tell him he could not think of this or that, anything being fair play. Oh, the beauty of it - letting his mind go.

But what would his fellow officers think of him, once they found out, if they didn't already know? Would they think of him as sexually twisted? Was he?

Who could he turn to? There was no one. He was on his own.

Now and then, though, when feeling exhausted and convinced there was no way out of his predicament, a stray thought would steal into his restless mind, playfully whispering to him daringly, with devilish delight, 'Why not tell your fellow officers the truth, right to their faces? Tell them the truth and dare them mock him. Dare them mock Buck Wilson.'

8

As Bravo Five was returning from breakfast, a fight broke out between two inmates in the yard and the alarm went off. There were no serious injuries but a short blade was found on the ground nearby and the entire yard had been put down for the officers to investigate.

Bravo Three had been quiet all day and the inmates had been fed in their cells. From the upper tier, section A, a lone feminine voice rang out. "Just want to let everybody know that my hormone treatment is coming along just fine. I consider myself a lady now and I want everybody to treat me like one. Just giving you the heads up." It was Chloe from 205.

"Can I move in with you?" said someone nearby.

"Thank you, that's very kind, but I have a friend already. I appreciate it, though."

"You're welcome."

"Put him on the list," bellowed out another.

Down below, officer Rivers exited the guard's office and walked across the day room. She climbed the stairs and went over to cell 225.

"Johnson?"

"What's up?" The cell was dark and he was lying on the floor, face up.

"Did Ms Granite come by to see you?"

"She did."

"What happened?"

"The usual."

"What's that mean?"

"Nothing."

Johnson turned on his side.

"Don't worry about it, I'm not suicidal."

Rivers had to strain to make out his features but she thought she saw him put something in his mouth.

"Are you sucking your thumb?"

"Leave me alone."

Rivers tapped twice on the door and walked off.

Down in 128, Joey had started to tell Legrand the story of his crime. He was sitting on the floor, back against the wall, while Legrand lay on his bunk, facing him, head propped up on folded arm.

"I touched her, that's true," began Joey, "but I didn't go in her pussy like she said at the trial. She made it up. It turned out she was 13, dressing like she was 21." Joey spoke in a light, breezy tone that Legrand found annoying.

"You'd be amazed what these girls can do. Anyway, I was going to college in LA, doing all right, I didn't think college was for me, though, but I was starting my second year while working nights at a pizza place. She'd come in with her buddies, all wearing their sexy little skirts and they'd flirt with me. I flirted right back. What's a man to do, right?"

"Ignore it," said Legrand, flatly.

"Easier said than done," replied Joey, chuckling.

Legrand had consented to hearing the story but was already having qualms. In his 31 years in prison he had not shared a cell with a child molester and had never heard a story directly from the guilty party. But though he thought himself a fair and mature man – he had never sanctioned brutality against child molesters or joined in the talk that sought to demonize them – he granted that the distance he had kept might conceal a measure of prejudice. So he wanted to confront it and hearing Joey out was an effort to do so.

"Penny for your thoughts – she'd say – and wink at me," continued Joey, "Then she started coming in by herself, told me she lived with an older cousin, that she was taking a year off from school and worked at a yogurt place."

"Who would hire her, she was 13?" said Legrand.

"Fake ID. You can get them anywhere."

The casualness in Joey's tone had stirred further Legrand's irritation. Could it be that Joey was feeding him a line of bull?

"So one night she showed up at closing time. She asked me for a drive home. I said yes. Once in the car, I suggested we go to a park I knew. We made out, nothing heavy. I knew I could've had her if I wanted to, but there was something odd about her."

"What was that?"

"Makeup. She wore lots of it. I thought she might be hiding some blemishes but I didn't think she'd be doing it to make herself look older."

"Writing on the wall," said Legrand, dryly.

"It's not like I was being dumb about it. I did ask her for her ID…"

"And?"

Joey shrugged. "I guess I should've taken a better look at it."

"So you took the bait, just like that, smart guy like you?"

Joey grew pensive.

"What about girls your age?" pressed Legrand.

"There was nothing happening."

"You're going to college, right? I never went but isn't it full of girls?"

"Actually, my father had kicked me out of the house and I had to drop out."

"Why?"

Joey hesitated. Here was a chance to get personal, to inquire into his truth, to start at least, but he passed. "Let me finish telling you the story, this is the best part…" Joey's face livened, ready to reel off the juicy details, eager to amuse. "So I pull down her pants but I keep a distance, you know what I'm saying? To protect myself…"

Legrand swung his legs off his bunk and sat up. Joey stopped, the hot glare of Legrand's eyes burning right through him.

"What's the matter?" he asked, weakly.

"I don't want to hear it," Legrand said bluntly.

Joey stared back, uncertain.

"Look, man, you're trying to entertain me."

Legrand's accusing words felt like a hard slap in Joey's face.

"I took you in out of respect for your humanity… and I have been impressed with your willingness to face those who want to demean and assault you, but as far as this story you're telling me … it's pure bullshit… and I expected something else from you, something honest."

Joey felt his mouth dry up instantly. Bowing his head, his heart sank. Legrand was holding him up to a standard he was not accustomed to. He was seeing right through him.

"I know you're determined to make it in general population…" continued Legrand, "that says a lot about you… but there's more to it, much more."

Joey listened intently, his head resting on bended knee, staring down at the toe of his boot - it needed brushing.

"You're welcome to stay, don't get me wrong, I don't have a problem with that. For me, it's a matter of principle: I refuse to let the mob dictate how I think, but if you want me to support you, you have to come clean."

Legrand sensed that Joey felt hurt and paused momentarily.

Joey didn't stir.

"There's no room for lying, Joey," the tone now gentler, even paternal, "All that does is lock you in. You've got good instincts… I see them. To fight back with your fists, that's beautiful, but you also have to fight back with your mind, to find your truth."

Joey glanced up, timidly… and Legrand saw that his eyes had moistened.

"Your truth. Nothing else will set you free."

Joey nodded with guarded anguish, the words 'Thank you' on the tip of his tongue, voiceless.

"All these men here are wounded people, with lousy childhoods, and all have come up angry and confused, quick to rage and destroy… hiding all the while as they run from their truth… do you want to be one of them?"

Joey shook his head slowly.

"Do you want to be stuck in that mode?"

Legrand was lecturing him and it shamed him but Joey strained to keep himself open. He felt he had to. He felt he needed to put up with the scolding because Legrand had something to say and no one had ever talked to him like that.

"I'm not sure what happens, how this madness to hurt child molesters comes about, but it's not hard to see how when along comes a person who's offended the innocence of a child, that these wounded men then take it personally, and every time they see you they're reminded of what was stolen from them… the brutality of the act."

Joey listened carefully. He had wanted to say to Legrand that he did, in fact, have a story to tell, a real one, a story that he had not yet found the courage to tell but there it was in him, hiding in his soul, sitting in a corner, cowering in shame… and if Legrand heard it he would think differently of him. But Joey could not conjure up the words.

He lifted his head and rested it against the wall behind. Would he ever be able to find a way out of his labyrinth? He closed his eyes. It felt like such an arduous task. Did he need a guide? He thought of his mother… his father… his sister Margaret. Then, unexpectedly, like a gentle breeze in summer, the face of Dr Jeffries floated into his mind. Had she not offered to see him again, even after he had been a bit rude to her? Yes, she had. But would that not be an admission that he could not do it on his own?

The question vexed him.

Could he, one day, not be like Legrand? What harm would there be in asking for an appointment? And to his surprise, by simply entertaining the thought, a ray of hope shone into his heart of gloom.

Little else was said the rest of the evening, Legrand wondering whether he had been too harsh with Joey and whether that might hinder their relationship. But every man was different. He knew, from his own life, that it was hard to get to the truth of who you were, and for some men, nearly impossible. But why was he interested in this kid, anyway? Did he bring out in him a desire to parent? He thought of the daughter he knew was out there, somewhere, and whom he was convinced he would never meet. And just who had parented her for him? Who had done his job? Maybe, by helping Joey, he would be repaying the unknown person who had parented his child… and may she live in peace.

Legrand had tried to sleep but could not. After a while he got up, crossed to the door and looked out.

From cell 221 the Vietnam Vet shouted, "I was in My Lai. I tried to stop it. I never got credit for that. The judge wouldn't hear it. I've got a Purple Heart. Why am I stuck in here? I can show it to you."

"I want to go home! I want to go home!" cried out Johnson, from 225.

No one responded.

First Watch had settled in and it was now near 1 a.m. Earlier, Legrand had seen Eddie Grisholt go up to the tower but now all he could see was that the grill to the rotunda was open. Legrand stayed by the door. Five, ten minutes went by, and his mind drifted. He thought of Joey, of what problems might have led him to his offense, and then the thought of his own father came to mind: the old man's long life in prison, his short and infrequent paroles. Now and then, his mother would surprise him and make the long drive up to San Quentin so they could visit. She had done it for him, not for her, since she had closed that chapter in her life.

Grisholt came out into the day room. He was carrying his baton, which he tapped evenly on the palm of his left hand. He eased his way over to the staircase and climbed up, turning toward C section, then strolling along the tier until he reached cell 240. It was Leroy's cell. Grisholt took a small pack out of his pocket and dropped it on the floor.

With his foot he slid it under the door. He then retraced his steps and went back up to his post.

9

Dr Gardner got a call from Lieutenant Griffith asking that he see Leroy Cadenas. There might be some trouble brewing and he thought Leroy had a hand in it since he had made a public threat to Joey Wilson. The Lieutenant had considered sending him straight to the hole but then chose to let the doc take a look. Gardner put him on his to do list: Johnson, in the same unit, was ahead of him. Ms Granite had reported that she had found him depressed.

Gardner called for Johnson but he declined, so he went up to his cell. He knocked twice before he got an answer.

"What do you want?" Johnson removed his blanket just enough to uncover his face.

"Gardner, psychiatry."

"You've got some Methadone for me?"

"Afraid not. Got a minute?"

"I'm kicking, man. Got goose bumps, cramps, nausea, diarrhea and I'm in no mood for chatting."

"Get up and move around, exercise helps."

"I know what to do."

"How long you've been hooked?"

"All my life."

"Want to start working on it?" said Gardner.

"The drugs or my life?"

"One and the same, you know that."

Johnson threw off his covers and jumped to his feet, flailing his arms and legs as he began to pace back and forth.

"Heard from your family?"

"Family? Prison system is my family." He sounded irritated as he continued to move, never glancing at Gardner.

"When was the last time you heard from anyone?"

"Forget it, dude, I'm not suicidal, go back to your paperwork."

"It's a simple question, Johnson, really simple. When was the last time you heard from anyone?"

"Two, three years... I don't remember."

"Who would you like to hear from?"

Johnson stopped and stared at Gardner. "The Pope. Can you get through to him? Collect?"

"I'm trying to work with you. Is there any relative you'd like to hear from?"

Johnson turned to the sink, opened the tap and splashed water on his face. He began to rub it dry but then stopped, his hands still pressed against it.

"Anyone?"

Slowly, Johnson lowered his hands. "My son," he said softly.

"Where is he?"

"Somewhere in LA."

"You have his number?"

"It's been a minute. He might have moved."

"And maybe he hasn't. You want me to put in a call to him?"

Johnson regarded Gardner with curiosity. "Sure." He then wrote the number in a piece of paper and slipped it through the porthole.

Gardner went back to his office and dialed it. A man answered. It was Johnson's son. After a brief introduction, Gardner got to the point. "You'd be surprised what a visit can do."

Johnson's son was not persuaded. "Look, doc, I appreciate what you're doing but this man was never there for me. Running around with the gang was obviously more important. It's taken me a whole lot of work to get something going for myself. I even spent time in the Youth Authority. But now I have a job and a roof over my head. I'm making it, making it, sir... and not breaking the law... on my own... so I don't see the point."

Gardner had heard if before: the struggle against the odds, the long held bitterness against the absent father who often had been fatherless himself or had not had a clue. But wasn't this situation different, the son fighting the good fight and winning? Could the son not be a father to his father and lend a helping hand?

"He may not have made a difference in your life but maybe you can make a difference in his," Gardner ventured.

Johnson's son was silent.

"You'd have to fill some papers to get permission."

"I've already done that. Has he even stopped using?"

"Just now he's going through withdrawal. Don't know much else, just met him today. He was transferred to my unit a couple of months ago and had been keeping a low profile. You've stayed in touch?"

"Not really."

"Why do you think he uses?"

"He's been like that most of his life. Look doc, I went to drug counseling myself, not because I was using but because I wanted to understand him and where I came from. He had his responsibilities and didn't meet them, and he felt like a failure and started using, all the while his judgment kept getting worse and worse. I understand all of it, but when does it stop?"

"When there's courage and hope."

Johnson's son was quiet for a moment. "I can help with giving hope but the courage… he's got to pull it out of himself."

"True."

"Don't you have treatment programs in there?"

"Barely, just starting. All these past years, zero," said Gardner.

"Why?"

"Because a lot of people still think the best treatment is punishment, and that to treat would be to coddle and pamper. And that belief reaches way up the ladder. The few programs that exist have a long waiting list, or give priority to those about to leave."

"You're serious?"

"Dead serious."

"But he's been locked up 12 or 13 years. Hasn't the untreated problem been worsening things?" The voice rang with exasperation. "They keep giving him piss tests which he fails every time… which take away privileges… or he gets into fights behind drugs, which add to his sentence. He got beat unconscious once. He's not a big guy, you know. He'll never get out."

"This is what we have now, Johnson. If we want to change it, we have to work on it. So call the governor. Complain. Organize politically."

Johnson's son let out a groan.

"I have to go now," said Gardner. "Do what you can but a visit might help."

"I'm going to try and go up this weekend. I'll have to check first to see if he's eligible."

"He'll really appreciate it."

"Thanks, doc."

"You're welcome."

Gardner went back to tell Johnson about the call and when he returned to his office the guard in charge told him that Leroy Cadenas was waiting for him in the holding tank.

The name was familiar. Gardner sat down at his desk, logged on, and brought up his record. He had seen him once before but then he had been transferred to another yard. He read the note. Leroy had been in the system since childhood, beginning at age 5. At age 9 he was caught shoplifting. Then he committed the same offense at 10 and 11. At age 13 he landed in Juvenile Hall on a burglary charge, then a second burglary count at 15, followed by an assault and battery at 17. From there he went directly to prison on his 18th birthday so he could finish his sentence. He paroled 3 years later and promptly violated the terms when he left the state without permission. On his way back to California he was found guilty of another assault and battery – this time on a security guard at a bus depot in Sacramento. While waiting for his day in court a cold case was discovered, a strong-armed robbery also committed at 17. Leroy had got two strikes for the offenses committed at 17. The assault and battery on the security guard earned him the third strike. And so, at the age of 22, under the three strike law, Leroy Cadenas was convicted to 25 years to life. He was now 28 years old. Since parting with his mother at age 5, he had spent his entire life bouncing around in the system, except for the one year he had violated parole and stayed up in Philadelphia.

Reading the histories sometimes made Gardner breathless: the dizzying pace of recklessness, the lack of guidance, the absence of nurturance, the volcano of dysfunction burning up the capacity to self govern.

When Leroy stepped into Gardner's office he was wearing his orange jacket. His hair was nicely combed, parted on the left side, where a one inch cut was healing on his cheek. He had a small star tattooed on the right. He sat across Gardner.

"Leroy Cadenas?"

"That's me."

"Gardner, psychiatry."

"I know you," Leroy said, learning forward with a thinly veiled sarcastic smile, "You're the guy wanted to pump me full of meds."

"Really?"

"Got me to feeling like a zombie, but I wasn't going to go for it."

"I have a different recollection," began Gardner, "I remember you telling me that you'd been in over 50 documented fights in the 6 years you've served on this term, the second one I believe… and I said, maybe, maybe I could help you think before you act so you could stop getting into so much trouble. That sounds familiar?"

"What do I care? I've got 25 to life, it'll be another 19 years before I go before the board."

"I'm sorry about that," Gardner said reflexively, as he always did when he heard of the long sentences.

Leroy made a wry face. "Sorry? What're you sorry for? You're not the one doing the time."

"I'll tell you why I'm sorry. When you were a child, did you dream of spending most of your life in a place like this?"

Leroy frowned.

"With mentoring, with support, you wouldn't be here but out there instead, in the world, making your contribution to society."

Gardner's empathic tone had surprised Leroy, leaving him momentarily at a loss.

Gardner leaned forward on his desk, "Want to heal, Mr Cadenas?"

Leroy drew back, eyes leveled on the doc. He found the question irksome though he didn't know why. He granted that in all his years in the system he'd never heard anyone put that question to him.

"Become a better man?" rephrased Gardner.

"What for? I can't get out," said Leroy, testily.

There was more to it than getting out, thought Gardner.

Leroy turned to look at the window. The sky outside was vast, limitless, but it belonged to others, not to him. He felt tired. Why open a door that you can't get out?

"There's also – Gardner began again – finding meaning in your life."

Leroy scoffed. "Is that what you called me in for, to tell me that?"

"Lieutenant Griffith wanted me to see how you were doing."

"He told you to talk to me about meaning?"

"No, that was my idea."

Leroy chuckled. "You guys in mental health have it easy, sitting around all day making up stuff." He shook his head, dismissively.

"Owning your story… transcending yourself… impacting other lives… acting in your world constructively," remarked Gardner.

"Without freedom?"

"You begin with what you have… then who knows?"

"What I have is nothing… and what you're talking about, without freedom, means nothing."

"I beg to differ," said Gardner.

"You can't possibly understand this not being free…" returned Leroy with a tone of irritation, "It weighs on you so much that some days it crushes you… doesn't let you breathe… so we find anything we can to distract ourselves from the pain… the anguish… and is it any surprise that we turn to beating up on ourselves to ease it?"

Leroy thought of telling Gardner that he had a long history of cutting on himself but held back. It was in his record, anyway, he could read it. "The games we play, sir… and we play a lot of them… they come from that emptiness. We come from broken relationships… and for us to heal we need healthy ones… everyone knows that… but there's nothing here… and it's by design."

Gardner listened.

"Have you ever felt trapped, doctor…?"

"Not like you."

"Young and trapped. What a curse. I was trapped when I was out there, too, I just didn't know it."

Leroy looked down at the ground and ran his fingers through his hair.

"Why did you surrender your freedom?" asked Gardner.

The question intrigued Leroy. Had he, indeed, surrendered his freedom? Had it been a conscious act? "There were things…" he began, but then shook his head slowly.

"What things?"

"Never mind. I want to go back to my cell." He joined his hands and closed his eyes.

Gardner took his pen and wrote a note on a form. Then he said, "That cut on your face, what happened?"

"Something I had to do."

"Had to?"

"Yep. I asked him for his papers…" Leroy stopped, touched his finger gently to the cut on his left cheek. The skin was turning color. "He's got a good right hand, real quick. I wasn't expecting it."

"A sex crime?"

"Yep. She was thirteen."

"How do you know that?"

"I have contacts. His name is Joey Wilson. Came down from Salinas, thinks he can tough it out. Well, he can't."

Gardner looked off. He felt dejected when he heard the absurd tales of revenge that had gone on in prison since forever; punishment without prior examination, vulgar, primitive. "So you're going to finish the job?"

"It's going to take a little while but we'll get there. Right now he's got protection."

"Who's protecting him?"

"C'mon, doc, you know that."

"I do?"

"Your boy, Legrand."

"My boy?" asked Gardner, incredulous.

Leroy gave a smug smile. "He comes to see you. We know what's going on."

Gardner had an inkling of where Leroy was headed but was not sure. "You got me. I'm clueless."

"He's your favorite, isn't he?"

"Legrand made up his mind a long time ago, way before I came to work in this prison, that he was going to turn his life around. Maybe you're envious."

Leroy chuckled. "Maybe. And maybe he wants to play the savior. But you'd better tell him he can't be protecting a child molester."

"He doesn't take instructions from me," said Gardner. "But put that aside, say he wanted to protect this man Wilson, for whatever reason, then why shouldn't he? He's putting himself on the line for what he believes."

"Look, man, you've been around enough," returned Leroy, "Prison politics is prison politics, and it's not going to change because you don't like it. He did it to a child."

"It's a horrible crime… but he's had his day in court and been deprived of liberty."

"Not enough," said Leroy, "but I didn't make it up, that's the way it's always been."

"And you just follow along, not daring to question?"

"Not exactly. I set some rules, too. I'm a shot caller. I get some privileges. I get respect. And people have expectations so I have to deliver. If I don't, someone else will. A B C, you feel me?"

"Do you know Wilson's story?"

"I don't need to."

"Why not? I'm sure he's had a troubled past. Like you."

Leroy kicked back in his chair, the smile wry.

"I'm sorry, did I upset you?" asked Gardner.

"Don't you go comparing me with that son of a bitch."

"All right, so you can't handle it."

Leroy clenched his teeth. "Why am I seeing you, anyway?" he said, defiantly.

"The Lieutenant doesn't want the problem with Wilson to get worse."

Leroy shuffled his feet impatiently, staring back at Gardner, "You done?"

"I've set aside this time for you. It's up to you if you want to use it or not."

Leroy got up, stepped to the door, grasped the knob but then stopped. He turned back to look at Gardner. "You know, except for that one year I spent up in Philly… I've been in prison 9 straight years. Nobody knows where I am or gives a damn, and I've learned nothing but bad habits. Now, tell me, where's the rehabilitation? Why do they keep us in our cells all day long, unless you're a fruitcake and in the mental health program?"

"I beg your pardon," said Gardner, "In my opinion every single man that steps into prison should get mental health."

"Everyone?" asked Leroy, puzzled.

"Everyone. We should be a therapeutic community, from the very beginning. A moment ago, you said you needed healthy relationships to fix the broken ones. That's what a therapeutic community would bring."

"What we need is work," countered Leroy, "every day... so we're not stuck in those cells thinking bad thoughts..."

"Like the thoughts of hurting Wilson," interrupted Gardner.

"That's right," said Leroy.

"But work won't help with that," continued Gardner, "For that you need to work through your anger... and I'm sure you will agree that you're a very angry man."

Leroy returned to his chair and sat down. He could talk to this doctor. He touched again the wound on his cheek and it reminded him of how much there was to tell. "I just want to scare him," he said, "and maybe his parents, who are at least middle class because they could afford a private lawyer, maybe they'll send him a little money so he can pass it on to me - a straight out screw-up - who comes from the lowest of the lowest of classes, how about that?"

"Extortion is not going to address the issue," replied Gardner, flatly.

Leroy stared back.

"I still don't get why someone with a brain, like you, would want to hurt Wilson?"

Leroy folded his arms, eyes softening as he looked straight at Gardner. "I was 5 years old when my mama got busted for selling dope and they sent me to protective services. That same night, while I'm lying there scared to death in a strange home, crying my heart out from missing my dope fiend mama, the guy taking care of the joint came over to my room and stuck his finger up my ass so he could jerk off. And he told me to shut the fuck up or he would whoop me."

Leroy searched Gardner's expression. Should he go on?

"The social worker didn't come back for another week... and when she came back I was seeing monsters and hearing things, and they didn't know what was wrong with me. I was too ashamed to tell them anything. 'Maybe he's just making it all up', I heard them say. 'Send him to the psychiatrist so he can sort it out'. And off I go to the good doctor who has a waiting room full of people and is too busy to hear my story. And I end up on some junk that made my arms jerk and got me all stiff so I was walking around like a little robot. Still, I could count my blessings, because for the next week the man went on vacation. When he came back I started screaming again and would not stop, so they had to take me to the hospital where they gave me more pills..." Leroy lowered his head.

"I'm so sorry," said Gardner, "that was horrible… did you tell them?"

"I never told anyone, anything. Nothing. I thought I was going to die… and it didn't matter to anyone."

His hands had begun to tremble and Leroy brought them together. "And no, I don't have anything in common with that son of a bitch, you're dead wrong about that."

It took Leroy a moment to calm down.

"I had to live with shame that didn't go away and I was scared of everything… scared of everybody. Didn't trust anyone, man or woman."

Leroy's wounds shone clearly in his eyes but there were no tears. "For the longest time I couldn't get rid of the thoughts; they would leave for a short while then come right back. But when I started to get stronger I thought I could get even. And one day I hit another kid and knocked him down and it felt good. It made me feel lighter. So I started to pick fights over anything. And they called me incorrigible and I suppose I was… but I wanted to feel better. They missed that. And I went on to other homes and juvenile hall and never spent one day of my life in a regular school."

Gardner listened quietly at the anguished recounting. "Weren't there some good people along the way… people who could see what might be going on?"

"There were… but I was so angry I'd scare them off. And I'd decided I had found the key to my recovery… to fight with my fists to erase my shame."

"And you're still fighting that fight," said Gardner.

"I suppose I am."

Gardner sat back in his chair. "That strategy of yours… it's eased the shame, lightened the pain… but it has also got you into a whole lot of trouble. As horrible as the injury was, your reaction to it is what has wrecked your life."

Leroy looked off, the expression glum.

"You have to work with the anger," pressed Gardner.

"It doesn't matter. I have too much on my record. No matter what I do, the courts won't let me out."

Gardner was a believer in taking small steps. If an inmate could try new behavior it would impact the interactions with his neighbor, and that in turn would affect the next interaction and so forth.

"What were the assaults and battery convictions about?" Gardner asked.

"There were two. The first one, I was drinking with this dude I knew from Juvenile hall. We were driving to pick up some girls he said were friends of his. It was dark. He pulled over to light a cigarette. We got to chatting, then he reached across and touched my crotch. I didn't even think about it, I just flashed on him." Leroy shook his head as he recalled the incident. "I'm not proud of that... I kept hitting and hitting... I was much stronger than him... I could've just said, 'man, I'm just not wired that way, just drop me off by the bus stop so I can go home'. That would have been enough."

"What damage did you do?"

"I fractured his jaw in two places. His nose, too. He pressed charges."

Leroy looked at Gardner. "There were other things I didn't get caught for. Once, when I was high on PCP... I beat up some guy out with his girlfriend. I don't remember much. Pure spite."

"Want to tell me about it?

Leroy shook his head.

"The second battery, what was that about?"

Leroy shrugged. He was tapped out.

But then his mood lightened and he smiled.

"What?" asked Gardner.

"There was this home I was staying in," started Leroy, "and every morning I'd see the children walking by on their way to school. I must've been 8 or 9. I'd knock on the window and wave at them. Some waved back. Then one day, the attendant left the door open for a moment and I snuck out and joined the kids passing by. And I went all the way to their school and sat down in a classroom. Of course, the teacher discovered me and called the police. They told me I needed a special teacher and so I had to be schooled at home."

"How'd you feel?" asked Gardner.

"A little sad. But I already knew I was different... that things wouldn't be the same for me."

"Did you talk to someone about it?"

"I don't remember. You want to hear about the shoplifting?"

"Yes, of course."

"There was this time when I stole books from the library... I didn't even think of taking out a card. Silly."

"Why not?"

"I don't know."

"What kind of books?"

"Kids' books." Leroy chuckled to himself, the expression rueful. "In the books I swiped - I had put a handful under my shirt - I discovered a copy of "Pinocchio," by a guy named Carlo Collodi. I began to read it and then lost it somewhere. Never finished it, didn't see the video either, I wanted to finish the book before I saw it. Did you ever read the book?"

"I did. It's a beautiful story."

"How does it end?"

"I don't want to ruin it for you," said Gardner.

"It's all right, tell me."

"I think I have a copy somewhere, I'll look for it and let you borrow it. That way you can finish the story."

Leroy grinned broadly. "I left off when the fisherman had covered Pinocchio with flour and had thrown him in the frying pan thinking he was a rare kind of fish, but then someone came in and scared him. I don't remember the details… but I was glad I didn't fry."

10

Most of the officers were searching for drugs and weapons in Bravo One and the entire yard was on lockdown.

From his cell in the lower tier of Bravo Three, 107, Butterfly, the 400-pound man with the beautiful voice, spoke out reaching clear across to the other side of the day room.   "Why are we in this shit hole, I ask you?"

"Because we have not seen the light!" said Chloe, the transgender with the naughty side, in for check fraud.

"So true," returned Butterfly, "And we have not seen the light because we're filled with blight."

"But how sweet is the night when your sweet ass is tight!"

remarked Chloe.

"That's for sure," put in Moonshine, the fellow in charge of cooking up the local brew, a nasty concoction of fermented leftovers that got you a buzz and uncertain consequences.

"Please, please, have some respect for the orator," said Casino, eager to get on with the show.

"Order in the house. Order in the house!" shouted one while banging on the doors. "What are we, animals?"

"No more than that," seconded another.

"Pray continue, my lord, ignore the rabble in the gallery," prompted Casino.

"Thank you, thank you, sir, you are a most kindly sort," bellowed Butterfly regaining the initiative.

"Come on, brother, tell it like it is, don't hold back," cried Bazooka.

"We are ignorant of the laws of the universe…" continued Butterfly.

"Read the bible!" called out Gumbo, who was serving time for GBI, great bodily injury.

"Go, Butterball! Let it all hang out!" prodded Chloe in her thin voice.

"Beg your pardon, my lady, it is Butterfly, not Butterball."

"It just slips out, sweetie, but I'll try my best."

"Do so. Thank you. We're all ignorant of the laws of the universe that tell us that deep down every crime is a cry for help, a protest again cultural, economic and political oppression, and therefore we are not just inmates, but prisoners of war."

A burst of applause sallied forth.

"Butterfly is on a roll!"

"I nominate Butter Baby for our representative to congress!"

"No, to the House of Lords."

"We are in America, you jackass."

"We are citizens of the world!"

"Hallelujah!"

"Yes, we are citizens of the world but, alas, we are prisoners of war," continued Butterfly, "a war on the abused, on the neglected, on the illiterate, on the uneducated!"

A heavy-set officer stepped out from his office under the tower and shouted to Butterfly, "Shut up! You're getting on my nerves!"

"With all due respect, sir, this is my duty and I take it very seriously."

The officer rolled his eyes and went back in his office.

"See how we upset the establishment when we protest?"

"I saw that," said Chloe.

"Will someone take note of this historic event?"

A raspberry rolled out.

"I'm serious. Will someone keep minutes?"

"Gentlemen, please, be serious, I'm on my period," said Venus.

Laughter rang out.

"See what I mean? We don't even respect our own, which is why we are in this sad state of affairs."

"Don't get off track, Butter Baby, keep going"

"Thank you, Chloe, I love you, sweetheart, even if you've assigned me a depreciatory moniker."

"Don't be doing the word thing, I have a dictionary too. And you're going to get Sparrow jealous."

"Sorry, dear, it's just that, well, when I see you saunter down the day room, after you take a shower, you do something to me. Like in that Brazilian song where the girl goes walking by and the guy says, 'Ahh!'"

"Shame on you, Butterfly, I had no idea you were of that persuasion. Oh my goodness!" said Gumbo.

"How can you expect that a grown man like me, 35 years of age, with all my artistry, in the bloom of my life, and yet serving a life sentence for murder, a gross miscarriage of justice if I may say so because I was only defending myself, how can you expect, I repeat, that barred by the laws of this land from having the company of the opposite sex, that I not be aroused by the grace and sweet cadence of Chloe's walk as she glides, no, not glide, skips daintily across the limpid, crystalline waters of the day room?"

"Oh Butter, you bring tears to my eyes, you man, you monster, you, you, that's sooo romantic, but I'm engaged to Sparrow."

"Alas, let me at least dream of you."

"Stop all this nonsense, get on with the agenda!"

"As I was saying, we are political prisoners but the powers that be, because they control the means of production, they label us criminals."

Another burst of applause erupted. "Hear! Hear!"

"Why are we deprived of education, of proper representation in the courts? Why does it take so bloody long to get anyone to revisit our cases?"

"Because we fucked up, that's why," cried out a disgruntled soul from section A.

"Please refrain from polluting, let alone interrupting the flow of this elevated discourse."

"Fuck you, you bastard, when I see you in the yard I'm going to whoop yo' ass!"

"You make my point, sir, that's why we're here."

"I'm a Gulf War vet! I'm being held illegally. I helped put out those fires in Kuwait!"

"Shut the fuck up!" shouted the irate officer, as he stepped out once more from his office. "Everybody chill out!"

As if on cue a number of cell doors began to rattle furiously in protest. The officer, exasperated, threw up his arms and went back into his office, slamming the door behind.

A round of laughter and applause followed.

"Since we're all here, and have all vented our bile, which we gather in abundance with every day that passes, and the officer is duly pissed off and unlikely to come out of his hiding place for a while, may we turn to an idea that came to me the other day."

"Let us all hear what Butterfly has to say, I pray. Everybody be quiet now."

"Thank you, Chloe. Ladies and gentlemen…"

"We're not gentlemen, we're fucking losers," cried Johnson from his upper tier.

"If you choose to see yourself as such, then, believe me, you will stay a loser."

"Whoppity Woo Woo!" shouted Casino.

"Gentlemen, please!"

"Let him talk."

"That's all he does."

"I don't want to hear any more bullshit," cried Horseshoe, serving life for killing his wife's doctor when he missed her diagnosis and she died prematurely.

Silence followed for an instant.

"I strongly believe," resumed Butterfly, "that if the good people of this great country had a chance to hear the accounts of our lives, from ourselves, straight from the horse's mouth, they would come to understand the injustices that have been committed…"

"Dream on, Bubba," cried out Robin Hood.

"Hear me out, please. I have a concrete proposal for you."

"Get on with it, man."

"He's revving up."

"I propose, therefore, that all of us write to our representatives in congress, and ask that a Prison Corps be created. Let me repeat, Prison Corps, after Peace Corps. And what would this body do? They would hear our stories, write them down and present them to the world. This Prison Corps would remind our more fortunate brothers and sisters of the old saying that the victors write the history, and that in the writing of it we have been forgotten while society at large has excused itself… because, ladies and gentlemen, I assure you… we were not born to fail…"

"Look up the word naïveté, Butterfly," cried out a man from Section C.

"Check out delusion," said another from the corner section below.

"… Now, we do have our share of responsibility for our actions and we must stand up and acknowledge it… and what that means is that we must speak the complete truth, no matter how much it hurts, and I mean everything, ladies and gentlemen…"

"Thank you," said Chloe in appreciation of being called a lady.

"… And if we do so, if we speak the complete truth, it will become plain to our more fortunate brothers and sisters that forces beyond our control played a strong role in the shaping of us, and though our own actions got us here there should be no reason whatsoever why we should be deprived of full rehabilitation and cultural enrichment. Ladies and gentlemen, I ask you and the world, why shouldn't prisons be universities?"

They all listened attentively as the mood seemed to change.

From their cell, both Legrand and Joey smiled in agreement.

"Why shouldn't prisons be vocational and technical centers?"

Some inmates clapped in approval.

"Why shouldn't there be more opportunities for intimacy with our spouses?"

"So we wouldn't be fucking each other!" said Bazooka.

"I don't mind," put in Chloe.

"Not just that, but intimacy humanizes a man," continued Butterfly, "and god knows we need a good dose of that."

"And who would make up this Prison Corps?" asked Culebra, Leroy's neighbor.

"Men and women fresh out of college, idealistic folks who want to change the world. Give us just one year of your lives, just one year!"

"I like it," cried out Leroy.

"Think of it… if our idealistic youth is attracted to the idea of helping the poor and disadvantaged in other lands, why not here in your own country?"

Scattered clapping.

"Thank you, Butterfly," said Chloe.

"Maybe they could even help us with our legal work? Some of us can't read,"
chimed in Horseshoe.

"That, too," returned Butterfly. "So, ladies and gentlemen, are we going to do this?
Are we going to write to our representatives in congress to ask that a Prison Corps be formed?"

No one said a word for an instant, but then Legrand jumped in and cried out, "It's a terrific idea. And I thank you, Butterfly, for taking the time and effort to think of the community. Because if we thought of ourselves as a community, a community of people with much disadvantage in common, we wouldn't be fighting with each other as we do. We would be helping each other instead. Think of it, folks, and remember the old saying, 'divide and conquer'. The more we fight against each other, the more we open ourselves to mistreatment. There's no reason why we should be separated by racial lines."   Legrand had often spoken in such terms but his calls to action had always been ignored. So he was genuinely pleased to hear Butterfly's proposal.

"I rest my case," said Butterfly, finally. "Good night everybody."

At about 10:45 pm, as Legrand stood by his window, two officers he seldom saw came in to relieve third watch. Joey had fallen asleep and was snoring away. Legrand was not the only one who routinely kept an eye on the comings and goings of the officers for this shift change; Butterfly did too.

Legrand sat back down and began to write a letter to an old cellmate that had gone home. 'Dear Lenny…' he began. He thought for a moment, got lost in reminiscence, then a smile came slowly to him. "I hope this finds you well in the company of your bride to be. Thanks for the package. I really appreciate it. You know you don't have to send me anything, just hearing from you and keeping our connection is what matters the most…" Legrand wrote well but took his time and it wasn't until a quarter to one when he finished the three-page letter. Writing it had brought back a stream of memories he enjoyed and valued greatly. He folded the letter and put it in an envelope. He didn't seal it: all correspondence had to be checked before it went out or came in. He placed the envelope on the shelf across, stepped over to the toilet, took a leak and flushed. He turned off the lights and looked outside again. The grille to the rotunda was open. He glanced over at Butterfly's cell. The big guy was still up.

Up in the tower, Eddie Grisholt was not visible. He might have been standing by the window to the yard or in the bathroom.

Down below, the day room's lights had been dimmed.

Standing there, watching, Legrand reflected that he had learnt to be patient: if only he had been so when he was 19 years old. He heard the rhythm of his breathing. What a price to pay for a moment of intemperance. He thought about it every day.

A strange sensation gripped his chest. It felt like a brief flip and he became aware of his heart's quickening. Something had happened. Never had he felt that before. He held up his wrist and felt his pulse; Gardner had taught him how to do it. He normally had a slow pulse, from all the exercising, but now he was at rest and the pulse felt fast and irregular. It took a moment before it settled down. What was that? He would put in a slip to see medical.

He remained by the door a while longer, saw the two floor officers exit the building and was about to call it a night when he heard a cell door being racked open. It was cell 240. Leroy stepped out, walked towards the section B staircase and climbed down the stairs. Legrand's cell was right under the staircase. Leroy crossed to the grille and entered the rotunda, disappearing from Legrand's sight.

At the end of the rotunda, by the door to the stairwell to the tower, stood Eddie Grisholt. Leroy walked right up to the officer. There were no greetings.

Grisholt spoke first, the tone hushed. "Want some more?"

"Depends."

Grisholt reached down and pulled out a sack from just inside the door to the stairwell. He left it at his feet. "There's two cartons of cigarettes and some weed. Super potent THC. Grown in the U.S.A. Humboldt County, California. Continued use guaranteed to lower your IQ."

"That's funny." Leroy noticed Grisholt wearing gloves.

"Interested?"

"What do you want?"

"Stall on Legrand."

Leroy frowned. "What's it to you?"

"He's acting like he's the king of Bravo Three."

Leroy smiled. "He's not acting, he *is* the king. You feeling intimidated?"

Grisholt let it slide. "You want the job or not?"

"I don't know. Have to think about it."

"I wouldn't dwell on it. That's not your strong point."

"Fuck you, Grisholt."

Grisholt smiled. "It would make you look good if you can pull it off."

"You don't think I can pull it off?"

"You didn't do so well with Wilson."

"I had an off day."

"I heard Legrand was there, so maybe he took you off your game."

Leroy grinned. "You're in rare form today. Okay... but I'll need help, especially now that Legrand's got Wilson with him. I'll see if Hyena's willing." Leroy motioned to the sack at Grisholt's feet and added, "I'll need more than the usual... plus the element of surprise."

"Got you. How much?"

"Crystal. Two hundred grams."

"What?"

"You heard me."

"What the hell's gotten into you?"

"I'm working on my self-esteem with Dr Gardner."

Grisholt chuckled. "What's he telling you?"

"That I'm a human being."

"Of course. What a nice gig those guys have."

"What, you don't think I am?"

"You're sensitive today. Would I be coming to you if I didn't think you were the best?"

Grisholt knew how to lather him up, thought Leroy.

Grisholt quickly turned toward the door behind. He looked through the window but there was no one there.

"Deal?" said Leroy.

Grisholt shook his head. "Too much."

"Then I'm not interested."

Grisholt grimaced. "I'll think about it."

The two men had been standing, toe to toe, eyes fastened on each other.

"Go on back to your cell. This meeting never took place."

"You're giving me the smokes and the weed?"

Grisholt handed over the bag at his feet. "A token of my appreciation."

"Nice touch, the gloves," said Leroy.

"Never too careful."

"Same here. Next time I'll wear a wire," said Leroy, smiling, in half jest.

"You're a funny man."

"You bring out the best in me." Leroy turned and headed back into the day room.

Legrand saw Leroy emerge from the rotunda, sack in hand, and a moment later the grille closed behind him.

Leroy went back into his cell thinking about the offer he'd been made. He unbundled the weed, rolled up a joint, lit it up and took a long drag. It smelled great.

Why did Grisholt want to put the hurt on Legrand? That he knew, Grisholt had never had a run in with Legrand, not because of Grisholt, but because Legrand was too smart to take the bait. So why now? Leroy wasn't afraid of tangling with Legrand or Wilson, but they both packed a punch, so if he agreed, the attack would have to happen in the middle of the night, when they were both asleep.

Leroy exhaled the weed slowly. The offer was risky but tempting. The thought of Gardner came to mind. He felt better from letting it all out and he wouldn't mind seeing the doc again for a friendly chat, but nothing was going to change. Prison was not going to change. He was not going to change. And he smoked the rest of the joint.

11

Poncho Sterling had no dreams whatsoever of a career in acting but he had a buddy from high school that was making his way in the casting business in Los Angeles and who had encouraged him to go out on some commercial calls. What did he have to lose? So about twice a month, Ernie, from the "Miracles Happen" casting agency, would ring him with an audition notice. Poncho had not been initially keen on the idea since it shortened the time he could spend with his parents who lived down in Westchester, but there had been some good experiences along the way and he kept taking the calls.

Today the audition took place in a studio near Manhattan Beach. The traffic from Lancaster had been difficult all the way in and it didn't get any better down the 405, but listening to Aretha Franklin's sultry voice had soothed his nerves. Ernie had emailed him the side. "This is an easy one – he had said – right up your alley." Indeed, he would be playing a prison guard who had only two words to say, "Death Row." Nothing else. It ought to be a slam-dunk.

He got off the 405 at the Rosecrans exit and traveled west for a short distance, past gleaming office towers. It was 10:05 and the audition was at 10:30. He had been on the road since 7:30. He went over the railroad tracks and just past, to his left, was the entrance to Paradise Studios. The compound itself was recessed from the road and Poncho didn't remember noticing it before, even though he knew the area. He drove down the winding lane right up to the guard gate. "Oh, shit!" he muttered to himself. Seeing the security officer inspecting the trunk of the vehicle in front, Poncho remembered that he had a shotgun in his trunk. It was a present for his mom.

The gate bar pulled up, the car ahead went in and Poncho drove forward.

"G'morning. I've got a shotgun in my trunk. I forgot it was there."

The security officer, pistol at his side, regarded him with a blank stare. "What business brings you here?"

"I have an audition at 10:30. Miracles Happen," said Poncho with a grin.

The Security officer didn't see the humor, glanced at the list on his clipboard, asked for Poncho's name, his driver's license and instructed him to open the trunk. He took the shotgun out and brought it in to the guardhouse. "We'll keep it here until you come out. Been here before?"

"I have not."

The officer handed him a sketch of the facility and put an X where he should go. "Take a left here and then a right. Park only in areas designated for visitors."

"Thanks."

The bar jerked up and Poncho drove through.

There were three people in the waiting room. Two were women, the other a tall man in his forties. He glanced at them to see what he was up against but they all had their faces buried in their scripts. Were any of them actual prison guards? He doubted it, which made him feel more hopeful.

He signed in on the laptop and took a seat.

The waiting area was a swanky room with shiny marble floors, diffused lighting and two thick piled, russet colored area rugs. A woman sitting a distance across glanced at him, flashed her large sultry eyes, then returned to her script. She wore a black, snazzy outfit and had a set of legs to kill for. It would be very nice to have her for a scene partner, thought Poncho. The woman uncrossed and crossed her legs again. Poncho sighed.

Right above her, a large, numberless abstract clock hung high up on the wall. It read 10:30 exactly. He liked being on time.

A heavy, floor to ceiling paneled door opened and a stylishly dressed petite lady called for the next person. "Dexter?"

A man stood up and crossed to the door. Dexter? There had been a Dexter when he had worked in North Kern for a stint, and that looked like him but he wasn't sure. The man had been a passing acquaintance - about three years before. He looked different.

Poncho stared at the woman across. She pulled down on the hem of her skirt.

Right after the audition, Poncho would be going over to see his parents and take them out to lunch. They were expecting him.

Ten minutes later, Dexter exited. Poncho was now certain Dexter was the same man. Poncho followed him into the midday glare and called out,

"Dexter!"

The man turned around.

"North Kern?"

"Sure was," replied Dexter. "Oh, hey, I remember you. I didn't see you come in." They shook hands. "I guess I was concentrating on the character."

"You get it?" said Poncho.

"Well, you know, it'll be a few days before they decide…"

"I mean, did you get the character?"

"Oh, sure. I'm taking some acting classes."

"Does it help?"

"I think so. It's a process."

"Where you working now?"

"Property management."

"No kidding? Left the joint?"

"Did my time," said Dexter, "Got married to this gal whose father is in real estate, so I go around and fix up the properties, do some maintenance. I set my own schedule. It gives me time to do my auditions."

"Sweet. You serious about this?"

"Oh, most definitely. I've already done a commercial and a couple of indies."

"Couple of indies?"

Dexter mentioned the names but Poncho had not heard of them. Still, Poncho acknowledged feeling a bit envious of the man's nice arrangement.

"Say, maybe one day I'll see you on the big screen?" said Poncho.

"Hope so. Got to run. Good to see, bud. See you around."

They shook hands and parted.

As he returned to his seat Poncho remembered that, as a child, he had had a small role in a musical where he had tap danced and sang with a group of other kids and even had a line to say. It had been a short run - the show hadn't gathered momentum - but it had been a lot of fun and he had got paid. So he was not exactly a stranger to the world of entertainment.

Fifteen minutes later they called his name. He strolled in with confidence and crossed to the seat in the center of the room. Facing him, from behind a long, stylish, glass and metal table, sat the lady who had called him in and a thin man with a pinched face, tousled brown hair and intimations of a goatee. They both had sleek microphones in front, so they wouldn't strain their delicate voices, thought Poncho, or else the acoustics were lousy.

They nodded politely at him. The young man leaned into the mike, "Whenever you're ready."

Poncho stared back at him and blurted out, "Death Row."

The young man said nothing for a moment, then, covering the mike with one hand, consulted with the lady in a whisper.

He looked back at Poncho, "Let's try again. If you could make it less dramatic, please."

Poncho was puzzled. He hadn't been trying to be dramatic at all, that was just normal for him. He looked down at the floor, thought of the shotgun he had just purchased, breathed in deeply, remembered a meditation class he had once taken, and softly exhaled as he let out the words, "Death row." The words flowed out like a mountain creek washing over a smooth bed of pebbled stones.

Both the man and the woman nodded. "Very nice." They covered their mikes again and whispered some more. "Now imagine speaking to an inmate who has spent 30 years in prison and is facing execution."

Poncho tugged impatiently at the collar of his shirt, then leveled a knowing look at the young man. "I got it," he said confidently.

"Take your time," replied the young man. "No need to rush."

"I got it," rejoined Poncho, "I've worked in San Quentin, I know the drill."

The young man paused for a moment. He asked the young lady for Poncho's list of credits. "I'm so sorry. I hadn't finished reading your credits."

Poncho bowed his head for a moment, then, with a cocky attitude said, "Death Row."

The man at the desk smiled and thanked him for coming out.

Poncho got back the shotgun on his way out and went over to see his parents. His father, a tall, white haired African American, greeted him with much affection. "Hey, man, you're a sight for sore eyes," and he gave him a hard squeeze for an embrace.

"Muriel!" he called over his shoulder, "Poncho's here!"

"I'm coming," cried Muriel in her frail voice.

And a moment later she was hobbling in holding on to a four-legged walker set on wheels. Her shoulders sloped down from her neck and her features were soft and kind. She gave Poncho the warmest of smiles and stretched out her arms for him to embrace her. He did and he kissed her on the cheek. Her eyes had turned rheumy with age but they were filled with excitement at the sight of Poncho, so much so that her lips broke into a quiver. Her skin sagged on her cheeks and under her chin but you could tell she had been a beautiful woman. She was African American also. Poncho was white. But Kyle and Muriel were his parents all right. He'd never known any other. They had taken custody of him when Social Services had required temporary lodgings right after he was born and he just stayed on. When he was 3 years old they officially adopted him.

Poncho knew little about his biological mother and nothing at all about his dad. In the birth certificate they had been listed as Jane and John Doe. She had been taking her last gasps when she arrived at the emergency room in LA County, rolling in on a gurney. A quick thinking nurse felt her tummy and cried out that there might be a baby inside. The surgeon skillfully cut into the abdomen and pulled him out. The bullet that had killed his mom had struck the aorta and barely missed him, but the nurse who saw him come into the world would become his mother.

"What am I going to do with this shotgun?" Muriel said to Poncho.

"Keep it in the closet. It's the simplest thing to use," replied Poncho. "I'll teach you. When dad's out on his trips and you're all by yourself, it'll give you a little protection."

"We have nice neighbors, don't we Kyle?"

"We do, Muriel, but he's right, it doesn't hurt to learn how to use one."

"And my sisters and nephews can come if I need anything," continued Muriel, not persuaded.

Poncho felt a little guilty that he was not living in Los Angeles to be closer to them. Kyle and Muriel had not had children of their own and, except for her relatives who lived in not too far off Carson, he was their only close relation. Poncho had wanted to come back to Los Angeles but there were no prisons in the city, only jails, and he had tried them all. For a while he had worked in Chino but the commute was about the same, and then other officers with greater seniority had bumped him. He had a college degree and could be doing other things, he often reminded himself, but something about working with prisoners would not let him go. Was he trying to help inmates find their way… or was he still looking for the murderer of his mom.

12

"We have been mistaken not to give the victim a key role in the rehabilitation process," announced Dr Gardner as he stepped into the office of Dr Lloyd King. It was a spare room with a couple of cluttered work stations, bare walls except for a calendar, and an imitation wood bookshelf with a scattering of manuals set against the wall. A coffee brewer stood on top.

Sally Roundtree, also a psychiatrist, had come in a moment before and taken a seat. Usually, after the day's work, they gathered for a quick, generally amiable chat, in what had been labeled the PM huddle.

Byron Gardner, 55, prematurely gray, a bit plump, with a youthful disposition, had knocked around in the prison system for a while. He liked what he did but now and then had thoughts of tossing the whole thing off and getting a job as a doctor on a cruise ship, where he imagined himself traveling the world, handing out pills for sea sickness, listening to beautiful unhappy women share their tales of woe and applying sunscreen lotion to their mounds and valleys. Surely such job existed.

"Say, Byron, you sound like you're ready to share one of your ideas," said King with a hint of mischief as he sat at his desk.

Gardner took the chair by the door, opposite his colleagues. "Do we prepare the victim to face his aggressor?"

"We don't," said Roundtree.

"Do we prepare the inmate to face his victim?"

"Not either," replied King.

"The closer you are to the inflicting of the injury the more likely the victim will be fuming with rage," said Gardner, "and the greater chance it will affect the judge and his sentence."

"So?"

"Why not allow for those emotions to settle?"

King and Roundtree glanced at each other.

"Don't the judges have the capacity to sort things out?" asked King.

"You really think they do?"

"Based on what we see around here, some do, and some don't," said Roundtree, "and when they don't the consequences are horrific."

"I've seen it, too," said King.

"Listen to this," said Gardner, sitting up in his chair and pressing his hands together. "A few days ago, I saw a 20 year old man who was tried as an adult at age 15 for shooting another gang member in the shoulder. With a gun enhancement and some other ridiculous stipulation, he was slapped with a 40 year to life sentence. Does it seem to you that a balanced man, judge or parent, would make that call?"

"They have a set of rules to go by," answered King, feebly.

"A 40 year to life sentence, Lloyd, think about it… 40 years. If the judge's following guidelines, like you say, then someone else is responsible for this kind of madness. Is it the legislators? Is it the public thirsting for vengeance? Someone did not process the emotions, someone over reacted and came up with these vindictive rules deprived of any common sense."

Sally Roundtree shook her head slowly. "If he had been a child of one of us, every shred of mitigating circumstance would have been summoned in the child's defense and the outcome would have been entirely different."

"Thank you, Sally," said Gardner.

"You were going somewhere with that," put in King.

"Sentencing ought to be done in phases, to allow for an interaction between victim and aggressor: an initial phase following the injury, and then a second phase, taking place *after* the victim has dealt with the rage of having been aggressed, and the guilty party has had time to show that he has evolved as a human being."

There was quiet for a moment.

"Closure would be delayed," began Roundtree.

"Closure at the expense of true justice deserves to be delayed," said Gardner. "In the trial of that adolescent, society was not called to the stand, and it ought to be, every time. How simple to just say 'he knew right from wrong,' without weighing the burden of dysfunction, the devastating effects of growing up without direction, without affection, and how it warps the mind."

King leaned forward. "Let's take one thing at a time. This parting of the sentence into two different phases, would allow mental health to play a key role, both with the offender and the victim. I get that. But do you think the public is ready for it? Because it would certainly expand our role enormously."

"The victim would have a huge say in the outcome of the second phase," remarked Roundtree.

"Bring the parties together, after proper preparation," said Gardner, "and attempt to facilitate the resolution of the emotional and physical damage caused."

"I see problems with the idea," said King, sitting back in his chair. "What?"

"Not every victim would want to be part of it."

"They would prefer a quick end," put in Roundtree.

"And think of this," continued King, "the victim would be vulnerable to pressures and   intimidation from the relatives of the offender."

"That could be an issue," granted Gardner.

"And then there's the matter of costs."

Gardner slid up to the edge of his seat. "If the inmate knows that his sentence could be modified by the victim's input during that second phase, he would have a powerful incentive to examine and improve his behavior. When he's finally ready to sit down with the victim, after working with mental health and not before, he would get to see, up close, the pain he's inflicted and the consequences of his actions. The victim, on the other hand, gets to understand his aggressor, his motivations, the changes he's undergone, if any, and then make a recommendation - for or against a reduction of the sentence."

"The advantages may well outweigh the disadvantages," said Roundtree, "cost being a factor."

"We do it in steps. Start a pilot program somewhere… work out the glitches," returned Gardner, undaunted. "Call it the Two Step Project."

"I don't think it'll go down well in Texas," began King with mischievous skepticism. "Look, I agree that the victim has been sorely absent in the process of administering balanced justice, but you may be asking too much of the victim."

"Much would depend on the victim's ability to process the trauma," said Roundtree.

"Mental health would have to be involved in assisting that person from the start," said Gardner. "The voice of mental health needs to get louder and louder, and we need to make the commitment to back it up. We have not done so."

"It's an uphill battle," said Roundtree. "I just saw a man this afternoon who's been in prison 9 years, with 2 left, but six months ago was caught with a stash of drugs. He was found guilty of possession with intent to distribute. The DA picked up the case and his public defendant just informed him that, with enhancements and other rules, he might get an additional 10 years. He acknowledges a history of depression and anxiety but never had a full encounter with mental health."

They said nothing for a moment.

"He could always take a plea and get only 5," said Roundtree, sarcastically.

"It's surreal," said Gardner.

King glanced up at the clock. "Time for us to go."

And they began to pack their things.

"To be continued," said Roundtree.

On his long ride home, Gardner thought of the ways that inmates could atone for their crimes, and a letter Legrand had sent to the governor came to mind. He had a copy of it. When he got back the next day, he emailed it to his colleagues.

"Dear Lloyd and Sally: here is a letter inmate Legrand wrote to the governor. Nothing came of it but I liked the idea.
Byron"

7/9/2012
Governor
Sacramento, California.

Sir:

I have an idea that may be helpful in crime prevention.

I am serving time in the LA County State Prison in Lancaster. I have been incarcerated 31 years.

During my stay I have encountered many inmates who, like me, have developed insight into the motivation that underlies criminal behavior. Maybe we could use our knowledge to keep young men from coming to prison.

The idea is this: creating a phone service whereby any person with criminal mischief in mind, could call and talk to one of us about his intentions. We would then assist the person in understanding his motivation and help him see the consequences of such an action. Even what appears to be an impulsive act, has needed time to hatch. Of course, we would have to be monitored by mental health and prison personnel to ensure quality of feedback.

"Crime on your mind? Please call 1800 xxx-xxxx for help in prevention. A Public Service of the California Department of Corrections and Rehabilitation."

The identity of the caller would need to be protected, of course, and I have no idea how this could be done or if it's even possible. But with IT advances it might be.

Funding for a program of this nature would be raised in the private sector. This may not be an obstacle, as there is no shortage of donors and institutions eager to be involved in social enterprises.

One of the saddest things in my life, aside from the pain and hurt I have caused and for which I am still atoning, is to see young men condemned to serve horribly long sentences for errors of judgment that contact with someone with maturity could have prevented. And it keeps happening all the time.

Thank you for the attention and good luck in your future endeavors,

LB Legrand
Inmate
Los Angeles County State Prison
Lancaster, California

13

*I*t was late afternoon in Bravo Three. At one end of the day room, a recreational therapist played dominoes with three inmates while, next to them, another read the newspaper.
    In separate adjacent tables, a psychologist and a social worker were busy meeting with their respective patients.
    Out on the other side of the room, a porter was wiping clean the steel tables.
    Nearby, the unit barber, clad in a white smock, worked his set of clippers to style the hair of one customer as another waited his turn.
    High above, on the wall, a TV set blared out a gruesome tale of adultery in a reality show.
    Legrand walked in and went straight to his cell. He had gone out very early in the morning to an outside medical facility.
    "How'd it go?" asked Joey, perkily, sitting up in his bunk.
    "Everything's all right."
    "Good to hear it."
    Feeling tired, Legrand went straight to his bunk. At 6 ft 5, being longer than the bunk, he had to pull up so he could fit. He closed his eyes and breathed deeply. His heart was aging, he reflected. He was 50

years old and had spent the last 31 in prison, barred from intercourse with the world. He thought of his mother, his father, the daughter he had never seen. Where would she be? Was she okay? It hurt him deeply that he had not been there for her, that she had had to find her way in the world without him. Oh, how it rankled him. He envied those men who got visits from their kids and got a chance to put their arms around them. And now this heart problem. Would he ever see her? He didn't want to dwell on it but since Joey had been with him he had been thinking about family more often.

The outside specialist he had seen, a lady, had examined him and confirmed that he had developed atrial fibrillation, an irregular beat that could occur for a variety of reasons. He had been started on meds in the prison but the rhythm was not yet back to normal. Some other things might have to be done. "Anything happening?" he asked.

"Nope," returned Joey, "Chewed the fat with Paytrell for a while. He's getting better."

"He should be, with all the time I've been spending with him."

"He thinks the world of you."

"Sometimes it works," said Legrand, turning on his side and closing his eyes. He had begun to drift off when Joey, eager for some gab, dropped down from his bunk and sat on the floor opposite him.

"What you do, today?" asked Legrand, lazily coming back to life.

"I'm sorry, you need your rest. I'll let you be."

"No, it's fine, really. If I sleep now I'll have trouble tonight."

Joey rubbed his arms and shoulders.

"You worked out?"

"Some. Just pushups. Feels a little tight." Joey was still puzzled that Legrand, having become such a model of restraint, courage and good judgment, would not be able to return to the outside world. He thought about what to ask to get a conversation going and then settled on a subject. "You think you deserve your sentence?"

"Yes. I do," replied Legrand without hesitation. "I took two lives, Joey. Two young lives. Ripped them from this world. So I deserve what I got. Life without parole. The way I see it, I took their lives and their children's lives… and their grandchildren's too. A willful act of mine, born out of a moment of emotional recklessness, severed an entire line of human development… caused untold grief to their parents and relatives…. all because I refused to suffer."

"Refused to suffer?"

"That's right."

The word had an odd ring to Joey. It reminded him of very sick people in a hospital, of folks with terminal illnesses, people with disabilities, men and women with afflictions that could not change. He, Joey, had a burden to bear, indeed, and had put up with a lot of grief, but he had not thought of it as suffering. Maybe it was his youth. "Is that what we're supposed to do here?"

"Suffer and heal," said Legrand.

The words gave Joey pause. "How have you suffered?"

"I've suffered and still do because I am not free."

Joey thought on this: he had a date to leave prison; Legrand did not.

"I was upset and had a few drinks," continued Legrand, "Say that I had decided to hit the fellows I ran into, just to get my misery off my chest. Fine. But did I have to beat them into a pulp? Once I got started I couldn't stop. I've asked myself, why didn't I?"

Legrand brought together his hands and rested his head on them. "What is remarkable is that there wasn't anything mysterious about my motivation. I couldn't stop because I was beating my father and my mother and my girlfriend, too. I was angry at everybody because I couldn't go to college and felt put upon. I would have been the first in the family. It seems so simple. And the thing is it took me years to understand it. Sure, my dad had bad genes and he drank and had a lousy temper and like the saying goes, the sins of the fathers are visited upon the sons, but it didn't help one bit to use it as an excuse. I began to heal only when I accepted the fact that it was my fault and no one else's. I could've slapped those guys; shoved them, made fun of them, humiliated them, called them names, scared them, you name it. But I didn't have to kill them."

"But, you didn't set out to kill them, from what you told me," said Joey.

"I didn't know my strength. Or did but ignored it. And that's my responsibility."

Joey thought about this. He, too, had ignored his responsibility.

"You asked me about suffering," resumed Legrand. "I suffer because I've had to tolerate the will of other men being imposed upon me. Lesser men who treat me like a child." Legrand paused for an instant. "All because I betrayed the love of my mother who had worked so hard to bring me up. All that work wasted. She died of sadness, you know... even though the doctors said her diabetes had gone out of control. But I knew what the real reason was."

Legrand adjusted the hands under his head. "I suffer, he continued, "because I denied myself the chance to blossom as a man, the chance to love a woman... be loved by her... be in her embrace... hold a child in my arms... guide her. And so I suffer, my friend..." – Joey took notice that this was the first time Legrand had referred to him as such – "...and am left only to imagine and accept."

Joey wondered how long it would take for him to accept his own offense. He knew he couldn't just turn a switch on, that it would take time, but he had a date to get out. He hadn't killed anybody. And that thought alone brought him comfort.

"And your victims...?"

Legrand turned to level his eyes at Joey. "They visit."

"Visit?" asked Joey in surprise.

Legrand smiled. "They come and talk with me. I extended them an open invitation a long time ago. At first I'd feel tortured by their faces. They would come and they would stare at me and we would relive the crime. I would hear every scream they gave, feel every punch I landed, the way the bone cracked on impact... I hit one on the head, just above his ear and cracked the skull. I have big hands." He pulled out his arm and opened his hand in front of him. Joey looked at it. It was huge indeed. Leblanc rubbed the stubble on his face, the eyes distant. "But then, one day... they started to talk. First it was Deshun... then it was Samuel."

Joey felt he was being taken on a journey deep into a man's mind and he was trying to catch every detail. He thought of a thousand questions to ask before settling on one... "Did you...?" he started but then pulled back, uncertain of the timing. But Legrand had anticipated him. "Ask for forgiveness?"

Joey nodded.

"I don't think it's up to me to ask. I leave it up to Deshun and Samuel. One day, I think they will. I'm hopeful. Fact is, the other day I thought I saw Samuel smiling. I wasn't sure. The way I look at it, I have to earn their forgiveness. If they haven't given it to me, it must be I haven't done enough."

Joey wanted to ask, what was it that had to be done and would be enough, but again he held back. The mood was not right.

"Did I ever tell you the story of Lenny," started Legrand again, his mood brightening a tad.

On the wall across their bunks were four photos of a couple. Above the photos Legrand had written, "Dream a little." It had made Joey curious from the start but never asked.

"Lenny and I shared a cell for 12 years. He's been free as a bird now for the last two. The woman with him is his fiancée. They look happy, don't they?"

"They do."

The background of some of the photos seemed from another country but Joey could not tell which.

"I like to dream a little, and it sure puts spice in my life," said Legrand. "For someone like me, pretending is important… pretending with a grain of truth."

"I could use some of that," said Joey, his mood livening also. He shifted his position to get more comfortable.

"I met Lenny in Old Folsom. We just hit it off. He was serving a sentence for bank robbery. They had pulled off the heist – three guys – and were lying low till the dust settled. Not one of them had been caught. They had worn masks and gloves and hadn't left a trace behind. Lenny kept going to his night shift at a hospital in Santa Monica -where he was an X ray technician - and didn't do anything different. When they parted, after splitting the loot, they said goodbye as they had agreed beforehand and did not meet again. And it all went well for almost two years. The only indulgence Lenny had allowed himself was to take a trip each year to Australia and New Zealand, so he could slowly take his share out of the country. He had been very disciplined about it. Then one of the other guys had a falling out with his girlfriend."

"Oh, no," said Joey.

"He kicked her out. He said she had cheated on him. That's what he told the police. Maybe she was just tired of waiting and wanted her cut, who knows, but the thing was he had broken the rules and told her who his partners were."

"What?" said Joey in astonishment.

"The cops showed up at their doors one night and that was the end. There was a reward for information leading to their capture. She collected."

"How much?"

"I don't know."

"What was Lenny's share?"

"All he told me was, 'enough to retire'."

"Did he get it all out?"

"No. He still had some of it and he handed it over. They gave him 25 years."

"Where is he now?"

"In France."

"Wow. You're French."

"Both my parents and grandparents."

"How'd he end up going there?"

"Lenny didn't like to read much but I do. So I'd send out for books about France. And I'd mix up some facts with a good bit of fiction and I'd tell him the stories. He was a great audience. He'd get excited and laugh his head off and we would have a great time together. Imagine my surprise when, on the eve of his release, he tells me, 'LB, I'm going to France. You've filled me with so many stories that I have to go there.' I was so excited for him. I didn't hear back for a good while and then, about a year later, I get a letter with a photo of him and this great looking woman beside him. They were both standing in front of a little building with a sign that said, 'Hotel Fleur de Lyon.'"

"He was using the money he'd stashed to travel around the world?" said Joey.

"Wait. He'd been staying at this hotel and was getting ready to move on when something happened that changed his life. The lady in the picture was working the desk. She was separated from her husband because he was beating up on her when he got drunk. She had put a restraining order on him but he wasn't letting that stop him. Then, this one day, when Lenny is sitting in the lobby glancing at a local paper, the husband walks in and starts smacking the woman. Lenny jumps out his chair, grabs the guy and throws him out. The lady is very thankful, treats him to a drink. She would've wanted to tell her story but they just looked at each other; she didn't speak much English, he didn't speak much French. Then the guy comes back, this time with a gun. He sees Lenny and comes at him. Lenny takes the gun away from him and gives him a whooping. The lady documents all of this. She calls the police and the guy ends up with a jail term. She then tells Lenny he can stay there for a month, free of charge. She's the owner of the hotel."

"Unbelievable!" cried Joey, excitedly.

"And lo and behold if they don't get into a relationship and voila! he is now her fiancé. She is fixing his papers and he's got a hotel to run."

Both men laugh uproariously.

"Amazing, truly amazing," said Joey.

"Who would've imagined? And it all started with me telling these made-up stories. So Lenny writes me back that the hotel is doing well and he can use a handyman... and Lyon is not far from Paris. That's where my grandfather came from, you know. He was Parisian. He fell in love with my grandma, Lilly Tambin, and followed her back to Guadeloupe."

Joey could tell that Leblanc was proud of having played a role in Lenny's life. And now he wondered whether this man, who appeared so at peace with himself, even though he was going to die in prison, would end up playing a role in his life also.

"Now and then I fancy myself walking down the Champs Elysees, near the Arc de Triomphe," began again Legand. "Down below you can see the Place de la Concorde and to your left are the Jardins des Tuileries, and then there's the Louvre, and the Grand Palais, to the right. And right across runs the river Seine... and you can walk on the Pont des Arts..." His voice had begun to trail off as he drifted into his dream life. "...And all kinds of people from all over the world go there. And they sit down and have a drink and they eat... and they talk about what they're going to do with their lives..."

"That's a great story, LB. Thanks for sharing," said Joey, feeling a profound sadness for Legrand, but hiding it from him.

Legrand was somewhere else, though. He had transported himself to Paris and saw himself walking along the Seine, looking at the splendid scenery, watching the beautiful girls go by, the boats sailing up and down the river, glittering with lights and filled with people having a good time... and with his hands pillowing his head... he began to fall asleep... smilingly.

14

At around 1 am, a call came in to the control room.

"What's up?"

There was the unmistakable voice again.

"Doing good," replied Grisholt. "What's up with you? Having trouble sleeping?"

"I catch a couple of hours here and there."

"Like the inmates," said Grisholt, jokingly.

"It rubs off on you, doesn't it?"

"Tell me about it."

"Anybody there with you?"

"No. Coast is clear."

"Anything to report?"

Grisholt sat down at his desk and lowered his voice. "You know how, working graveyard, I hadn't had a chance to see him, well, today I was covering third shift for a buddy of mine and he came out to evening day room. Looks like a nice kid, chip of the old block."

"He's not. And you've just insulted me, Eddie."

"Sorry, Buck."

"He took advantage of a 13 year old girl."

"That's bad. Were there any mitigating circumstances?"

"What's there to mitigate in a crime like that?"

Grisholt stayed quiet.

"But according to his mom there was nothing the kid could do wrong. The moment I'd try to put my two cents in she'd be all over me. It's like he was her little prize, keep daddy out of it no matter what."

Grisholt remembered Buck as strong and forceful, but here he was talking about having yielded to his wife in the raising of their son.

"Like I said before – continued Buck – he should get what's coming to him."

"You wouldn't want to protect him at all?"

"Hell, no."

"Isn't that kind of sick?" offered Grisholt, "not wanting to protect your own? I mean, he's blood?"

"There you go insulting me again."

"I'm sorry, Buck. It's just that I've never seen this happen before," Grisholt added hastily.

"All my life I've never stood in the way of these monsters getting their due. Why start now?"

"You've got a point," said Grisholt, feeling a pang of cowardice. But that was all right, he reasoned; he had an axe to grind. He was still undecided on whether to exact his revenge on Buck, albeit indirectly, but the possibilities were becoming more and more enticing. The greater confusion there was in Buck's heart and mind the more likely he could get away with it. He relished the thought.

"How would that make me look in front of all the other guards?" said Buck.

The word 'human' entered the periphery of Grisholt's mind and, for an instant, he thought of sharing it with his old friend. But no, the hell with him. In fact, screw Buck. His old mentor had let him down when it counted and apparently had forgotten the embarrassment he had had to endure, the veiled mockery from his fellow guards up in Corcoran, after being beat in a fair fight with an inmate. Sure, Buck had warned him not to do it, not to accept the inmate's challenge. Okay. But all he had wanted after the thumping he had got was a little help in getting revenge. A little help in giving the inmate something to remember; maybe a broken arm or a leg, something; a little deformity to take home with him as a souvenir. But Buck had opposed it, and Grisholt remembered it like it was yesterday. So, yeah, fuck Buck.

"You've got a point," said Grisholt again, this time without feeling cowardly at all, but enjoying the duplicity, reveling in the malevolence.

"Now, if he came right out and said he was my son, then I don't know what I'd do. Disown him, probably."

"You'd do that?"

"Yes, I believe I would… or just…." And Buck halted.

Or just what? thought Grisholt. Say it Buck! Have him killed? Yeah, snuff your own son. Do it! Oh, revenge could be so sweet. Buck Wilson having his son transferred down to Lancaster and to Bravo Three specifically, so that he could count on him, Eddie Grisholt, to do whatever needed to be done. Buck not suspecting that his old protégé might still be harboring enormous resentment against him. But maybe he did know and didn't care. Or maybe Buck was just stupid. Oh, cruel fate, thought Grisholt as he entertained the possibilities and felt the cold sweat fill his hands. He could get his revenge while giving Buck what he wanted. Lovely.

But take it easy, thought Eddie in the quiet of the pause. Relax. He had waited and now his patience was being rewarded. Of course, Buck might just be speaking in anger and might change his mind, but why not prepare the ground, giving Legrand a good scare to push him aside, making it easier for others to pounce on Joey and exact their jungle justice. One step at a time. Yes. Breathe.

"You know, Buck, right now your son is getting protection. I thought I'd tell you."

"What?".

"His cellie."

"What do you mean?"

"When he arrived he got housed with an old timer, a lifer, and this guy's looked up to by other inmates."

"What's his name?"

"Legrand, LB."

Buck laughed out loud. "Oh, the world is small, indeed. The old Frenchie coming back into my life."

"You know him?"

Buck snorted. "We go back a while, all right. He's got a couple of brain cells floating around in that mush of his he calls a brain and thinks he's better than us. Let me tell you about that coon ass. When he was up in Old Folsom he got his hands on a book by Aristotle and before long he was going on about how the inmates ought to demand they be addressed as citizens, citizen this or citizen that. Imagine that?"

Grisholt chuckled at the thought but that would be Legrand.

"He was to be addressed as citizen Legrand and so should everybody else. And if they didn't they were not going to cooperate. Somehow, the jerk got one of the crazy psychiatrists to buy into that nonsense because it would raise their self esteem and a lame Associate Warden got to thinking it would be a good idea, too, revolutionary in fact, until Sacramento got wind of it and they put a quick stop to the bullshit. It wasn't long before they sent old Frenchie to the hole for fomenting insubordination – he got a year for it – on top of his life sentence, and the AW was demoted and sent off to run AD Seg (Administrative Segregation) in Indio or Calipatria, whichever is more unbearable in the summer."

"Wow," Grisholt had stood up from his seat and walked over to the front of the room to eyeball the unit.

"What're you doing about Legrand, had any problems with him?"

"No. But I don't like him, either. Sonofabitch's got a swagger about him that pisses me off."

"Walks around like he owns the joint. Yep, that's him."

"I've got an idea to make him eat some humble pie."

"Whatever you do, don't kill anybody. It's a hassle, all that paperwork."

Eddie Grisholt laughed and felt lighter. Not just yet, that's what you really meant, right, Buck? And then he said, "You're one of a kind, Buck." Yeah, why not, share a laugh with old fatso, grease him up a little before giving it to him nice and good.

"I try," said Buck, "Just remember to keep me posted on what he's saying. I don't want my name dragged into the mud."

"No, we don't want that to happen. Our reputation is very important." And Grisholt wanted to add, 'Do you not remember what you did to me?'

"But he's got to get what's coming to him," continued Buck, without a clue as to where Grisholt's mind was going.

"Gotcha. Say, Buck, what happened to the psychiatrist who was keen on the citizen idea?"

"He got a swift kick in the rump. He must still be sore, wherever he is. Kicked him right out of the CDCR, for life."

Grisholt gave a hearty laugh. "Well deserved. I'm for kicking them all out. Get back to the old days."

"Those days are gone, might as well face it. Good night, Eddie, it's been good talking to you."

"Good night, Buck."

Right after he hung up, Buck paused for a moment. He had called from the garage of his home in Pomona where he felt he had the privacy he needed to speak his mind. Janice was safely tucked away in her bedroom on the other side of the house. He was still mulling over what to do if Joey began to speak of him and reveal personal details, which he would eventually do, no doubt. But there was something else that had just entered his mind: for an instant, when he had heard Eddie Grisholt talk of Legrand sharing a cell with Joey, Buck had felt a glimmer of relief. And it both surprised and disturbed him. Was the protection Legrand was offering Joey getting Buck Wilson off the hook?

Buck went to bed but could not sleep. Next to him Janice slept soundly. No matter what her worries, the woman had a way of rearranging things in her mind so that her sleep went undisturbed. That was another thing he envied about her.

Buck kept thinking of the feeling of relief he had noticed when he heard that Legrand was protecting Joey. Did that one instance reveal something about him really wanting Joey spared? Was all his talk about being ruthless with Joey a front? Had he been running off his mouth because he could not think of himself capable of standing up to his peers?

He hadn't had a drink in a long time but now he was craving a shot of scotch. He had given up booze because it had become a compulsion but he had kept a bottle nicely hidden on a shelf in his daughter Margaret's closet so Janice couldn't find it. And Margaret was out to college plus she didn't call him often anyway, so the hell with her. He got up, went and got the bottle of liquor and served himself a full glass. He wanted the whole thing but he had to work the next day.

The great majority of child molesters in prison, knowing the odds of being seriously harmed or killed were high, opted to be housed in what was called SNY, Sensitive Needs Yard, where extra attention was given to shield them from the wrath of other inmates, though you still could get hit. Not Joey. He had chosen to tough it out in general population and face whatever came his way. It was the boldness of that move that stirred contradictory feelings in Buck. Sipping on his scotch he even admitted to feeling a glimmer of admiration for Joey: maybe he wasn't a sissy after all. But that was as far as he was willing to go. A pervert was a pervert.

Buck had learned of the two knifings Joey had survived up in Salinas and still hadn't moved a finger to do anything to prevent any further attacks. He had felt guilt over it – enough that he had gone into his garage and rocked himself back and forth until he made himself sick and thrown up – but he had managed to suppress it. What he did do, working at the highest level possible for him and in great confidence, was to put a word in requesting that Joey be transferred down to Lancaster so Janice would have an easier time with the visiting. That was it. And it had not been by design that Joey had landed in Eddie Grisholt's unit. Buck remembered their dealings all too well, but he was not about to ask for a change.

The news that Legrand was now Joey's cellie had come to muddle things up. Buck recalled that, not long before, Janice had brought up that a cellmate of Joey's, a lifer of French descent, was not letting him get away with his tall stories. Buck had thought about Legrand but dismissed it. What were the chances that that pairing would take place? But it had, and now it rankled him that he would have to owe an inmate for any kindness extended to his son. Legrand of all people, and Janice saying that Joey thought of him as a father. Fuck Joey! Fuck him and Legrand, both.

Buck was now certain that Joey had told Legrand all about him. Lies, of course. And he could only imagine old Frenchie gloating about sheltering and guiding his son, doing the job that he, Buck Wilson, had not been able to do or simply refused to do or had felt inept to handle or had just been muscled out of the way by Janice and her possessiveness.

Buck took another swig. Scotch gave him a nice, cuddly warmth. If Janice found out he had drunk that would be another fight right there. Screw her, too. He felt his shoulders tightening and took a deep breath. He said to himself that he had better calm down, though; surely there was a way out of the mess. And Janice had not been in a mood to fuck and she knew that was his big release and that bugged him, too. Why was she in a withholding mode? Oh yes, he knew why. He felt too emotionally reliant on her, and she knew it and she clobbered him with it. And he was going to do something about it, by golly he was; it was long overdue. He took another swig. Maybe now he'd had enough. The scotch was good, though, very good. The best he'd had, maybe. And to think he'd just bought it at the local store. Ah, yes. One more swig. He began to feel sleepy.

Back in Lancaster, Grisholt thought about his relationship with Buck: it had definitely gone through some phases. Before becoming a guard, Grisholt had been knocking around from job to job, not going anywhere fast, when a friend mentioned that prisons were hiring. The thought of becoming a guard had an appeal to it: the swagger and the telling people what to do was most attractive to him. He had always admired that about cops – in his mind he had already equated guard with cop - and on top of it, the girls loved the uniforms and he would be able to tell stories instead of feeling like he was a stick in the mud, which was how he felt most of the time. He liked the idea that the job would give him an air of instant authority, although the thought that there must be something more to it made him uneasy. But he needed a steady job, the pay was good and the creditors were calling. So he went for it.

He got a passing grade at the academy – barely - his instructors letting him slip through while holding their breath. But it wasn't until the night before his first day on duty that it dawned on him that he wasn't ready for the task. And it had nothing to do with the academy's training. He was ill prepared for the job because his character was not developed enough.

Buck had spotted the troubled soul right from the start and had taken him under his wing. Buck was fond of 'breaking in' new recruits. It was his way of getting back at a system that refused to promote him, plus it allowed him the chance to form a little group of admirers, whom he would instruct on the old but true ways of doing business. A guard was a guard; he barked out the orders and expected to be obeyed. He had no tolerance for the cuddly style that the mental health people were trying to bring in, all the bunk about understanding emotions. Burping and babysitting was what it was - stealing from the taxpayers - and he was one of them so they were stealing from him, too. If people out there really knew what was going on inside prisons they would be appalled. Inmates knew what they were doing when they committed their crimes and had to pay for it. As far as Buck was concerned, his job, his contribution to the community, was to rub the inmates' faces in the muck because that was the way you learned. So that was all that rehabilitation ought to be about. Simple. Straight forward. A no-brainer.

Furthermore, he knew darn well, because he had seen it with his own eyes, how inmates lied to mental health all the time, how they pretended to be suicidal just to get a ride out of the prison; lied to escape punishment and hide in comfy hospitals where nurses ran around all day wiggling their fannies so that inmates could jack off. Everybody got a thrill out of it, except the taxpayer. The inmates faked symptoms and tricked the naïve doctors into prescribing a host of pills, manipulated them by making stuff up that had never happened, just so the do-gooders would pamper them with sweet talk. So Buck considered it his civic duty to fight back because the whole thing was revolting. And though he knew that some of his fellow guards, particularly the young ones, thought of him as a dinosaur, Buck just laughed. 'Look – he would say – they keep coming back, don't they? That proves my point.'

It was about 1:30 am when Eddie Grisholt and Buck had hung up. Rivers and her fellow officer had motioned to him that they were going out on break and they exited the building through the side door. As soon as they did, the figure of Leroy in 240 had shown up at his cell door window. He had been waiting.

Grisholt took notice and began to rack open his cell door but then stopped. He didn't know why but he was now leery to proceed. Not having enough room to squeeze out, Leroy waved impatiently. Grisholt looked down at his briefcase; the stash was in there. He had got away with crap like that before so why was he now having a sense of foreboding? Was he thinking of his career? Did he really give a rat's ass if Joey got or didn't get the beating he was due? Did it matter that Legrand had an infuriating swagger? Did he give a shit about Buck? What was the problem, then? What was wrong?

His hand, resting on the control board, was shaking. His heart was racing. A lump had formed in his throat.

Then he saw the door to Leroy's cell resume opening. What? He gasped. He looked down at the board. He had pressed the button.

15

*I*t was 9:30 am when Joey exited his cell and crossed to the podium. Officer Bealey checked his I.D. and motioned to the tower to open the grille. Joey had expected a catcall to blast from the tiers broadcasting his crime but none came and he felt a ripple of relief. Not that he should lower his guard, he reminded himself.

The grille finished opening and he walked out.

The glare of the morning sun thrust hard upon him and he squinted as his step livened.

When he walked into Dr Jeffries' office he found her leafing through a notebook.

Without looking up she asked him to take a seat. She was all business, thought Joey, just like the first time. She calmly turned a page on the notebook. Joey felt more relaxed this time and he noticed her staid femininity, the gentleness of her features, the blonde dye in her hair fading off a little. His eyes went to her hands: he liked seeing women's hands, the comforting, soothing power they suggested. Her nail coloring was chipping. Interesting: she didn't seem to fuss over them, maybe too busy for such things. And he couldn't help but wonder, whether one day, as he matured into a more sophisticated person, he might have a chance at a woman like her.

"How are you?" she said as she raised her eyes to him. There was a faint smile on her thin lips.

"I'm fine. Are those notes about me?"

"No."

"Have you seen my file?"

"I have."

"So then you know everything?"

"Your file is only the surface. My task is to go underneath it all… to go into the world of your motivations… what shaped you… only then will I be able to help you."

"Maybe I don't need any help. I've already been incarcerated 3 years and…"

He let the sentence hang, unsure as to how to proceed, while Dr Jeffries calmly raised her hand to her face, thumb to her chin, the slender fingers fanning gently across her mouth.

"You were an amateur actor in a community play," she began, "and the young girl, Melanie, 13, developed a crush on you. There was one instance of oral copulation."

She was trying to pin him down, he thought, and he felt an urge to resist.

"That's not accurate," he blurted out, pushing back on the hind legs of his chair. He needed the distance.

"Her sister found the two of you on the sofa."

"I was going out with Darla, her older sister. We broke up and she set me up. Framed me is what she did. Darla was 20, had her own apartment and Melanie would sleep on the sofa in the living room…"

Joey stopped and looked off. Why in hell was he rattling on anyway? He didn't know this doctor. Would she keep his confidence? He had heard of clinicians sharing the inmate's information with the guards. Joey turned to stare at her. Her expression hadn't changed but for a slight arching of her eyebrows. There was that firmness about her... same as he had seen in his first visit... but there was more... was it a willingness to listen to him, not simply to judge? He felt a pull towards her... but no. He mustn't give in, he barely knew her. It was entirely up to him to proceed, wasn't it? Exclusively up to him to take a chance on this unknown person. Should he?

It was a long pause but it hadn't felt that way to Joey when Dr Jeffries began again, "Maybe you'd rather wait..."

He leveled his seat, cupping his hands in front of him, peering into her eyes. "I got up in the middle of the night to go get a glass of water in the kitchen and there she was..."

"Melanie?"

"Yes. She had a blanket over her but her breasts were uncovered. I knew she was awake. I got an erection the moment I saw her but just walked by, didn't say anything. I was naked, too. I suppose I could've turned back to the bedroom and put some clothes on. I didn't. I get my water and head back and... there she was... her eyes open... not embarrassed at all. She says, 'Hi,' I say, 'Hi.' I thought of just moving on to the bedroom but something stopped me. Without looking at my erection she said, 'You look... exposed,' and she smiled. I smiled back and sat on the edge of the sofa, right by her feet, which she pulled up just enough to make room for me. My heart was pounding. Something told me I shouldn't be sitting there, feeling all that I was feeling, but I didn't want to get up either. I figured we could just talk... you know, a friendly thing."

Dr Jeffries tilted her head slightly.

"I notice she has freckles on her cheeks," continued Joey, "So she says, 'You're looking at my freckles.' I say, 'Yes. I like them.' 'I don't,' she answers, and pulls up her knees a bit more so she could make more room, her feet rubbing against my skin when she does. The thought of what was under the blanket was driving me crazy; the way she had tugged at it had left a little dark opening under it. My cock was throbbing."

Joey and Dr Jeffries locked eyes.

There was an air of impudence about Joey and Dr Jeffries thought he was taking pleasure in the telling of the story. Was he trying to push her away?

"Then I notice Darla standing by the door to her room looking daggers at me. It might have looked like something was going on but no… we were just chatting."

Dr Jeffries drew up her shoulders, lifting her chin slightly. "That's not what the file says."

It had been a matter of fact statement but it felt to Joey like a judge slamming down her gavel. "Nothing was happening," he objected, "I was just going to get up to return to the bedroom." He halted. "You don't believe me, do you?"

"No," she said tersely.

She had seen right through him, he thought, just like Legrand had, and he felt cornered, the heat of her probing eyes insisting on an answer. But heck, no, it would be him doing the pushing instead. He pulled his seat forward, closer to the desk, and said brashly, "See, you have to understand… have you done Meth, doctor?"

She shook her head calmly.

Joey gave a smirk. "That's all right, doc, you don't have to tell me your personal life. See, when you do Meth you see things differently and sometimes you get paranoid. Darla was high because she'd taken a hit a few hours before and still wanted to go on. I'd begged her to quit but she would not. I told her there was no more, which there wasn't."

"Were you using also?" asked Dr Jeffries.

"I'd snorted coke at the beginning. That was it. I liked seeing her go wild… but one of us had to stay in control." Joey wondered whether he should have shared this bit of information but the hell with it. "By then she had run out of cigarettes and she asked me to go get her some. It was the middle of the night and I said no. That pissed her off. Then she says, 'I'll let you do anything you want if you go get me a pack.' I still said no. That's when I went out to get the glass of water."

Joey lowered his eyes and stared at the single carnation in the slender vase on her desk. Nice touch, he thought. It reminded him of Caprice. She liked to have flowers around the house, too. Again Joey felt Dr Jeffries' eyes on him and he looked back. "Of course, I didn't have to go all the way to the kitchen to get the glass of water. I could've gone into the bathroom right next to the bedroom."

He ran his fingers through his hair. There was that manner of hers, again, that way of looking at him that made him feel vulnerable. He reminded himself that he wasn't in a court of law, that he didn't have to spill out the whole truth. In fact, he wasn't ready for it… no, not yet. Anyway, it should be on his terms not hers… but why had he come out to see her? Was it to impress Legrand… or had he come out just because he liked her… because she had made an impression on him that first time they had met… because the thought of her offered hope.

"Melanie didn't want to press any charges…" he continued, "she had a crush on me, I knew that… in fact, she wouldn't have minded…" and he checked himself.

"Wouldn't have minded… what?" said Dr Jeffries.

Joey averted her eyes. But he knew he had crossed the line. He had let her glimpse what had been his real intent and it shamed him. And the truth was that if he hadn't got caught he would've continued the affair, mindless of the consequences, impervious to Melanie's circumstances, simply because it gratified his appetites. He was thinking as much when she interrupted.

"We've got a lot of work to do, don't we?"

Joey felt defenseless.

She leaned forward, her expression warmer. "You know why you came in today?"

"I'm not sure now."

"Because there's a part of you that wants help."

Joey stared back.

"But there's another part that's getting in the way, isn't there? The part of you that prefers to keep hiding… escaping."

Joey sat very still as he listened.

"But you came in and that's what counts. You dared to come in not thinking that you'd feel vulnerable here with me… but you did… and that's a step forward."

Joey bowed his head slightly. He appreciated the words of encouragement. He needed them.

"Every day I call for people to come in," continued Dr Jeffries, "and every day only a few are willing. Those who don't are afraid to even begin to look at themselves, afraid to question their views, pretending they don't even have to."

Joey heard her but still didn't feel that he was that different from the rest of the inmates. If it hadn't been for Legrand he might not have made the appointment. "I think there's another reason I'm not ready for the whole truth."

"What's that?"

He shook his head. "Never mind."

"It's important to be open and say what's on your mind," said she.

He had held back because, though he wanted to tell her he found her pretty and warm and kind and that she turned him on, he was now also seeing her as someone of value, and he did not want to scare her away. And in this simple acknowledgment he found the impulse he had lacked the moment before and now said, "Maybe I don't want to own up to the fact that I'm a total screw up… and that I'll never be able to have a woman like you… and that going into detail about how I messed up so badly will make it utterly clear that someone like you is totally unattainable. And that hurts." He felt his head swimming, beads of cold sweat now sliding down his temples. He wiped them off with his hands and dried them against his denim pants.

"You're a young man, Mr Wilson… there's no telling what you can do with your life if you're honest with yourself."

Joey closed his eyes for a moment. Could that really be true? He desperately wanted to believe her. Then, glancing at the carnation on the desk, he said, "I like the flower."

"Thank you."

He raised his eyes to hers and said, "Don't ask me to give you up so soon. I'm barely getting to know you."

"Give me up?"

"I'm not sure I know what that means," said Joey, "You bring up something in me that's gentle and generous… but there's a dark side, too…" He rubbed his face slowly with both hands. "I knew what I did was wrong and I did it anyway… and the thing is… what's really scary is…"

"Go on…"

He shrugged his shoulders dejectedly.

"You would've kept doing it," Dr Jeffries said softly.

And he nodded slowly.

"It's your shadows, Mr Wilson… and we need to walk through them."

Joey liked that she had used the 'we', making him feel that a real partnership was being forged. "I need a guide to go through my shadows?"

"Yes."

She closed the notebook on her desk, folding her hands over it. "One more thing: there are boundaries that must be in place for our work to proceed, boundaries that have to be observed at all times."

"I understand. I'm sorry that I spoke the way I did before."

Dr Jeffries assented.

"But maybe…" he glanced up at her, a flash of hope in his eyes, "… maybe I can be the best patient you have and I can have you that way."

"Being the best patient you can be… the hardest working… will let you have yourself sooner… the whole fullness of you… not me."

"Ever?"

"Ever."

He felt the sting of the disappointment and yet, right alongside, and perhaps even stronger, a sense of welcome hope rising in him. Boundaries, yes, it was boundaries that he had not perceived and observed that had landed him in prison. Boundaries that had not been there to check his recklessness. And he understood that he had to trust her, and let her peer into his heart and mind.

He righted himself in his seat and clasped his hands behind his head. He thought of Legrand, how now he had something to tell him, something that his cellmate would approve, something that would begin to redeem him in his eyes.

There was quiet for a moment as he sat shuffling his thoughts.

And he saw that Dr Jeffries was not hastening to end the session, and it occurred to him that she was okay with the silence between them.

There she was, sitting in front of him, firm like a rock, hands folded, eyes unafraid, with no hint of wanting to escape. And it comforted him that this physically frail looking person whom he could destroy with his fists should he ever want to, would have the intellect and emotional strength to hold his madness.

16

*P*oncho Sterling worked second watch most of the time. He was there in the day room, distributing mail along the lower tier in section A, when Joey returned from his session at about 10:30. Joey ambled in, head down, minding his own business, leisurely heading straight for his cell in 128. Five other inmates, on the way back from mental health and medical, strolled in with him.

Officer Tanpuro was at the control room. He glanced down at Joey and felt nothing but disdain. On the second tier, in cell 234, Hyena happened to be at his cell door when Joey entered the unit. He, too, was bothered that Joey had not yet been brought down to size. Unable to contain himself, he fired off a blast of insults. "Say, child molester! Yeah you, crapola! You can't hide all the time, I'm telling you right now, first chance I get I'm going to punk you. Right in front of everybody, and I mean, I'm going to pull down your pants and I'm going to slam it to you!" He was throwing down a heck of a challenge and each word came out like a bullet. Poncho Sterling turned to see where it was coming from. He made a mental note of it but just then another inmate called to him. Joey had almost reached his cell door when he stopped. He had had it.

Officer Tanpuro racked the door open for him to go in his cell but, instead, Joey stayed put. He wanted to scream but held back. He slowly turned around, glanced up at cell 234, saw Hyena staring down at him, and right then and there made up his mind. He backed up a few steps to the staircase and began to calmly climb up. Up in the control room, Tanpuro had got distracted with opening doors for the other inmates coming in and two others being called to go out. Joey was already on the upper tier landing when he called out to Tanpuro, "234! Open up!" He said it with the same tone of authority that officers used and Tanpuro fell for it. He pushed the button for 234 without looking.

Down below, Poncho Sterling quickly recognized that Hyena's cell was being opened as Joey approached and instantly called out to Tanpuro to correct his move. It was too late.

The cell door had opened wide enough to let Hyena through. Sterling pressed the alarm. Hyena squeezed out and saw Joey barreling straight for him. Joey ducked his head and went for Hyena's legs. Hyena tried to dodge him but Joey dove into him, seized him by his crotch and the collar of his shirt, lifted him off his feet and swung him over the railing. But he didn't let go. Stunned, speechless, completely at the mercy of Joey and his incredible strength, Hyena found himself dangling from Joey's arms. Hyena thought of reaching for the railing but then heard his tee shirt start to rip and desperately clung to Joey's arm. Joey was looking at him, seething with rage. Not a word came out of Hyena's mouth, his face pale as the white of his eyes.

At the control room, Tanpuro had got his rifle – the one with live ammo – trained on Joey.

Poncho Sterling had rushed to the scene, the packet of mail he was distributing still in his hands. "Wilson! Do not drop him," he commanded. "Hyena's got the message. You will do some serious damage if you drop him. You've made your point."

"No, he hasn't," cried out an inmate from a neighboring cell.

"Drop the bastard!" said another.

Other boots were rushing in to the unit in response to the alarm, sergeant Howitzer at the helm. The sergeant quickly appraised the situation and ordered the incoming officers to split up and go up the stairs on either side of Joey and the dangling Hyena. A few others, reluctantly, heeded his instruction that they position themselves underneath the hanging Hyena, like a safety net, just in case he was dropped. But the clamoring for blood continued – "Drop him! Drop him now!" - some called out angrily as they kicked their doors.

The officers were now up on the tier and were carefully approaching Joey, inching closely as they spoke to him. "We're just going to get close and we're going to grab him and bring him up, all right?" said Officer Thompson, a former medic in the Navy, speaking to both his fellow officers and Joey. And then, in one quick move, Joey pulled the dangling Hyena up and over the railing and unto the tier. The officers rushed in and grabbed them both, thrusting them to the ground, and the unit exploded in loud cheers.

"Woo Woo Woo!" some chanted as both Joey and Hyena lay prone and were handcuffed.

Butterfly couldn't restrain his excitement and started to belt out, "Fly me to the moon... and let me play among the stars..." the old Frank

Sinatra tune, in perfect pitch, while a disgruntled inmate yelled out to the guards, "You're finally earning your pay, you no good bums!" while another shouted "USA! USA!" and the bang and rattle of cell doors rose to a deafening roar as the feuding men were escorted down the stairs and whisked off the unit.

The alarm was turned off and the reinforcing officers began to clear the scene. Sergeant Howitzer crossed to the podium and called Officer Tanpuro up in the tower. They spoke for a moment.

Poncho Sterling had returned to distributing the mail but, as soon as the sergeant had gone, he signaled to Tanpuro that he wanted to come up and have a chat with him.

Tanpuro wasn't keen on discussing anything with Poncho but the matter had to be settled. He pushed the button to let him in. He figured he would take the initiative and fire off first. He was sitting at his desk looking out into the day room when Poncho Sterling walked up. Tanpuro swiveled back to face him. "I had him, Pancho. Had my finger on the trigger," he said blithely. "I was ready to take him out."

Poncho said nothing, pulled up a chair and sat across from him. "It's not Pancho, it's Poncho."

"Yeah, sure."

'Why'd you open the door for Hyena?"

"You asked me to," Tanpuro deadpanned.

Poncho couldn't believe the gall. He stared at Tanpuro, weighing his words carefully before letting him have it. "I don't know where you've been... what kind of trouble you've had... but we don't lie in here."

"What you talking about? I heard you clearly."

"No, you didn't. I'm in section A doing the mail, the call to open 234 came from Section B, right near the cut. Hadn't you heard the insult? Have you got plugs in your ears?"

"'234, open up'. That's all I heard. I thought it was you," said Tanpuro.

Wow. The man thought he was stupid. Poncho's anger rose. "Is that what you told Howitzer?"

"The truth, man, nothing but the truth, so help me God."

Poncho hung his head and took a deep breath. What on earth had made this man think he could run over him? He had to be dense.

"It wasn't you?" said Tanpuro.

"What?" The insolence to ask, thought Poncho.

"When I heard you ask me to close it back up I thought you'd recognized your mistake. But don't worry, stuff happens," said Tanpuro with a grin, insisting on making light of it. "When you write your report, you can say that you thought Education had called for him - I don't know what for - and wires got crossed. No one got hurt anyway, just a little excitement and some egos bruised. Sergeant will understand. Why sweat it?"

Now the clown was telling him how to write his report, too. Poncho felt an urge to slap Tanpuro silly. "Why sweat it? Because I'm not a liar, that's why. And you are." Poncho felt the blood rushing to his head and he remembered that he had high blood pressure and was only 33 and his doctor had told him to try and find another line of work. And he brought his hands to his head to rub his temples when he thought he heard Tanpuro snicker as he swiveled his chair back to the desk.

"Don't you turn away from me, I'm talking to you!" Poncho snapped.

Tanpuro bristled. He had the impulse to give Poncho a good tongue lashing but feared his response. He was seething, though. "You might as well know that me and captain Driscoll go back a long way," he boasted, instead. Poncho couldn't help but laugh as he shook his head. "Really? Look man, I'm going to keep trying hard to think you're not an idiot... but don't push me."

Poncho got up and began to cross to the stairs when Tanpuro, his cockiness melting, said with a whimper. "I don't want any trouble, okay?" He was pleading now, Poncho could hear it. "I just want to do my job, get my pay check. I got a family, all right. I have two kids heading for college."

'Don't you start blubbering on me now, you dunce', thought Poncho, but he left it at that. He had said what he needed to say.

Wilson and Hyena were questioned at the Program office and signed the required marriage Chrono saying that everything was okay and they were willing to put the whole incident behind. Neither of them wanted to be moved to another unit and, more importantly, the feud between them was heating up and had to be resolved.

17

*P*oncho Sterling had met Dr Gardner years ago, way before he had gone to work for the prison. Growing up, his parents would take in 1 or 2 foster children for the extra income and Poncho would tag along with his dad when the children had to see the psychiatrist. Dr Gardner was at the time working for a mental health center near Playa del Rey, right by the Los Angeles airport. To encourage Poncho to come, his dad promised that after the visit with the doctor, they'd pick up some burgers and then go to a spot where they could see the planes land and take off. Poncho never refused.

All the kids who were assigned to the Sterling home had had a rough time growing up, what with their parents struggling with drugs or with domestic violence and the resulting neglect or abuse, but when they came to the Sterling home something special began to happen. Little by little, and in the most unexpected ways, the children began to be more trusting. Poncho was always looking for the first sign of their getting used to their new home. 'The first sign is a smile, mom,' he announced one day when she was in the kitchen preparing dinner, 'the very first one. Even if they're still sad, if they smile at me I know we're on the way up.' And his mom had called it the Poncho sign. 'Have you seen any Poncho signs yet?' she would ask. Poncho would get a small allowance for interacting with the children, but for him it was more fun than anything else. He was 11 years old when his mom and dad began to do foster care for the county and it lasted until he went away to college.

Poncho remembered how Dr Gardner took his time with his patients. After seeing them a few times and confirming that their new environment was to their liking, he would begin to reduce the medication. In fact, many of them went off completely. And it happened that one day, at the end of a visit, after his dad had told the doc how much Poncho enjoyed interacting with the kids, that the doctor had put his hand on his shoulder and said, 'You're making a difference in their lives.'

A couple of years later Dr Gardner moved on.

Poncho didn't see him again until some 12 years later, when they met again in Lancaster.

Poncho had wanted to talk to Gardner about his quest to find the killer of his mother. He had searched the available hospital records from the day of the shooting. They had fingerprinted her but he had found no match for her after a nationwide search. There were no identifying documents whatsoever. She had been buried at the county's expense but there was no record of where she lay. They just didn't know. All he knew was that she had died on September 3rd 1982 at County Hospital, after being found crumpled over in pain, gasping for air on the corner of Sixth and Grand, near Pershing Square in downtown LA, at 4 in the morning, right after being shot at point blank, from the side. No witnesses had come forth. She was described as brunette, in her mid to late twenties and she had all her teeth. If he had known where she lay buried he could have had her body exhumed to check them out, maybe they could offer some clue. He had a copy of her photo, lying lifeless on a steel table in the morgue, one eye partly open and the other closed, as if she were winking at him. He thought she was pretty, with a slightly upturned nose, small ears and a long neck, her stringy hair brushed back by the nurse or someone. The lips were thin and the upper one crested in the middle. He imagined her a country girl, growing up in a farm, who then had taken off to try her luck in the city. Her hands, which were not photographed, were described as calloused. So she had done manual work. Somewhere. Sometime. And then there was that final entry: no needle tracks had been found in her arms. Her blood had been negative for drugs. He thanked her for that.

Poncho Sterling wanted to talk to Gardner about letting go. He had felt a duty to his mom to try and find the murderer. There might be a brother also, or a sister. The pathologist had been careful in his examination and had observed that she had undergone an episiotomy. So she had given birth at least once before. But he might never know.

18

*I*n the crowded visiting area, Joey and Janice embraced, glad that they were to see each other again. He drew back to hold her face, "You look beautiful." She smiled but looked away. It was early December and she was wearing a brown coat over a tan colored dress, and a yellow scarf around her neck.

"Everything all right?" said Joey.

"Everything's fine. I mean, not quite fine…"

"Why not?"

"Because you're here, Joey."

"Thanks, mom, but aside from that?"

She didn't reply and they sat down. She seemed a bit tired, thought Joey, but he attributed it to the travel.

"What did we do wrong, son?"

Joey wondered if she would ever ask the question but there it was. "I'm still thinking about that. You guys played a role but I did, too. You made some choices and I made mine. Maybe it's too early for me to answer that question. I just need to understand. I don't know what else to say."

Janice closed her eyes and nodded slowly. He knew her well and she seemed to be struggling with something.

"Go ahead, mom, what is it?"

"There was a time… when you were 6 or 7… that you had a fight with your dad and you ran to the neighbor's. Remember that?"

"I had lots of fights with him and spent lots of time at the neighbors."

"This one time you insisted they call me and I rushed back from work. Something had happened with your dad. You'd had a dream… then you'd gone into the kitchen. You remember?"

Joey shook his head, uncertainly, his memories vague. "No, I don't."

"You don't remember why you called me?"

"No."

She took his hand in hers.

"I didn't think I was like the other kids, that much I recall. Something was missing…" said Joey.

"What?"

"Not sure... but I wish we would've talked more."

"Talked about what?"

Joey gave a slow shrug. "Everything."

"I thought we did," said Janice.

"We skimmed the surface. Glided over things in our own special way. When we got to the feeling part we jumped to something else. But I did the same thing, too."

"Maybe I should've talked to you about girls."

"Why didn't you?"

"Why? Boys and girls are the same at that age," said Janice.

"No, we're not. I had a weenie and the little girls didn't."

"You were children..."

"In fact, I wanted to have a bigger weenie, like the one dad had."

"Joey, what's this?" she said, taken aback by his candor.

"Just plain talk."

"Is that what you talk about with your psychologist, the size of your weenie?"

"Actually, it hasn't come up. Not yet."

"Wait, is she saying I did something wrong?"

"We haven't got to you, either."

She stared at him. "Why are you being disrespectful?"

"I am not disrespecting you. I was just trying to be open. Maybe we should talk about the weather, instead."

"The weather is just fine," said Janice, brusquely, while pulling the ends of her yellow scarf into a knot.

Joey gave an apologetic smile and putting his arm around her pulled her to him.

"I'm sorry."

"I didn't like that language. But we can keep talking." She looked at him with doleful, inquisitive eyes. "What would you have wanted to talk about that we didn't?"

"That I thought you kept me from dad."

Janice looked front and was quiet. She rested her head upon his shoulder.

"Even after Margaret had come along," added Joey.

"You resented that?"

"Yes."

Janice righted herself in her seat. A worried, searching expression had come over her.

"It was like you wanted me to be only yours," continued Joey.

Janice nodded. "I did do that."

"Why?"

Janice was silent.

"You must have some idea," pressed Joey.

She folded her hands on her lap. "Your father and I were having problems… and I had been thinking of leaving him."

"It went on for a long time."

"It's complicated. I'd rather not go into it." She felt restless and stood up. She needed to move. "Is there anywhere we can walk? I've seen some visitors going around behind a fence…"

"Yes. We can go outside." He led her to the small, fenced patio outside the building where other inmates and their visitors were going around in a circle. Joey and Janice joined in.

"I was feeling stifled in there." She took his hand. "We had some difficult times at the start. But we've worked it out."

He sensed that she wanted off the subject and he let it go. He was glad she had come all the way out to see him. Legrand, by contrast, got no visits. Zero. Joey glanced at the other inmates doing the circle with their moms or girlfriends or children. Everyone was living his story. Mom by his side was living hers. Dad his own. Everyone had some suffering to go through. No one was spared. And like everyone else, he had to try his best and manage his burden, dodge the bullets, heal the wounds. "I resent dad for not fighting for me."

Janice didn't answer.

"I was talking to LB the other day about suffering…"

"Shouldn't priests be handling that?" returned Janice quickly. "What are his qualifications? He's not getting out, you are."

"Why are you getting upset?"

"I don't understand how they put a nice boy like you with a person like that." And the instant she made the statement she realized she was glossing over Joey's offense – again.

Joey stopped. Pulling her to the side, off the circling path, he placed his hands on her shoulders and said to her, "Mom, look at me, really do look at me, please. I'm not a nice boy. I took advantage of another person. I'm struggling to accept it and you have to do it, too."

Janice frowned and shook her head.

And Joey thought of how only a few days before he had let Hyena push his buttons and he had snapped. And if Hyena had slipped from his grip when he was dangling him off the tier, he would have been facing an attempted murder charge and forget about getting out. And it all had happened in an instant. But there was his mother calling him a nice boy. "That's one thing," he continued, "and the second is that I couldn't have asked for a better cellmate than LB. He's been in prison more than 30 years and may never get out, and he knows more about suffering than the priest or any man of the cloth."

Janice shot back, testily. "I know about suffering, I've had to put up with your father, and I did it for you… and for Margaret, so we could all stay together. So don't tell me I don't know about suffering." She spoke forcefully, feeling fully entitled to her words.

Joey didn't like the turn the conversation was taking any more than he had liked holding Hyena over the handrails. "Look, we've got off track. What I meant to say earlier is that I wish we had been able to talk more freely than we did."

"I didn't tell you not to talk."

There was no point in fueling the flames anymore. She could have the last word. But he acknowledged that the conversation, prickly as it had been, had been another step forward in their learning to dialogue. So maybe there really was hope for him after all. And Joey wanted to tell Janice that, as a child, when he had felt something was wrong, it had come on as a vague and oppressive feeling that he had been unable to put into words, and that he had secretly yearned for someone to translate for him, someone to read his little mind, so he could be put at ease. But not know, thought Joey, not now. He would wait to say it later.

"You always could count on me," said Janice.

And Joey gave a slow nod. "I kept a lot of things inside, mom. And it was hard to bear. I just didn't know it then."

"I suppose that for some things I wasn't there for you," acknowledged Janice.

"For some things you were, for some you weren't," said he.

It had taken a long time to begin to speak openly and they would need more.

The thought of Dr Jeffries floated into his mind. Was he borrowing from her? Yes.

The spirit of his therapist had come to be there between Janice and him.

19

Mary Jane Jeffries had come to psychology late. Now 45, she had started out as an art major and then taken a turn to performing. Born in Laramie, Wyoming, where her parents had had a ranch before cashing in and becoming missionaries in South America, she had spent a good part of her youth immersed in a variety of cultural settings. She had grown up in Panama, Ecuador, Peru and Bolivia, and had become fluent in Spanish, which always surprised the people she met. Along the way she had developed an independent streak and a keen sense of resolve, which both pleased and frightened her parents. And so it should not have come as great surprise when, on the very day she turned 18 and living in the outskirts of Lima, she announced that she would be leaving home to take up with a young man, 7 years her senior, who enchanted with her charms had decided to renounce the priesthood and together set off to sail around the world.

She wasn't going to marry Norberto, mind you; she was going to venture off with him. No vows were being taken, no promises of life together in the future; all she wanted, she said, was to go off into the world and explore, and the friendship with Norberto had promise. Her father, who had become very attached to his daughter, nearly fainted when Mary Jane broke the news, having to be perked up by his wife with a shot of cognac, ordinarily reserved for special occasions, which indeed this one was.

"But you don't know anything about sailing?" said her exasperated father recovering from the shock.

"We can't support you, darling," added her mom, who was equally aghast at the boldness of her daughter but secretly admiring her courage.

"I'm not asking you. Norberto speaks French and Russian, I speak Spanish, and we plan to make our money by teaching. He has enough to get us to Japan."

"Japan!?" her dad exclaimed nearly fainting again.

"Oh, God! You're not going to try and sail across the Pacific?" said her mom with real alarm.

"No, no," said Mary Jane, shaking her head with a hint of amusement, "we'll fly there. Norberto has friends in Osaka with enough room in their home to put us up for a while. They give sailing lessons for a living. We'll take lessons from them and teach languages to pay our way." It all sounded deliciously fun to Mary Jane. And why not?

"But will you be able to work, you'd be tourists?"

"His friend Masashi says you can make money under the table. Other people do it."

"But that's against the law."

"Oh, mom."

Two weeks later Mary Jane and Norberto flew to Japan, learned to sail, taught languages as predicted and eventually, well after their visas had expired, set sail for South Korea. There they plied their trade with success and, after only two years, had saved enough to invite her parents to stay with them for a month even paying for the plane tickets. Shortly after, Norberto was hired by the US Army as a linguist and a year later they had their first child, Gracie Kim.

It was around that time, when Mary Jane stayed home to care for their daughter, that she began to develop a serious interest in music. And it fell to baby Kim to begin to show her the way. When the child cried Mary Jane would sing to her and, as if by magic, the baby would stop and smile back radiantly.

Mary Jane began to sing along to tunes on the radio and soon discovered she could retain melodies, one after the other, with their exact pitch, and not get them mixed up. She sang to Norberto, also, who wondered why in the world she hadn't sang to him earlier.

But what proved to be the turning point was what happened one morning. After singing to baby Kim, they stepped out of the apartment to go for a stroll. A handful of neighbors had gathered on the walkway outside. They all chimed in with their good mornings and said they had been sitting there just to hear her sing. And they did it every morning. What a pretty voice she had, said the neighbors, did she sing at a club?

Three months later, Mary Jane Jeffries was sitting at a club in Seoul that had an open mike night every Wednesday. Norberto was next to her, ready to nudge her on, if needed, the mesmerized baby Kim dandling on his knee. She had arrived early, signed up on the list, spoken to the band and offered the sheet music for her song. Of course they knew it and asked what key she wanted to sing it in. When her turn came up Mary Jane didn't blink and went up on stage. Standing in front of the mike, under the glare of the lights, she looked out at the audience. The room was full. In the darkness she couldn't see the detail of the faces except for those in the first few rows. She wanted to hold the mike but her hands were sweaty and she thought she might get shocked if she did, so she kept it on the stand and got very close instead. The band waited. All was quiet suspense. Mary Jane dried her hands on her skirt. Then Norberto cried out, "Go, muchacha!" She smiled, looked back at the band and nodded. The music started. For a second, right after the first strains began, she drew a blank and forgot all the words, but then the first line came up and she remembered everything again. And the song flowed. "People… people who need people… are the luckiest people in the world…"
And the audience swooned with delight. She had chosen the Barbara Streisand hit for her debut and it went off smoothly to warm applause.

20

Leroy Cadenas was still debating whether to go ahead with the job Grisholt had offered. He had got half the Crystal Meth he had asked – the down payment - so the ball was in his court. He had thought of the possibility of triggering a racial riot, since he would be targeting a black man, but Leblanc had enough authority with blacks to check the retaliation. He had done it before. He had let it be known that whatever pertained to him was his only, not the black community's business. And then there was the fact that Leroy was half black – from his mother.

His father had had an on and off relationship with his mom, a high school sweetheart, but then she got pregnant. 'He told the gang that he now had a son, that he wanted to move on,' his mother told him, "but they wouldn't let him go. He held you in his arms, Leroy, he made you smile,' she had said. Baby Leroy was three months old when father was gunned down on the front porch as his mother looked from the window. 'I begged him not to step out, begged him that we go live somewhere else. But he insisted that he needed to face them, and if he didn't they wouldn't leave him alone.'

Leroy didn't even have a photo of the man.

Faced with difficult decisions, Leroy sometimes cut himself. His arms and thighs bore the scars of those struggles: long and short thick lines arranged transversally on his skin. He did not like to do it but, sometimes, pressure would overwhelm him and he would yield to the impulse.

He always tried to hide the scars, but covering up the evidence was a hard thing to do when you were incarcerated; your body was simply not yours. At the discretion of the guards a man could be frisked at any time of the day or night, the ostensible reasons being the need to search for weapons, drugs or other possible contraband. Worst of all was the stripping down you had to undergo when you went through Reception as you entered a new pen. Then you were asked to take your pants and shirts off, drop your shorts, turn around, bend over, spread your cheeks, bare your butthole and give a cough! cough! cough! just in case you were hiding something up your tail - all under the cold stare of the guards.

The cutting had started after he turned 15 and in Juvenile Hall and had been moved into a cell with an older and stronger youth who, from the start, wanted to bully him out of his food. By then, young Leroy had been schooled by his peers not to be a snitch: to solve problems on his own, regardless of the odds.

At first, reluctantly, he gave in to the bully, but then the memory of his first day in a foster home began to come back and he could not find peace. He'd wake up in the middle of the night flailing his arms, shouting as he fought off and struggled to get away from the man who had molested him.

Leroy was making a lot of noise and his roommate didn't like it. He warned him to settle down - it was disturbing his sleep - and if he didn't, he would get a stiff stomping.

The night following the warning, dreaming again and thrashing about with greater violence, he struck his elbow against the sharp edge of his bunk and drew blood. It was a small cut, but as he stared at the wound and saw the blood ooze he felt a sense of calm. The next night he didn't have a bad dream but the following night it came back. The stronger youth grabbed him by the throat and slammed him against the wall, "I don't want to hear it again, you feel me!? Crazy mother fucker!"

The big stomping seemed imminent and Leroy had to think quickly. He thought of waiting till his roommate fell asleep and then go off on him, but he would have to hurt him badly to prevent the bully from retaliating, and surely that would bring new charges and extend his sentence. Snitching was out of the question. But if he saw some blood oozing again… would he get relief from it…?

That night, before going to bed, young Leroy took the handle of a toothbrush he'd sharpened and kept hidden, and cut his thigh. He did it carefully, starting with a scratch at first, then pressing again on the same groove till he saw the first blood seep out. The sense of peace returned and he didn't have a bad dream that night, or the next. The bully – Clive was his name – grinned at him. Slowly waving a fist in his face he said to Leroy, "All you needed was a little shock therapy," and he let out his mocking laugh.

Leroy had seen his mom sporadically since their initial separation and each time she seemed like she had aged much more rapidly than her years. She wrote occasionally. She had been in jail for drug possession and had returned for a brief spell on a violation. But when she was assigned to a drug rehab center she had made the most of it. Then came the final letter. In the letter his mom had told him that she was determined to make things right for herself. She had a plan to go back east, to Philadelphia - where she had relatives - enroll in school and start a new life. She had learned how important it was to be honest and she was writing to tell him just that.

She was 19 when she had got pregnant with him and she loved him very much but she had come to realize that she was not really cut out to be a mom. She had tried to but failed. The stress was just too much for her. Surely it would have been different if dad had been around but God had other plans. So she was writing to say goodbye. She knew he loved her and she hoped he would understand. Some of the words in the letter were smudged and Leroy imagined that his mom had shed tears as she wrote. He would have wanted to hug her as he imagined her crying, holding her to tell her that everything would be okay, that because he loved her so much he would let her go so she could straighten out her life. 'You go and do something with your life,' he heard himself telling her, 'I'm a big boy. The State's taking care of me. It's like if I have been adopted. After the group home I may go to prison but the guards will be like my parents. Don't worry, you go. Go and make something of yourself.' There was no return address on the letter, but young Leroy kept it and guarded it with his life.

Shortly after Clive's threats had intensified, Leroy dreamt of his mother. She was very happy to see him. She wore a green dress that seemed made of silk and her hair was nicely done. She had got a job in Philadelphia selling products to supermarkets and had got herself a car and had money in the bank. There was a break in the middle that he couldn't remember but in the next fragment he had returned to his room and was trying, frantically, to gather his things. He couldn't find them. It seemed like mother had changed her mind and was now sending for him. "But where are my things?" He had to hurry. "I've been here all this time and have nothing!" He ran back to tell his mother to please wait another moment, so he can look again for his things. To his relief she was still there, standing by the door, but then she said, "You don't need anything, Leroy, just you. That's all you need, just you." "What?" And he woke up with a deep sadness.

Young Leroy was accustomed to exercising twice a week but now began to do so daily. Clive – who was only two years older than Leroy but looked like a fully developed adult – eyed him suspiciously. A few days later he told young Leroy that he shouldn't exercise anymore, that he was fine just like that. The instant Leroy heard this it sent shivers up his spine. He thought to himself, 'I knew it would come; he wants me for his bitch.' And he decided to put a stop to the bullying, even if it cost him his life.

That very night his mom returned in a dream. She was dressed in a business suit and was busy stacking goods in a shelf at a supermarket. She looked older, her hair gray. Leroy walked up to her, 'Mom, I'm going to kill him tonight,' he said. 'Why, Leroy?' she answered calmly. 'He wants to punk me.' A worried look came over her. 'Can't you scare him off?'. 'He's bigger than me,' pressed Leroy. 'Try scaring him off, son, it might work,' and she returned to stacking the shelves. The word 'son' reverberated in his mind. He smiled.

That evening the unit would not go out to chow but instead would eat in the cells. When the food came around to the porthole, Clive was the first at the door to get his tray. There was a serving of red beans, rice, the usual non-descript meat, a piece of cornbread and a small carton of milk. Clive slept on the lower bunk, which was assigned to Leroy, but Clive had appropriated. Young Leroy picked up his tray and turned to put it on his upper bunk.

"Pass the cornbread and the milk," said Clive.

"I'm hungry today, you can't have it."

Clive stopped. Leroy pulled himself up unto his bunk fully aware that he would not be eating his meal. Something else was about to happen.

"What did you say?" said Clive with a look of amused astonishment.

"I'm eating my cornbread," Leroy repeated in a defiant tone.

"Like hell you are…" replied Clive and he jumped up from his bunk and tried to grab Leroy's tray. But Leroy was ready. In one quick motion he kicked at Clive landing the foot squarely on his face. Trays flew and young Leroy jumped on his foe. They grappled and punched, falling to the floor, Leroy on top of Clive. The officer who had passed the tray was only a cell or two away and, upon hearing the noise, quickly sounded the alarm. Leroy and Clive were socking and bruising each other when the cell door opened and the pepper spray rained in. Still they fought while more spray was doused on them. But soon the sting of the chemicals overwhelmed them and both stumbled out the cell. Clive held his upper lip, now split in two all the way up to his nose, his two front teeth missing and blood flowing profusely from a gash that laid bare his upper gum. Young Leroy came out grinning: he was bruised and he was bloodied, but he had scored against the bully.

That had happened thirteen years before and he had never been bullied again, although some people had tried. He returned to a group home at seventeen but then got into trouble again - an assault with battery - and was back in Juvenile Hall for a spell. Then the trip to the pen for his 18th birthday so he could finish the sentence and finally the parole back to Inglewood in Los Angeles at 21.

They gave him a month's supply of medication to control his mood, a sleeping pill, a referral to a mental health clinic and some pocket money.

It was a fresh start, but he could not stop thinking of his mom. What had happened to her? What was she doing? Was she alive? He had not heard from her since that last letter.

He found work with a roofing company, then a waste collecting outfit before moving on to hosing down and cleaning outdoor toilets, all the while saving what money he could, the insistent thought of meeting up with mom tugging at his heart. No, he could not be at peace without making the effort. He had to do it. He had to go up to Philadelphia and search for her.

He tried to get his parole agent to transfer his parole up to Pennsylvania but the agent said that, unless he heard from his mom, he could do nothing about it. 'But that's the reason I want to go,' insisted Leroy. The parole agent was adamant. And then he made his decision: he would go anyway, even if it meant incurring a violation.

To save money he hitchhiked his way up and it took him a week to get to Philly. He slept in shelters, worked part time for a pet store cleaning cages and walked the streets inquiring at every supermarket he could find. He showed the two faded photographs he kept but no one seemed to recognize her. He sought help from public librarians and even put an ad in the paper. He found a private investigator and did errands for him in exchange for his help tracking her down. But that didn't help, either. 'Maybe she didn't come to Philadelphia,' said the investigator. 'Sorry, man.'

Going to the police was out of the question since they might run a check on him, nab him and drag him back to California. And so, nearly a year went by before Leroy concluded that mom had vanished, and that he had better return to California and make good with the law. He would have to serve a year or two at most for the parole violation. Then lovely Tiara stepped into his life.

All these thoughts went through Leroy's mind as he sat in his cell, looking at the stash that Eddie Grisholt had given him for the planned assault on Legrand. That Grisholt wanted a hit on Legrand knowing that he shared the cell with Joey still troubled Leroy. Grisholt wasn't doing it as a favor to him, that was certain. The man was strictly business, tit for tat, no favors for anybody. He liked that about him. But something was amiss. How could you open the door for an attack on Legrand and not expect that Joey Wilson be a target also?

Leroy thought of the reputation he had to protect because that's all you had in the joint, and wasn't his first board appearance 19 years away? He might not even be alive when it rolled around. Plus, everybody knew the board shot you down the first time up, so he might never see the streets again. Ever.

He thought of lighting up a joint but decided against it. He needed to have all his brain cells firing at full blast for the planned assault.

He thought of Dr Gardner… their talk… still… 19 years before board… fuck… how do you live with that? And his mind turned to whether he should carry a shank for the assault - just in case.

Up in cell 225, Johnson had been quiet. Ever since his son had come in to visit he had stopped shouting that he wanted to go home and had started going out to yard once again. He walked, then ran around the track till he was exhausted, all of which helped fight back the recurring cravings for heroin.

With the new surge of energy came a commitment to clean up his act so he could take advantage of whatever changes in the law took place. The robbery he had committed had not made him eligible for Proposition 36 – which he lamented every single day - but California had been passing laws to reduce overcrowding and new bills to modify sentencing were in the works. It was in that spirit of renewal and hope that he had put in a request to medical to get checked since he had been sharing needles when he injected the drug.

Officers Morelos and Rivers had paid him a visit at cell side and were pleasantly surprised when he told them that the nightmares had stopped the very next day he had seen his son. Human contact was a powerful medicine indeed.

21

Leroy didn't have a cellmate because he had beat up so many of them that word got out that if you stepped into his cell, that same day you would have to fight him. No honeymoon or let's talk about this or that to see if we have anything in common and are compatible. Nothing. He would tell the incoming inmate, even as he approached the cell in the company of a guard, that he better be ready to slug it out, so be prepared. And it worked. The approaching inmate would balk, preferring to put up with a rules violation for refusing a cellie, than go in and have a fight with an uncertain outcome. And if the officer gave Leroy the rules violation instead, he would say, 'go right ahead, pile it on, buster. Want to send me to the hole, suit yourself.' And so Leroy was, unofficially, single cell.

It didn't help his state of mind that he had no visits. An old aunt who had sent him money occasionally, had died of a stroke two years before and since then there had been nothing more for him. Nor did he expect anything.

Except for Tiara, the pretty prostitute he had met up in Philadelphia, just after he had given up searching for his mom and was getting ready to return to California. He had her address and had thought of writing but had not mustered the nerve. What if she didn't answer, or worse, that she answered and rejected him?

He had gone 34 times with her – he kept a detailed diary of each encounter - before she told him that it was best if he didn't come around anymore, that it was plain that he wanted something different than what she could offer. She had her man and was spoken for. Leroy had got attached to her and she to him but it was not good for business. Mack, her man, who pimped and monitored her closely, had told her so. 'You're a nice looking fellow – Tiara had said to Leroy- why don't you find yourself a good girl? You shouldn't be having to pay for it.' To which he had gamely answered, 'Don't charge me, then.' They laughed but Tiara was serious.

But was Leroy any different? She had heard his story, touched his scars. His behavior reminded her of her own self destructive impulses. A part of her wanted to break up with her pimp and fly off on her own.

Leroy aroused in her the desire to nurture and she had felt a bond to him that gave her strength. She felt it the most when she saw him sucking voraciously at her breasts. 'Slow down, baby,' she'd heard herself whisper to him with affection, while looking into his big brown, needy eyes… could he be the one? And he would gaze up at her, longingly, her breast still firmly in his mouth, and wink. And she would wonder, could they go off somewhere, just up and go? Yes… why not… but then she would have second thoughts. She knew so little about Leroy. He had told her about the offenses that had landed him in prison. But was there more, was he telling her the whole truth?

Leroy did not take well to the notice to give her up. He had longed to be loved by a beautiful woman like Tiara, to hold her in his arms, be held by her… and now there she was, finally, his dream fulfilled. He had first seen her in a photo posted outside a strip joint not far from downtown Philadelphia, a small club in the basement of a three-story building. To him she looked exactly like the pin up girl he had taped on his wall while in Juvenile Hall in California and to the sight of which he had masturbated a thousand times.

With the money he had saved he bought new clothes, and for the next 5 consecutive nights was first in line when the place opened. It took that long before she gave him the time of day and they had their first encounter. The girl was popular, all right. But it was worth the wait because it had been wonderful, so much so that for the following six weeks he forgot all about the failed search for his mother. He worked whatever jobs he could find to have enough money to see Tiara - again and again.

He had fallen in love.

Tiara knew it and liked it. It made her think of going back to school. But what if Leroy got tired of her? What if he had a temper? What if he was possessive? She needed time to sort things out but knew Mack stood in the way.

Mack had always treated her well. He had taken her in, groomed her, counseled her. She was 17 when he had picked her up during a trip to Jersey, where he found her hitchhiking after she had run away from her drunk and abusive father. What would she have done without him?

On Mondays he took her shopping, on Thursdays he took her to do her hair. Every single week. A portly type, well known in the trade, Mack had made a nice living of it and knew which palms to grease to keep the gig going. But he was now getting on in years and had become attached to Tiara. There were other women in the stable and he nurtured them all but Tiara was the star. Only she knew of his waning potency and only she knew how to make him feel as manly as ever.

The night that Tiara told Leroy to stop seeing her, that Mack had said so, Leroy had answered curtly, 'I'll think about it.' But he had barely contained his fury.

"It's for real, Leroy," said she.

Burning up inside as he was, they had sex a second time, and a third. He did not want to leave. "I'll pay to spend the night."

"I can't… he's raised the fee."

"Again?"

She nodded, anxiously.

"I'll pay."

"It's five hundred."

"What!?"

Tiara saw Leroy's muscles tighten. "I'll pay it!"

And she let out an anguished sob as she looked him in the eye.

"I can't… Mack's waiting for me." And turning away to hide the pained expression, she said, "It's his night with me."

Leroy lay very still for a moment, then shook his head slowly. But what else can I expect of myself, he thought in silent reproach… and then, abruptly, got out of bed. As he dressed he glanced at her for a moment. Lying there in bed, blanket pulled up to her chin, she said she was sorry. That was all. Nothing else left her lips after all those nights together. And it filled him with enormous disappointment just as his anger kept rising. But no, he would not vent in front of her. No, he didn't want her to see that side of him.

At the door they looked at each other, one last time, and he left. But he had walked less than a block when he suddenly cracked and could hold it no more. It was past midnight and the street was deserted. Seeing a luxury car ahead he thought of Mack and curled his hands into fists. Nearing the vehicle he thought of smashing a window. But when he reached it - a late model Jaguar - he leapt up onto it and, jumping up and down on the hood put a deep dent across it. The alarm went off instantly but what did he care. He climbed up onto the roof, jumped on it furiously, putting in another serious dent before stepping down to the trunk and unto the street beyond, walking off calmly without an effort to pick up the pace, secretly waiting for someone... yes... for Mack to come out and confront him. But no one did and Leroy kept walking. And just as he was ready to round the corner and drop out of sight, he turned and looked back, and there she was, his Tiara, looking lovely in her nightie, up in the apartment above the club, staring down at him from her balcony.

As he recalled the events, now six years a memory, Leroy sat silently in his lower bunk. He was holding the sharp toothbrush handle he used to cut on himself but he had not cut, nor did he want to. Instead, Joey would get it. The new regulation toothbrushes came with a short handle, to avoid their being turned into weapons, but he had bought one with a long handle that had been smuggled in. And that was the one he was going to use with Joey. Yes, Joey... who had had the nice family to grow up in and who had chosen, out of his own free will, to take advantage of an underage girl. Joey, who had defied prison rules and who would not run scared from threats to put some harm on him; Joey, who had the gall to knock him down and then dangle Hyena from the top tier railing; Joey, who had visits from his mommy who put money on the books for him to buy goodies from the canteen. Someone had to show the boy a thing or two and Leroy thought it fell to him.

How different his life would have been if he had stayed out, if he had been able to persuade his beloved to go off with him, if Mack hadn't been jealous. After that one last time he had seen her, Leroy had walked back to the room he rented, nearly 45 minutes away, cursing all along that his life had been one betrayal after another. The moon was out. He cursed the moon. Police cruisers went by. He cursed them, too. And he kept walking, crossing paths with other wanderers in the night and entertaining thoughts of striking one or another, not for any reason in particular... just because. But he restrained himself.

Just as he was preparing to return to California, he heard through an acquaintance that a company was looking for strong men to work the oil rigs in Siberia. The excitement shook him out of the doldrums. A new beginning beckoned; he would go off, make a pile of money, then come back and lure Tiara away. So what if he'd have to wrestle a few bears in the frozen wilderness. Emboldened, he marched to the office and interviewed. They liked him but there was one catch: he needed a passport. His heart sank. With his violation of parole, he didn't stand a chance. Still, he spent 100 bucks for a fake one. Not good enough. The guy handed it back to him and said he was sorry. Disconsolate, Leroy decided that it would be best to face the music and make good with the law. One year at most, he thought. Maybe two. And he could always return. He had a whole life ahead of him.

On the way back, while at a bus depot in Sacramento, tired and still thinking of Tiara, he lay on a bench and went to sleep. A security guard came by and asked him to move along, the depot was not a shelter. Leroy was pulling himself together to do so when the guard asked him for his ID. Leroy didn't have one.

"Man, I'm just down and out. Can you give me a break?" But the guard was a stickler for the rules. He stared at the tattoo Leroy had on his right cheek, the little star, then got on his radio to ask for help. Just like that.

Miffed, Leroy rose, stepped up to the guard and snatched the radio from him. "Can't you give me a break?"

"Give it back," said the startled guard, retreating a step.

And Leroy reached over and grabbed him hard by the throat, the man nearly choking as he squeezed.

"Can't you give me a break?" said Leroy again.

The guard had peed in his pants. Leroy released him and began to walk away, throwing the radio in the trash as he exited the building. Leroy didn't run or look back, just walked on. A few blocks away he went into a café and ordered a latte and a pastry. He would have enough time to finish. When they came in for him he was sitting quietly thinking of Tiara, the thoughts of her making him feel calm. He didn't want to run from the law anymore. He was through. Just a year in the pen, maybe two at most, he kept reminding himself, that should be all, and the job in Siberia might still be there when he finally went off parole.

But the security guard and his superiors had decided to press felony charges.

And then, to seal his fate, a cold case emerged that Leroy would now have to answer. A strong-armed robbery charge committed at 17.

Right out of Juvenile Hall, he had gone to stay with a foster family that didn't do much supervising so he had plenty of opportunity to roam the streets. He began to hang out with the neighborhood gang that was pushing an extortion racket on the business owners of a local strip mall. Everyone was cooperating, except for the Chinese owner of the 'Elegant Taste' donut shop. Young Leroy, anxious for recognition and eager to move up the ladder, offered to take care of business.

He cased out the place and found out which car the owner was driving. It was a black SUV. The Chinese man parked it in a small square lot behind the store. Leroy waited for night to fall and snuck up to the car and hid under it. He thought the Chinese man might be packing a gun so he would have to act fast.

A little after midnight, as usual, the Chinese fellow left the store and began to walk to his vehicle. As he entered the lot the man stopped for a moment. He looked about. The light was dimmer than usual. He was right. Leroy had knocked out one of the lights. The Chinese man, of slender build, thought of going back into the store but, glancing at the lot again, decided to go forward. Speaking in Mandarin, he cursed the landlord for not keeping up the property but kept heading straight toward his vehicle. He got to it and clicked open the door.

Leroy reached out with his powerful arms and seized the man's ankle, jerked him down and dropped him to the ground. The Chinese man fumbled for the weapon he was, in fact, carrying, but Leroy's forceful pull was so strong and disconcerting that the weapon fell out of his belt and out of reach. "What the hell!?" the man had managed to sputter in Mandarin as the irresistible force dragged him under the vehicle. Leroy took hold of both ankles so he could better pull on the man while simultaneously sliding out from under the car himself and coming out on the other side, so that it was only the Chinese man left beneath the vehicle. As he was being pulled the man forgot all his Mandarin and was now cursing in excellent English "Fuck you! Fuck you!" which he repeated, again and again. "I don't want to hurt you," said Leroy to the fellow. And the man stopped cursing. Leroy pulled on both his legs and dragged him out from under, then he stood him up against the side of the SUV.

Holding him firmly he walked him over to the driver's side so he could pick up the gun. Leroy found the weapon and put it in his pocket. "Now listen to me," said Leroy as he kept a tight grip on the man, "we figure you make 10 grand a week, so we need one grand, just one grand… you understand… one grand a week and we'll keep you safe." The man started cursing again in Mandarin. "Stop!" cried the exasperated Leroy. The man kept cursing. Leroy slapped him. The man stopped and grew very still. "Listen carefully… a young girl, about 6 or 7, will come to see you sometime this week. She will ask for a donut. She will have three short ponytails on top of her head. When she pays for it she will ask you for a donation for a trip her school will be making to the San Diego Zoo. Give her the money, okay? One thousand." Then the man slapped Leroy across his face. Leroy slapped him back. "Don't do that. I could kill you." The Chinese man just stared at Leroy, no longer afraid and instead glaring with rage.

And just then another car entered the parking lot. Leroy turned to look and the headlights blinded him. "Robbery! Robbery!" cried the Chinese man as he tore himself from Leroy's grip and began running right into the lights. The car slammed the breaks. The man's quick response took Leroy by surprise and he had no option but to bolt.

The agile Leroy bounded down the dark alley next to the lot and soon had disappeared into the night.

The Chinese man pressed charges and no little girl came by to ask for money for a school trip, although the man stayed forever suspicious of little girls with three short ponytails.

The Chinese man, a clever fellow, had scrutinized Leroy's features. He had been a portrait painter in Beijing and had a photographic memory. Leroy would forever be wary of artistic types.

22

*E*ddie Grisholt had called Leroy Cadenas to the rotunda in the middle of the night and told him that there were to be no weapons involved in the assault. All he wanted was for Legrand to get a good whooping. Joey was to be spared. It was not about him. And Leroy had answered that he was not to worry. They had the surprise factor in their favor; they would go in, land a few, and get out. Simple. He had got the instructions down pat. Hyena would hold Joey while he put the hurt on Legrand.

Understood.

"I know you have a grudge against the other one," said Grisholt, "but this is just business, I'm paying you for it. Stick to the plan."

"You got it."

"And you'll test your self-control," added Grisholt, slyly.

Leroy didn't tell him that there was already talk on the tiers that it would be best for him to move over and let someone else call the shots on their side of the unit, that he should step down and be a regular soldier instead. And it didn't help one bit that Leroy had seen Dr Gardner, which branded him a cuckoo, since visits with Mental Health were frowned upon, more so if you were Hispanic, or partly so. Never mind that getting loaded with drugs or the prison booze, was okay. Seeing a psych was not.

At 12:30 am, Eddie Grisholt's cell phone rang. It was Buck. Grisholt thought of not answering but relented.

"How's everything going?" said Buck.

"It's going."

"How come you didn't get back to me?"

"Been busy."

Grisholt had left Buck a brief text the night before, "Flowers for the man – tomorrow," and Buck had called several times. But Grisholt had ignored him.

"It's going down?" asked Buck.

"Flowers for the man," said Grisholt.

Grisholt could sense, in Buck's voice, the concern that his son might end up a casualty in the planned assault. And he had noticed it, too, when Buck had wondered aloud how trustworthy was Leroy. But Grisholt had told him that he could vouch for the man, that he had a long standing relationship with Leroy. Trust an inmate willing to hit another one? Absurd. But Buck had stayed silent.

Then Grisholt had assured him that no weapons would be involved, just your average - you better get the message prison pounding- 'Flowers for the man'.

"Legrand is the target, not your son," said Grisholt.

Buck's unease kept gnawing at him but, again, he said nothing.

Later, when he thought back on the conversation, Grisholt acknowledged that he would have turned around and cancelled the strike had Buck objected, but his silence had sealed the deal. It had taken three times of his being knocked down by the inmate up in Corcoran before Buck had stepped in and stopped the fight. Grisholt had felt so humiliated by the defeat, that soon thereafter he had put in for the transfer. Four years and he was still smarting from it like it was yesterday. But now things were beginning to shape up. Get Legrand out of the way, scare him off, then Joey would be a clear target for the rest of the demented assholes he had to work with day in and day out.

"Just have to wait for the right moment, Buck, when my buddies go out on break. They're very predictable. It could happen any time."

"Good," said Buck, still fighting his apprehensiveness and reluctant to put it up front.   "I don't want any appearance that I have been protecting him."

"No one will question you," returned Grisholt. "Frenchie will get it that he has to do the right thing, move out of the way and let prison politics be what they are. Actually, I know Frenchie's more bark than bite."

Buck held his tongue for a moment, then said. "No, he's got bite. I don't like him but he's got bite."

"I don't think so."

"Trust me, he does."

"Well, we'll see after tonight."

Though Buck knew that he had trapped himself with all his talk about having to protect his reputation, he had not counted on Eddie Grisholt having any initiative of his own. Where had that come from? And Buck allowed that Grisholt might still resent him for that beating he had got up in Corcoran. He had warned Grisholt not to fight the inmate. He had seen the young man scrap on the yard and knew he could punch and dodge like the best, but Grisholt would not take the advice. It had all started with a simple incident, something that happened every day in the unit: at the close of day room, Grisholt had ordered the idling inmate to take it to his cell and the inmate had ignored him, instead deliberately crossing to another fellow's cell door to chat it up. When Grisholt had insisted that the inmate obey him, the man turned around and called him the B word, right in front of everybody. Another officer would have taken it in stride - another day in paradise, call for help if needed - but not Grisholt. The public insult had stayed with him, rankling and eating at him, and the following night he had gone to the inmate's door and challenged him to a fight in the gym: one on one. He was sure he could take him.

No, it couldn't be, thought Buck. There might be some sore feelings, sure, but Grisholt and him had been friends. Why hold a grudge for that long, and worse, let it play out in a matter of this seriousness?

Buck tried to dispel his doubt but it would not go away. Was he kidding himself that Grisholt owed him anything? Of course not, something still had to be there. Hadn't he broken him in as an officer, led him by the hand, burped him, offered him support and advice in just about everything? Yes, he really had done that. He had treated the man like the son Joey could not be. And everything had turned out well, except for the fight. Sure, in hindsight, he could have stopped it after the first knockdown, but Grisholt himself, boiling with rage, had wanted to go on. It was not that he hadn't some good moves and even landed a few blows, he did, but it was simply that he had been outmatched.

It was the third knockout that dislocated Grisholt's jaw.

Buck had warned him, Grisholt granted, but he had not tried hard enough and that was the difference right there. That's what good friends do, they go the extra mile. After the first knockdown, Buck should have told him to cool it, that it was over, but he didn't do that. So no, he would not forgive him. Buck had betrayed him and he would answer it with another betrayal.

Grisholt felt a wave of loathing for Buck and thought himself more justified than ever in carrying out his designs. Would Joey Wilson get hurt? Anybody's guess, really. Prison was prison. If he tried to come to Legrand's defense as he suspected he would, then he would be attacked also. True, Joey was getting a reputation for being hard nosed and was likely to hold his own but Leroy and Hyena would have the advantage of surprise. He would see to that.

A good whooping, that's all. Nothing more. Did his conscience bother him? Maybe a distant twinge but nothing else. Anyway, Leroy had assured him no weapon would be involved.

"Everything will be all right," said Grisholt into the phone, confidently.

At the other end Buck Wilson, his approval for the assault dwindling fast, still could not persuade himself to put a stop to it.

"There's a nice moon out tonight here in Lancaster," said Grisholt.

"If Ansel Adams were around he would've taken a photo. He would have titled it, 'Moonrise. Lancaster'."

The tone struck Buck as a little too lighthearted and he wanted to tell Grisholt to go fuck himself. What the hell was he thinking, that he was a werewolf?

"Call me after, all right?" said Buck.

"Of course."

"You know…" began Buck again, the thought to call off the whole thing right on the tip of his tongue.

"Buck… we're doing the right thing," said Grisholt, interrupting him. Yes, he could taste the feeling of control and, oh, how he enjoyed it. Here, at last, he would be sticking it to old Buck Wilson, the famed Corcoran warrior, the Central Valley he-man, the son of a bitch who had let him down.

When he heard the phone click at the other end, Grisholt felt a sense of relief. No, it was better – it was a feeling of triumph.

23

Legrand had stayed up till midnight, as always, carefully watching for signs of something unusual but, having noticed nothing, had gone to sleep. Joey Wilson snored.

In his cell, Leroy Cadenas did some light flexing and stretching of his well-built muscles as he focused on the imminent combat. It felt like he was oiling a weapon or tuning a delicate musical instrument. No drugs would be needed. In fact, in anticipation of the cell search that would follow, he had passed his stash over to Culebra and others for safe keeping. He was over his drug phase, anyway. All he did was a little marijuana, now and then, and he planned to phase that out, too. But he didn't mind selling the junk. The more he could weaken the brains of those around him the more he would have an edge. It was a battle for survival. The thought of Dr Gardner came to him again. What would the doctor think once he learned of the incident? Did his opinion matter at all? Leroy acknowledged that it did. Somewhat. But he had not known the doc long enough.

The toothbrush he had prepared for the occasion lay on top of the shelf. He looked at it. He had filed it down to a razor sharp edge. He could kill with that thing so maybe he should use it only for back up, only in case things didn't go well. He could not come out a loser. That was clear. Once he went into the cell he would go straight for the upper bunk where Joey slept and he would give him a good pounding. Put out his lights at least. No knifing. Hyena would be in charge of restraining Legrand.

He wished they could spare Legrand but it was unlikely. The old man would get in the way. That's who he was. Leroy acknowledged that he respected the old Frenchie. At 50, he did not have to hurt anybody to prove anything. He already had a solid reputation and with it came the privilege of not having to give a damn about what low ranking punks thought of him; and he dared everyone by doing the unthinkable and protecting a chester - right in everybody's face. Just what kind of shift had occurred in the old man's brain that he had arrived at that position? There was a gulf separating them and Leroy felt envious. He had hoped one day to make friends with him but Legrand was standoffish, keeping to himself most of the time: reading, writing, exercising, taking whatever classes were available, volunteering for every kind of work, not a lazy bone in his body. Leroy reminded himself that physically he had the advantage, being over 20 years younger and there being no arguing with the law of nature, but he would have to act quickly because just one solidly landed punch by Legrand could put him away. As Joey had shown, Leroy's jaw was not the greatest.

Then the doors cracked open. That was the signal.
Leroy poked out his head and looked toward Hyena's cell. It, too, had been opened. The day room was dark. The office down below by the entrance to the building was dark, too, the officers having left for their break. Leroy took a deep breath. He slunk out of his cell and headed for the stairs, Hyena following, two silent figures crouching in the shadows to avoid being detected by other inmates in the vicinity - there were a few insomniacs.

Grisholt watched their movements carefully, at the ready to rack open the cell door to Joey and Legrand's. He could still back off, he said to himself, his heart pounding, the thrill coursing through his veins, but hell, no!

Leroy and Hyena stole down the stairs as cats on the prowl. Staying low they quickly reached cell 128, squatting into position on both sides of the cell door. The element of surprise was crucial. And there they were, holding their breaths, just waiting for Grisholt to open it.

From the booth above Grisholt had the men clearly in sight but for some reason was hesitating. Hands drenched in sweat, he could still back off.

Leroy and Hyena stared up wondering what the hell was Grisholt waiting for.

His cell phone rang. He had forgot to turn it off. He glanced at the screen: it was Buck Wilson.

From his garage, in Pomona, frantically pacing up and down, Buck Wilson, desperately expecting Grisholt to answer the call - he had finally made up his mind to call off the attack – shouted at the top of his lungs, "Pick up the phone, you asshole!" But Grisholt ignored it. And Buck shouted, as loud as he could, "Pick up the phone, you bastard!!" And the moment he did, as if his voice had suddenly found wings to sail for miles and miles, up and over the mountains, Butterfly, in cell 107, gave his cell door a loud kick and instantly launched into a rendition of America the Beautiful. "Oh beautiful, for spacious skies, for amber waves of grain…" At one thirty in the morning!

And Eddie Grisholt impulsively pressed the button to open the cell door.

With Butterfly's banging and singing, Legrand had jumped to his feet and immediately roused Joey just as the cell door cracked open enough to let Leroy squeeze in, Hyena right behind.

"…America, America, God shed his grace on thee…"

Legrand was the first man Leroy met. Leroy lunged into him but the old Frenchman was ready. Fists flew back and forth between the two as Hyena flashed past and jumped on top of Joey. Two hard blows to the head dazed Leroy and he backed off. Another shot nearly took him off his feet and then, fearing defeat, he reached for the blade and swung wildly toward Legrand, landing it to the left of his neck, sinking it into the lung below. Legrand recoiled. Now Leroy's powerful fists smashed on Legrand, blood spilling every which way, Leroy tearing into him, while Joey and Hyena, next to them, on the bunk, stayed locked in fierce combat, wrestling and crushing each other.

"...And crown thy good with brotherhood...from sea to shining sea..."

Butterfly was now shouting the words of the song while banging as hard as he could on his cell door to awaken everybody he could.

Inside 128 the feuding men were so tangled up with each other that Leroy and Hyena could not pull themselves off from Joey and Legrand to make their getaway.

"Pick up the phone!!" Buck Wilson kept shouting from his garage in Chino.

Lights were being turned on in the cells to the rallying call of Butterfly's voice,

"Oh beautiful for heroes proved in liberating strife..."

Hard hits and muffled groans filled the cell, heads and bodies crashing against cement and the sharp edges of the bunks.

"Lock them in!" cried a lone voice. "Let them kill themselves!" shouted another.

"...and more than self their country loved... and mercy more than life..." sang Butterfly.

Leroy burst out of the cell, stumbling and falling to his knees, Legrand stepping out right after him. On his left neck, just above the collarbone, a small wound oozed and gurgled blood, spraying out like a geyser each time he let out a breath.

Leroy got to his feet and sped off, running up the stairs, but Legrand was unable to give chase, his breath failing him. Gasping for air he stumbled to the foot of the stairway and hung on to it so he could lower himself and sit on the steps.

"...America, America, may god thy gold refine..." belted Butterfly.

Hyena freed himself from Joey's grip and shot out of the cell, face bloodied and torn, whizzing past the dazed Legrand and leaping up the stairs.

"...till all success be nobleness and every gain divine!"

Most of the cells were now lit and the collective banging of the cell doors had turned into a slow and mournful march while, incredibly, in the control booth, Grisholt sat frozen in his seat; he had not imagined this ghastly outcome in full sight of the entire unit.

"Sound the alarm, you dimwit!" cried one inmate. "Hit the alarm, you punk!"

shouted another. "Legrand's dying!"

"...Oh beautiful for patriot dreams, that sees beyond the years..."

Legrand was fading but still sat at the bottom of the stairs, his head leaning against the railing, the wound spraying blood with each exhalation.

Joey emerged from the cell. Dazed, unsteady on his feet, face soaked in blood, he saw Legrand and crossed to him.

"...America, America, god shed his grace on thee..."

Bewildered and confused, Grisholt had yet to press the alarm.

"Hit the alarm!" came again the roaring chorus of voices.

And Grisholt finally did. Then, quickly, seeing that Leroy and Hyena were safely in their cells, closed their doors.

"... and crown thy good with brotherhood... from sea to shining sea!"

Joey stood in front of Legrand, his head buzzing, the vision blurred by the walloping he had caught from Hyena. "I can't see," he blurted out.

"The blood... wipe it off..." said Legrand, haltingly. And Joey did but he still couldn't see straight. He sat next to Legrand. "What's that blood on your neck?"

"Don't know... something... went in there..." Leblanc said between gasps.

Joey looked at him. "I owe you," he said, looking at his friend whose image was now becoming clearer. "Whatever went in there... it was meant for me."

Leblanc smiled back. "Comes... with... the... territory," said he, faltering, every word an effort... the breathing now shallow and fast. "Got my... lung... you all right?"

"Yes," said Joey.

The doors to Bravo Three opened and the guards rushed in. Joey and Legrand were immediately commanded to lay prone on the ground. "He can't breathe, he got it in the lung," protested Joey.

"Down! Down!" shouted the first officer, waving a baton at him, ready to strike. Joey lay on the ground as ordered. Legrand was barely breathing now. "Let... me... sit up... please," he implored.

"Let him be," said Sanchez, a seasoned officer.

And just then, two nurses rolled in with the gurney.

"He's got that nasty chest wound, he'll have to sit," said Sanchez.

He helped place Legrand on the gurney, while the nurses lifted the head of it so Legrand could lie in a semi recumbent position. They turned around and raced across the yard to the medical building from where he was dispatched by ambulance to an outside hospital.

Back in Pomona, Buck Wilson sat dispirited and dejected on the edge of a stack of boxes, the cell phone still in his hand. He felt exhausted, wiped out. And then he saw Janice standing at the open door staring at him.

"Who were you calling?" she asked.

Buck shook his head slowly.

"It has to do with Joey, doesn't it?" pressed Janice, advancing towards him.

He shook his head again.

She got closer and extended her hand. "Give me the phone."

Buck, pouting his lips, shook his head again, though more slowly. He didn't want to lose control but his volcano had been rumbling.

"I need to know who you were calling. Give me the phone."

And Buck lost it. He threw the phone against the garage door and the cover flew in one direction, the body in another. Janice rushed to try to recover it but Buck grabbed her and shoved her aside. Enraged, he picked up the body of the phone, reached for a hammer in the shelf and keeping Janice away from it, shouted to her, "You want the phone? Here it is!" And he dropped the phone on the ground and, falling to his knees, slammed the hammer on it. Furiously, once, twice, three times, four times, each instance sending bits and pieces flying off. Janice wasn't giving up and tried to struggle with him but he held her off with his strong arm. "You still want the phone?" he said, tauntingly. And he hammered again at the small broken parts cracking them into even tinier pieces. And he hammered and hammered until there was nothing but a black dust left of it. But still he kept hammering away, pounding at the concrete floor beneath and tearing it up, the splintered pieces scattering about.

"Stop!" cried out, Janice. "Please, Buck, stop!!"

Buck halted. Hammer in hand, arm cocked for yet another blow to the shattered concrete floor, he stared at her for an instant, his body swaying ever so lightly, eyes raging with a fury she had never seen, a wrath that brimmed with self-contempt, and yet, in the pained and tortured midst of it, shone the glimmer of a desperate plea for forgiveness.

Buck lowered his arm slowly, his body following, crumpling to the ground.

Two paces away stood Janice, her face pale, transfixed - wondering what other horror had been visited upon her son.

In Lancaster, in the moonlit night, Joey walked in the direction of the triage room, his arms handcuffed in back, two guards beside him. A light breeze blew in from the west and the throbbing in his face became more noticeable. He had been hit hard. His mouth was so dry it was painful to swallow. Blood still trickled from the open wounds and he could taste it, too. He opened and closed his mouth. His jaw seemed to be working but there were some sore spots on the right. A tooth or two might have been loosened from the powerful blows. He had a buzz in his left ear that wouldn't go away and he couldn't hear well from that side.

He owed Legrand big time, thought Joey, if it hadn't been for the Frenchman it would've been him in the ambulance, or worse, and they both owed Butterfly and his America the Beautiful, the warning having given Legrand a chance to jump to his feet, flick on the light and rouse him. Who knows what would've happened if it had not been for that timely signal.

As he walked along Joey cursed in silence a prison system that allowed such assaults to take place. The handcuffs were too tight and were cutting into his wrists and he cursed the system for that, too.

The officers had offered him to ride up in the electric cart but he had refused. He needed to breathe the air, to feel alive. He wondered how Legrand was doing; Legrand, the friend who had been given a choice to change cells and had not. Would he make it? And he realized that, at that very moment, he wanted nothing more than to be at his side so he could watch over him. Oh, the madness, the madness of it all.

Buck Wilson was still lying on the floor of his garage, the hammer next to him. He lay on his side, the legs pulled up, the head resting on his hands, his eyes wide open. The storm had passed. Janice was sitting on a crate nearby, watching him. Half an hour had gone by. Then Buck stirred. He calmly stood up and went inside the house. Janice rose and followed.

Buck went into his daughter Margaret's room and opened the closet.

As Janice looked on, he reached up to the highest shelf, pulled out a shoebox and took out the half finished bottle of scotch. He sat on the edge of his daughter's bed and took a swig from it. Janice pulled up a chair and sat across. She knew what was coming.

"Why did you take Joey away from me?"

Janice stared back. Buck had never asked her the question, not directly. She gave a slow shrug. "I suppose I needed something really my own. It was my insurance."

"Insurance?"

"I didn't think we'd be together very long."

"Horseshit!"

"Please don't curse, I hate it when you do that."

"Did I ever give you the impression that I was looking at other women?"

"You looked, you just didn't act on it. Not that I knew, anyway."

Buck's face was drawn, mortified, and it was this that worried Janice the most. What had the call been about?

A wave of self pity rose in Buck and he closed his eyes. Why had he not stopped the assault an hour ago?

"Give me the bottle," said Janice reaching over with her hand.

"I'm going to drink as long as I want."

"Buck…?"

He held on to it but felt like a pouting child.

"Are you working tomorrow morning?"

"Not anymore."

"What was the call about?"

He could not bear to tell her.

"I need to know what the call was about."

"I'm having an affair."

"I don't think so, and if you are, I don't give a damn."

He laughed.

"Why did you take Joey away from me?" The question, the question: the one that he should have asked 20 years ago. Now it rang hollow because he knew the answer, had known it all along. She had taken Joey away because she could.

"If you knew what I was doing, why didn't you stop me?"

"I didn't realize it till it was too late." He said it and, this time, he felt no shame, like he had so often before. In fact, Joey had solved the problem himself. He would be neither Janice's nor Buck's. He had taken off when he was thirteen.

Buck looked off, his jaw slacking. Janice reached over and took the bottle away from him. He offered no resistance. She put the bottle down by the side of her chair. They looked at each other. "We thought about ourselves, not him… and we both lost," said she.

"He lost," said Buck.

They were quiet for a moment. She stood up and crossed to the window. All was quiet, the neighbors tucked away in their own worlds.

A dog barked.

A cat chased after another.

24

Gardner learned of the incident the moment he walked into the mental health building at 8 am the following day. Bravo yard was in lockdown mode. He made a few phone calls to see about the status of Legrand and was relieved to hear that he was in stable condition. The punctured lung had been addressed and he was resting. Now the task fell to custody, to see that the culprits were dealt with. He found out that Captain Driscoll was in his office and headed over to speak to him.

Sam Driscoll was in his early forties, bright, diligent, part of the budding movement to see the prison system improve and aware that there was much baggage to cast off.

Gardner stood outside his office waiting for the man to get off the phone. A minute later Driscoll waved him in.

"Have a seat, doc."

"Good morning. Don't know if you're aware of it but Legrand is my patient."

"Didn't know that. Sorry about what happened."

The Captain told him who the alleged assailants were and the approximate time the assault had taken place. Gardner was stunned.

Filled with disappointment, he dropped his face in his hands for a moment. When he looked up at the Captain again he told him that Leroy Cadenas was also his patient.

"Lieutenant Griffith asked me to see him and I did. I thought we were establishing rapport. I really did think that I had a chance of making an impact."

"We can only try, doc, that's all we can do," said Driscoll.

Gardner reviewed in his mind if he had had grounds to have given a specific warning to the victims of the assault. But no, Leroy had made his threat public, everyone knew about it. What Gardner was angry about was that his work had meant nothing, accomplished nothing.

Staring down at the floor, Gardner questioned himself in silence as the Captain looked on. Driscoll felt tempted to say a soothing word but he knew the doc was a veteran and held his tongue. The doc had to deal with his own limitations as a psychiatrist just as he, on the custody side, had to deal with his own.

"What details can you give me?" said Gardner.

"Nothing more. Regulations, you know. An official investigation is under way and Sergeant Krause is in charge. It's really out of my hands."

"Krause?"

"Just transferred in from Folsom."

Gardner shook his head slowly.

"Why in hell were those cells opened in the middle of the night?"

"The investigators will get to it," said Driscoll. He shared Gardner's concern. "Doc, you know I'm with you on this."

But Gardner could not be shaken from his gloom. "Who is this sergeant Krause?"

"Don't know her but have heard she's capable, on track for a promotion, sees the job as a career and wants to do well."

"You really think we'll get to the bottom of this?"

"I hope so."

Gardner left the Captain's office but felt no better than when he had gone in. Never very certain as to the impact of his work, he now doubted even more his ability to get to the essence of his patients. Could he have probed further? But the more he thought about it the more he acknowledged that he had barely started to work with Leroy and the work took time. A bond had not been established. Still, he was angry with

Leroy and decided to go directly to Ad Seg (Administrative Segregation, a.k.a. the hole), where he was now being housed, to confront him with his behavior. He found out his cell number and went straight to it.

The cell door window had been papered over so he could not see inside. He rapped on the door. There was no response. He rapped a second time. "Cadenas! This is Dr Gardner." Again, no response. Gardner knocked a third time.

"Go away," came the voice from inside, finally.

"I need to talk to you."

"I don't."

"I cannot believe you did what you did."

"You don't know anything about being a prisoner."

"What on earth gave you permission to dehumanize Legrand? You, knowing that you yourself have been dehumanized, why did you choose to treat someone the same way, even worse?"

Leroy wanted to tell Gardner that he hadn't really set out to intentionally stab Legrand, that things had just got out of hand, that the whole thing had to do with reputation and survival, as reasoned by a man who had lost hope of ever regaining his freedom. But that was no excuse, was it? He had made a choice to carry the weapon. Yes, he had. And having done so, he had gone past the point of no return.

Gardner stood there for a long minute, quietly waiting for Leroy's answer. He was about to leave when, from a nearby cell, a calm and reassuring voice flowed out.

"Leave him alone, doc. He needs time to himself. He'll come around."

The voice sounded familiar. Gardner stepped over to the man's cell, two spaces down from Leroy's. He recognized an old patient of his, a lifer, a man with whom he had worked for a short time a while back.

"Fillmore. Remember?" said the inmate, smiling.

"I do. What're you doing here?"

"Got in a fight. You know how it is. Fellow tried to put one over me. I'll be all right. If I get a fair hearing, I'll be back in Delta pretty soon"

Gardner remembered the story. The man had been cultivating marijuana on a large scale up in the sierras when a band of thieves decided to help themselves to part of the crop. In the shootout, two of the men were killed. Fillmore had got 18 years for it but he was appealing his case hoping for a sentence reduction. Chances were that he would get one. He was a smart fellow, Gardner recalled. He wished him good luck and walked off.

Legrand spent three days at an outside hospital and, as soon as he returned, Gardner called him in to his office.

"My lung had collapsed so I couldn't breathe," said Legrand. His face was still lumpy and discolored from the thrashing he had got, the upper lip swollen, a cut healing across his nose, another on his eyebrow. "In all my years of fighting, when I was younger, I never got hit this bad. It's just that, when I got stabbed…" And he stopped. "It could've been worse."

"I'm so sorry," said Gardner. "One of your assailants is one of my patients."

Legrand looked off. "You know I won't mention any names."

"Driscoll told me."

"You know who opened the doors?" asked Legrand.

"No."

"Grisholt. And who do you think was up in the control room when I came in from the hospital yesterday?"

"Grisholt?"

"Exactly. Now how is that possible?"

Gardner was baffled. "I've been assured that there's an investigation going on," he said, apologetically.

"Even if there is one, that man shouldn't be allowed to be in charge of letting people in and out of their cells," continued Legrand in exasperation. "Why isn't he off duty while he's investigated?"

"I can't speak for custody…"

Legrand shook his head. "Nothing changes, man." He took a breath but then flinched from the pain. The wound was still fresh.

Gardner knew he had to be there to listen to the anger, but he knew, too, that it would reach a zenith and then subside, for Legrand had long ago become a rational man. Still, it was his task to grasp the depth of his patient's protest.

"So what do you have to say," said Legrand, leveling his challenging gaze at Gardner.

Gardner felt that he was being reproached. "The system is slow and unfair and cruel," he began, "But there are good people here, too, at every level: committed people who want to understand what happened in your lives that caused you to wreck them; real people, willing to put in the time and energy; sound people, who want to move the prison system forward, knowing full well that it's an uphill struggle."

Legrand closed his eyes for a moment.

"And it's a war we're fighting every single day," continued Gardner, "A war between those who give a damn, who think that we ought to and can do better, and those who believe that you are a lost cause, beyond hope. And as hard as it may be for you to stomach the notion now, those of us who give a damn are winning. We may lose our battles, and there will be many more we'll lose, but we will win the war."

"Where the heck do you get all your optimism?" said Legrand, in frustration.

Gardner said nothing.

"This is not the first time he's done it," pressed Legrand. "An inmate blows him off and he can't handle it and then he turns to another to settle the score for him."

"Have you reported it?"

"C'mon, doc, what do you think they're going to do with my report?" Just as he said this he grimaced from a shooting pain on the site of the wound. He slowly shifted his weight in the seat. "We watch these guys all day long. We know who is weak and who is not. And it's the strong who're always the fairest."

And so it was in the universe, thought Gardner, the weak behaving like brutes to hide their perceived weakness, even from themselves.

"Word is that the attack was meant for Joey Wilson," said Gardner.

Legrand looked off.

"You still want to be in the same cell with him?"

"Yes."

"Why?"

"Because I can help him. He may have molested a child but there's a human being in there, and I'm making it my business to help bring it out," said Legrand.

Gardner held Legrand's gaze. He had grown to admire him and here was another reason why he did. Still, he offered, "there may be more attacks…"

But Legrand was firm. "It's what I have to do. Let that be my way of making amends, of giving a sense of purpose to my existence."

25

Dinner had come and gone and the unit had settled down for the evening business. Those not on restrictions had come out to play card games or chess, get a haircut, walk about, chat with the neighbors. But Butterfly, as usual, did not step out. Except for showers, he never did. And he had not for the past year, ever since he had been in a fight and had been slashed across the face, from the right forehead clear down to the left chin, a deep cut that miraculously skipped his eye but traveled deeply over his nose.

Witnesses said he fought bravely but there had been three to fend off and it had been too much. While gallantly out boxing them, a knife had circled in the air and sliced into him. He had glimpsed it as it neared but it was too late.

That he had been using Heroin was no secret, and neither was the fact that the drug had slowed him down. The agility he was known for, despite his size, had not been there when needed. He had been targeted because he had been late on paying his drug debt. In fact, he still hadn't, arguing that his facial disfigurement had settled the score. His creditors thought otherwise and a contract was still out on him, so Butterfly stayed in his cell and read, practiced his singing and put on the weight. One estimate ran that he had packed 100 extra pounds on his already oversized body, putting him at over 400. He was reluctant to set foot on a scale.

No one knew much about Butterfly's past, either. He came from northern California, exact location unknown, though some people placed him somewhere in the vicinity of Eureka, near the border with Oregon, and that he had worked in logging for a while. Some said he had even finished college but no one would confirm it. He was vague about his offense saying only that he was serving life for murder but had got a bad deal. He had shot back in self defense.

On occasion, when Chloe was out in the day room, and she was getting along with her boyfriend and could afford to flirt, she'd come by his cell door and chat with him. Butterfly looked forward to those moments. The sight of Chloe, her slender, feminine figure, her budding breasts, always gave him a kick. He knew that she belonged to Sparrow but he loved the attention she gave him.

Today was one such special day.

"It's good to see you, Chloe. I don't know what I'm going to do when you leave."

"Oh, listen to you," she answered coyly, with a little lift of her head. "I'm sure you'll find someone else to come check on you."

"It won't be the same and you know it. Sparrow okay with you coming over? I don't want to get you in any trouble."

"Of course he is. He knows we're just friends."

Butterfly sighed dramatically. "What're you going to do when you get out? It's coming up, isn't it?"

"Three months."

"Dang! You lucky bitch."

Chloe laughed. "I feel like one, too." She opened her mouth wide when she laughed and he could see all her teeth which he thought were perfect. She put her hands on her slender waist and thrust her hips forward. She enjoyed the way Butterfly took her in. It was hunger in his eyes, she could tell. "I'm going to go work in a hair salon my cousin just opened."

"I can only imagine all the action you're going to get. Like in a candy store, right? I'm jealous."

"Don't be silly, I wouldn't do that to him."

"You're going to come visit?"

"Of course. We're getting married so we won't have any hassles. But enough about me. I worry about you, Butter. I worry about you being stuck in there all day long and putting on all that weight."

"I'm going to cut back on the bread, the pasta, the meat."

"Oh you poor thing. Starting when?"

"Tomorrow. You inspire me."

"Be serious. That weight is dangerous. How much do you owe?"

"Nothing. They cut me, didn't they?"

"That's not how they see it. How much did you owe?"

"Three hundred."

"That's it?"

"Yep."

She leaned a little closer to the gap on the side of the door and whispered, "Once I get going out there, I'll send you the money."

"No, I can't let you do that."

"But I want to. You're my friend. But you have to promise me you won't use again."

"I'm done. The day I got sliced I stopped," said Butterfly.

"Oh, god, I remember that day." She brought her hands to her face and closed her eyes. "Just horrible. I thought you were going to die."

"Things happen," said Butterfly.

"They did a great job stitching you up."

"Yeah, that's true, except for the nose."

"It makes you look dangerous, like Brando. But when you get out you can get a nose job."

"Really?"

"You'll look so debonair."

Butterfly laughed.

"I can see you swaggering down Hollywood Boulevard on Saturday night, or up and down the Strip, a bitch on each arm."

Butterfly gave a good, hearty laugh.

She smiled, glad she could do that for him. "Okay, I have to go now. I told him I'd be here just a few minutes. Be strong."

And she leaned at the gap again and whispered, "I love you. In a friendly kind of way."

"I know. Thank you, Chloe, that means a lot to me. I love you, too."

And she sauntered off, swaying her hips like Butterfly imagined the Girl of Ipanema had done, when she inspired Jobim to pen the famous song. He looked longingly after her and thought that one day he would write a song for her.

Half hour later, day room ended and everybody was asked to lock it up.

But the interaction with Chloe had stirred up Butterfly and he now wanted to sound off. He waited a few minutes after the last man had gone into his cell and then bellowed out into the empty day room, "What about drugs?" The rich baritone voice shot through the unit and could be heard in every corner. No one answered right away so he waited a moment.

"What about them?" came back the voice of an inmate in section B.

"Why do we use?"

"To pass the time," cried out another.

"That's the problem right there... passing the time," returned Butterfly. "That's all we do in this shit hole we live in. When we first come to prison, does anybody tell us, 'you're expected to find out why and how did you become the person you are now.'"

"There are no expectations," replied Bazooka.

"None whatsoever," rejoined Butterfly.

"We're supposed to know. We're all grown assed men," shouted Bellevue, a New Yorker who had come down to the Southland on vacation but lost his way.

"But we're not, Bellevue. When we come in we're not grown assed men but failed and incompetent people, unable to solve conflicts, emotionally immature and unable to have satisfactory relationships with other human beings... or simply incapable in some instances."

"Lighten up, bro, I just had dinner and you're going to make me throw up," yelled out Baby Face.

"Just so everybody knows, I've switched parties, I'm now a Republican!" shouted another inmate.

"From the Tea Party, right?" said another.

"Go, Butter baby, go," shouted Chloe from her cell she shared with Sparrow.

"When we come in we have no identity of our own... and yet we call ourselves men," said Butterfly.

"Ah, shut up, you motherfucker. Just a little while ago you were doped out on Heroin, now you think you can preach to us," shouted Gator, who claimed he had once made a living in Florida capturing and skinning the reptiles.

"I was doped out, you're right... and it took almost losing my life for me to begin to see the light."

"I don't mind the singing but you can stuff the preaching," continued Gator.

But Butterfly would not be discouraged. "Gentlemen... I don't speak to offend... not in the least. My intention is to begin a dialogue... to help us find a path so we can emerge as human beings..."

From their cell, both Legrand and Joey listened attentively.

"... Why do we keep hurting each other?"

TV sets were turned down and the men went to their doors to listen.

Leroy had his ear pressed to the crack of the door and so his neighbors Culebra and Casino.

"We are doing so because we're not being personally responsible for our lives," continued Butterfly, "because no matter how much pain a man has in his life, no matter how much hurt he keeps in his heart and mind, it is his pain alone and not his brother's. So don't pass it to anyone else. Butterfly's pain is Butterfly's only and no one else's. And I should never give it to another person."

"If you give it to another person then you're escaping your freedom," said Paytrell, who rarely contributed to the discussion.

Legrand and Joey, next door, smiled when they heard him.

"Thank you, brother Paytrell," said Butterfly, "and if we follow that logic, then we should stand firm and not let others give their pain to us… it is their pain and they have to deal with it. You can hear it and choose to help because we're all brothers and sisters, but it is their pain."

"I love you, Butter!" cried out Chloe.

"I do, too!" seconded Venus, who was particularly adept at hiding cell phones. For a fee.

"I became an addict because I couldn't bear my pain… and I indulged in all sorts of poisons to escape from myself… only to find that I had injured my beautiful body and brain and made things worse."

"Why couldn't you bear your pain?" Bazooka asked from the far corner.

"Because I couldn't accept who I was… couldn't live with myself just as I was. I looked at everybody and thought everybody was better than me. I couldn't look myself in the mirror and say, 'I am who I am… and it's okay'… I couldn't say, 'sometimes I'm weak and it's okay, inadequate and it's okay, less than manly, even cowardly and it's okay… and it's okay… incompetent and it's okay…' and if I accept and bear it I will then start to work to make it better… for even if I'm feeling trampled and squashed, humiliated and shamed… even if I'm flawed or disfigured to no end… I can still rise… and I can because I have breath… and if I have breath I have worth… and if I have worth I have an obligation to live my story… and when I choose to live my story I will give my heart wings for it will be a story of becoming… that man can always, always, no matter what he has done or where he has been, rise to redeem himself… and perchance to soar."

Johnson, the heroin addict on a path to recovery, had listened carefully and nodded in agreement.

"Nothing original about that," someone shouted.

Another rolled out a raspberry.

"Heard it before," cried yet another.

"I know you're a pussy, you motherfucker," interrupted the twisted soul from cell 118.

"Every man has a seed in him that he must nurture..." replied Butterfly, "the man in 118 has just not found it."

In their cell, as they stood pressed against their door listening, Sparrow began to caress Chloe's tush but she removed his hand gently, "Not now, baby."

"We know that there's no proper rehabilitation or therapy in this shit hole we live in... or there is for the few," resumed Butterfly, "But there's nothing keeping us from helping each other grow, is there? So let us stop hurting each other. Let us stop giving grounds for the authorities to think we're idiots. Let us stop asking our relatives to smuggle in drugs for us."

"Pay your debt, you piece a shit," cried the man from 118.

"Take the yet to evolve individual who just spoke..." replied Butterfly.

"Fuck you."

"... That one, precisely... is willing to be a party to the injuring of a man for three hundred dollars..."

Leroy listened carefully.

"... But did his dear mother want him to behave in such ornery fashion? Of course not. Because no matter how troubled the dear lady may have been, I can assure you she never wanted her son to get stuck at such low level of personal development."

"You piece a crap, don't you mess with my mother."

"But circumstances intervened and he got all twisted up," replied Butterfly, "I understand, and because I do I can forgive him."

"I'm going to fuck you up bad," insisted 118.

"Please do hear me, sir, I just told you I forgive you."

"I'm gonna fuck you up and then fuck you, too."

"Oh, dear, it gets worse. So ladies and gentlemen, I beg of you that we unite... I beg of you that we pull together and summon the best we have in ourselves... because no one will do it for us... certainly not the American citizen who doesn't want his taxes raised anymore and wants prisons built as far away from his home so they won't affect his property value... and who can blame him, he obeyed the law."

"Butter baby, your heart is a rainbow!" said Chloe, excitedly.

Some cells banged and rattled in approval.

"Don't escape your truth! Don't give up your power! Don't escape from freedom!" cried Paytrell.

"He's taking his meds," said Joey to Legrand.

"There's no reason why we cannot tutor our brothers," resumed Butterfly, "the one who can read teaching the one who can't. God knows I could learn from those who have beat drug addiction on their own. And let us begin to build a community."

"Eat my bird!" shouted a disgruntled sort.

"You know, in the time I've stayed in my cell, for no other reason than to preserve my physical integrity..." continued Butterfly.

"You mean so they wouldn't kill your ass, you coward," cried 118.

"... As I was saying, in my isolation, I've taken to reading as much as I can to nourish my developing mind... and I came across a man who lived more than two thousand years ago... two thousand years ago, ladies and gentlemen, think about it... and while I cannot say that I understand all that this wise man said, this much he's made clear to me... the irrational separates us... the rational unites us."

Butterfly paused for a second, waiting for a reply, but there was none.

"I love you all, even those who have harmed me and wish to do so again. Good night!"

26

*I*t was a Saturday evening, back in Los Angeles, when Gardner went to see Mary Jane Jeffries perform. Through thick and thin she had kept it up, become a competent pianist on the way, and was enjoying a steady following. Gardner had heard her play a variety of tunes but he enjoyed most of all the love ballads. She played only on Saturdays, in a little Italian restaurant east of Hill on Colorado Blvd in Pasadena.

Tonight it had been raining and the attendance was sparse. After an hour or so into her show she turned off the mike and walked over to join him.

"How're you," she said as she sat next to him.

"Enchanted by your singing."

"Thank you."

The waiter came to the table and asked if she wanted something to eat, but she politely declined.

"A glass of wine?" said the young man.

"Sure. Pinot Noir, please."

"The gentleman?"

"I'm fine, thank you." Gardner had ordered earlier.

The waiter walked off.

"They treat you well?"

"They barely pay anything, but I get to do my songs and enjoy the audience."

"Your voice is growing richer."

"You're too kind."

"I am serious. In fact, I was sitting here enjoying your magic when I remembered that night, about a year ago, it happened to be raining also – something about you and rain -when I strode in at around 9 or so. There were a few scattered customers sitting around, like tonight, and I stopped in the middle of the room, wiping the wet off my shoulders and looked at you and said, 'Stormy Weather, please', and you didn't miss a beat and launched right into it.

"It was a lovely moment. Were you breaking up with someone?"

Gardner hesitated and she immediately checked herself. "I'm sorry, I didn't mean to get personal."

"No, not all. I was just feeling romantic that night. Rain does that to me."

She averted his eyes. "It's a pretty tune."

"The way you sing it."

"Thanks."

"How's your daughter?"

"Gracie Kim? She's working for an NGO in Bolivia. They promote the welfare of women in the developing world. She teaches English."

The waiter returned with the glass of wine.

"She happy?"

"She seems to be. Just talked to her yesterday."

Gardner had been sweeping the breadcrumbs on the table with the butter knife. He swept them one way and then the other.

"Something soothing about that," observed Mary Jane, pointing to the traveling breadcrumbs.

"Maybe telling a story," smiled Gardner as he let the butter knife rest. "Want to get lunch tomorrow?"

"I have plans." She said it a shade too quickly and she saw Gardner flinch.

"Another time, maybe?"

"Sure." Again, her reply was not warm and she sensed she was putting more distance between them than was called for. She asked herself why. She enjoyed his company.

"Just wanted to chat about various and sundry things."

"You spend a lot of time with your patients," she said. "What is it they do for you?"

He peered into her eyes before answering. "That's a big question, my dear, one I will be glad to go into when you have time for that lunch with me." He reached over and squeezed her hand, lingering an instant.

She grinned. "I've been a little busy lately."

"You sing in Korean?"

"I do." She brushed back her hair as she met his gaze.

"I suspected you did. I have never heard you."

"When Korean customers come in. It surprises them and they leave nice tips. One day I'll sing one for you."

"I'm looking forward to it."

They talked a few more minutes and then it was time for her to return to the keyboards.   She had drunk only a few sips of her wine and she slid the glass toward Gardner. As she did she rotated it slightly so that the edge with her lipstick was away from him.

"Here, you can have the rest of mine".

Gardner took notice but then rotated the glass back so he would be drinking from the side with the lipstick. He raised her glass, "Till next time."

"Till next time."

He stayed for a few more songs then left. He had felt a bit hurt that she had turned him down on the lunch offer but it was not the first time. So far, it had always been mixed signals with Mary Jane.

He got home, read a few pages of an American history book and turned off the lights. He fell asleep right away but soon woke up. He tossed around for a few moments but sleep eluded him. He got up and checked the time; it was 1:15 am. Padding over to the living room with the intention of reading he changed his mind and decided to step out into the balcony instead. He slid open the door but as soon as he did, the sound of it disrupted two lovebirds, a man and a woman, who had quietly been cuddling in the deep end of the pool below. Ah, how delightful, thought Gardner.

Startled, the couple had pulled apart as they looked up in his direction. Gardner did not recognize them. They were young, probably guests of someone in the building.

He sat down in the shadows, lamenting the interruption he had caused, as much for them as for him. The light in the pool outlined the shape of their bodies without betraying their features. She seemed to be naked, her long hair falling unto the water and fanning out, the shapely legs wading invitingly beneath, as if readying to wrap around her lover and squeeze his nectar. But would they carry on, would they let him be their witness?

The water lapped gently around them and the light from the pool bounced up, playfully, unto the balcony above.

She giggled nervously for a moment, whispering something in her lover's ear that made him laugh, and then they both turned to glimpse in Gardner's direction. They were deliberating.

She giggled gain, caressing her lover's hair, taking her time to fiddle with his chest, then tilting up his chin. Holding himself up on the pool's edge, he slid his free hand under her so he could lift her to him. She let herself. They kissed. Long. Sultry. Meant to be remembered, thought Gardner. He felt he had been invited to the occasion.

The man leaned back against the coping as she slid both her hands down to free him… and raising herself slightly moved smoothly into place. Meant to be remembered. Yes. She pressed down on his shoulders and rose gently, sweetly, just enough, then lowered herself, ever so tenderly, slowly relishing the joy of the fit, two lovers in the night.

Gardner had closed his eyes. He had let his mind take him back to a time, not long before, when it had been his turn to love in the open.

She was from Nashville but didn't sing, although, true to her roots, she loved to hum along to a country tune. She worked as a traveling nurse and had crisscrossed the world, even spending time in Saudi Arabia where, if she was to be believed, an elder member of the royal family whom she had tended to had courted her lavishly. After indulging him a bit, she had turned down the offer and made her way to Los Angeles where she had met Gardner at a bar on Vermont Ave in Los Feliz, just east of Hollywood. She was two years older than him but looked younger, the most unusual circumstance being that she had been born exactly on the same date that he had, March the 11th. Gardner was amused and took the initiative to strike up a friendship. Her French name, Genevieve, enthused him further. Though she preferred to be called Gen by intimates, Gardner relished the mouthing of the name, Gen-e-vie-ve. He had been a lifelong student of French but had never made it to fluency and had given up hope of ever doing so. Genevieve, on the other hand, spoke the language fluently and had even picked up Arabic while juggling the entreaties of the wealthy Saudi prince. Language was part of her charm.

Despite occasional flare ups, their relationship had moved along. They had played tennis on Saturday mornings in Burbank – her choice – but that hadn't lasted, her powerful serve being too overwhelming for Gardner, although he consoled himself with the notion that it was the way she looked on the court, her statuesque figure and the short, dainty, frilly attire, that distracted him and made him lose his grip.

She rented a home in Topanga Canyon with a beautiful pool shaped like an oyster with lighting that suffused from blue to magenta and in whose warm waters they had indulged each other till the wee hours. She was a wonderful swimmer also and, in her youth, had been in the Olympic tryouts for synchronized swimming.

One night, after they had seen each other for about 5 months, she invited him to a Latin nightclub in the Mid-Wilshire area in Los Angeles, an upscale spot she had heard of from a fellow nurse.

They took a small table to the side with a good view of the floor. The place was trendy and filled with young, svelte, flashy women but it didn't take long for Genevieve to make her move. Though in her forties, she boldly took to the floor and dazzled from the start, her steps graceful and precise to the percussive rhythm of the Cuban congas. She gyrated fluidly, skirt swirling teasingly, allowing a full peek of her carefully chosen undies, let alone her perfectly toned legs.

Gardner had never seen her dance this way and was in awe. A crowd of beautiful people had circled around, swaying to an unceasing beat that roused the blood, lured the feet to fly and bodies to rub against each other.

Gardner could not rival the skill of Genevieve. He went through the motions of keeping up but it was pointless, she was way out of reach. It was her show.

There had been no malice on his part, as he recalled, but pulled by the surfeit of pulsing flesh that surrounded him, he had let his eyes go wandering and they had settled on a lush, brown, petite Hispanic beauty that stood in the circle. She smiled back.

As Genevieve did her pirouettes on the floor, the Hispanic woman winked at Gardner, her dark, glistening eyes beckoning. He knew better but it was divine to lock eyes – if only for a moment - with an enticing woman who couldn't care less whether he could keep up with Genevieve or not.

And then he felt the intense glare of Genevieve. It burnt right through him and it was unforgiving.

She kept dancing but did not look at him again. Instead, she stared at the Hispanic woman in the circle. It must have been a murderous expression because the woman instantly lowered her eyes and, turning around, disappeared into the crowd.

The tune ended and Genevieve, in a huff, headed straight for their table. She was clearly incensed but was straining to compose herself. When she could bear it no more she pressed her hands down on the edge of the table and glowered at him. "I want to leave," she announced, the words biting.

"Why?" asked Gardner, playing innocent, not having grasped the depth of the insult, "Aren't you having fun?" It was the wrong thing to say.

"How dare you?" she lashed back, her face suddenly flushed.

"What?" His tone was calmly inquisitive, even an effort to appease, but there was no turning down Genevieve's rising rage.

"Don't you dare look at another woman the way you did while you're with me," she said.

A flurry of thoughts came back to him. He knew she had a quick temper – little things that had happened between them had told him so – like the time he had forgot to take off his shoes when he walked into her carefully decorated living room with the white, lush carpet she had just steam cleaned, but they had been able to work things out. But something about this flare-up he was now witnessing had the potential of being seismic.

"I did nothing wrong," he said to her, a note of pleading in his words.

She threw the glass of wine in his face.

Stunned, he closed his eyes. He felt the wine run down his face, the tracks cool as the liquid coursed down to his chin, then dripping off onto his new velvet jacket. He had to steady himself, he knew as much. He had not intended to smile – and if he did, it was a private smile, not meant for her – but he did and she turned to him with renewed anger, the poisoned fingers jabbing in the air, eager to wound and to provoke.

"Say something, you sonofabitch!" she shouted, each word the stab of a knife.

"I look at a woman but it means nothing," said Gardner, "And I do not deserve the treatment I'm getting from you. I do not deserve any of it, not an iota of it..." and as he spoke he felt a flash of rage begin to rise in him and he thought he needed to stop, that it was he who needed to leave, that words weren't going to do it, that he had to leave to protect himself. But he couldn't get up from his chair.

"Bastard! Sonofabitch!"

Had he had too much to drink?

"How dare you insult me in public!" she continued.

Her words were pounding and pounding on him.

"And let me tell you something..." he began again. He could still get up and walk away, couldn't he?

"Coward!" she lashed again, "Say something!"

And it got away from him. "You may be pretty but you become an ugly woman when you carry on the way you have."

Her response was swift. She stood up abruptly and yanked up the table, tipping it toward him, the cloth, glasses, bottles, plates and cutlery all sliding onto his lap, and she stormed out.

Gardner remembered getting up from his seat, being aware of all the neighboring tables having their eyes fixed on him… then reaching calmly into his pocket, putting two hundred dollars on the bare table and, as he walked to exit the cordoned off area where they had dined, a man who was seated in the last table raising a glass of wine toward him in offer. Gardner stopped, looked at the man. He had a young, chunky, affable face. "Do you need it?" said the man presenting the glass. And Gardner waved him off. "I've had enough, but thank you, anyway. Good night."

Outside the club, Genevieve had asked the attendant to call a cab. She was standing near the curb, facing the street. The club's neon lights splashed dizzyingly on the sidewalk as the traffic whizzed by. It was past midnight and more people were queuing up to come in and join the fun. Gardner handed his parking stub to the attendant and stood at a distance from Genevieve. In a conciliatory mood, he approached her. "Let's go home, okay. We can talk about this later." She had behaved insolently and he would have to reconsider continuing in the relationship but he was glad the pang of anger he had felt was subsiding. The attendant brought up the car and opened the door for Genevieve. She got in. Gardner sighed with relief, paid the attendant, got in and drove off. But it wasn't over.

Inside the car, the windows rolled up, she began to go at him with untamed fury. "How dare you?" she said to him, over and over again, each time with more venom and now slamming her fist on the dashboard.

"Please, Genevieve, please," he begged of her, but she continued.

"Look, maybe we should just end this, all right, let's call it off," said Gardner, "Obviously, I'm just not right for you." The words inflamed her instead. Turning abruptly, she hauled off and struck him. She had intended to hit him in the shoulder but miscalculated and her fist slid over and got him in the neck. The blow stung Gardner and the vehicle swerved out of control for an instant. Gardner reflexively grabbed her wrist and brought it down hard against the gear console. She shrieked. They were traveling down Wilshire, heading west and unbeknownst to Gardner, the swerving and the waving and Genevieve's flying fist had attracted the attention of a vigilant police squad who had started to track their vehicle without turning its overhead lights on.

"You hurt me!" screamed Genevieve. And she turned again on Gardner and smacked him. She was strong – remember her power serve at tennis – and accurate – and now every blow was hitting the mark. The one that struck his right ear had set his head abuzz; the one that landed on the jaw had made him see stars. Gardner was trying desperately to parry off the blows but could not while simultaneously attempting to pull over to the side of the road.

"Stop it!" he kept saying. He turned the signal lights on to pull over but the distracted drivers on the next lane were not letting him. Genevieve landed another blow. And another. Gardner missed that the traffic light ahead had turned red. When he saw it he slammed the brakes but the car rolled well unto the crosswalk. Gardner grabbed Genevieve's wrists and held them down. "Stop!"

"Bam!" went the startling sound and both Gardner and Genevieve stopped.

Standing in front of their vehicle, an intensely irate man stood staring at Gardner. He had just slammed his fist on Gardner's hood. Heavy set, with a ruddy face, looking bloated or drunk, he shouted, "You punk! Look where you're going! You almost run me over, you prick!" Gardner didn't remember seeing anyone near him when he had slammed the breaks. The heavy-set man pulled a flask out of his back pocket and threw it at the windshield. Miraculously, the flask bounced off and over leaving only a small crack in the glass. But it was too much for Gardner. He flew out of the car, ran up to the man and punched him in the face. Where he found the strength to land a blow like that Gardner never could figure out but he was clearly beside himself. The man wobbled back, dazed, then seemed to recover and lunge at him. Gardner recalled hearing a voice commanding him to stop but he only saw the drunken man charging like a bull. Gardner moved swiftly out of the way and let the man trip on himself and fall to the ground in front of the vehicle. He landed hard, face down. All traffic had stopped and a few vehicles honked while passersby stood to gawk. A man in a Dodgers' jacket pulled out his cell phone and began recording the scene. The man on the ground lay still, very still, a trickle of blood oozing out of him. That's when Gardner noticed the boots of the police officer coming up beside him.

"Pray that he's not dying," said the cop flatly. And he switched on his transmitter and called for an emergency response.

Wanting to repair the damage done, Gardner dropped to his knees to assist the fallen man but the cop shouted, "Stay back! This is the scene of a crime!"

What? A crime? A feeling of panic seized Gardner. "But I'm a doctor," he pleaded.

"Stay back! You're a suspect. Possible homicide," commanded the officer, and Gardner retreated to the front of his car, the words 'you're a suspect, possible homicide' resounding in his addled brain.

He needed desperately to get back to his senses. He remembered that he had not been meditating as often as he should and now the graveness of the situation was galloping out of control. The man in the Dodgers' jacket was pointing his camera phone directly at him. The action struck Gardner as sheer effrontery. He would have none of it and he advanced toward him. "Hey, listen, you jerk, I'm not giving you permission to photograph me." The man in the Dodgers' jacket sneered at him while backing off a step. Gardner wanted to leap over and seize the camera when he felt a hand on his shoulder, and now the soothing voice of a cop, a second one, "Look, buddy, cool off, that's the least of your problems right now."

And he was right. The cop then told him to turn around, he would have to cuff him up and put him in the patrol car. "Can I stay here, please," pleaded Gardner. The cop vacillated. "I may be able to help this man... I'm a doctor," and the cop consented.

Seeing the man on the ground, motionless, Gardner imagined the worst. If the man died from the injury, then Gardner's life would be over. Just like that: a moment of intemperance, pure and simple. Forty minutes before he had been on the dance floor with a beautiful woman and now he was handcuffed and having a charge of homicide hanging over his head. Beads of sweat had gathered on his temples. He thought of his daughter, a junior in college, what was she going to think of him? Who would be there for her to lean on? He thought of his ailing parents who relied upon him to assist with their expenses. He thought of his own life, all the roads he had taken, all the dead ends he'd encountered, all the projects unfinished. Would he lose his license to practice medicine? A wave of dread surged in him, the beating of his heart ringing loudly in his ears. "Breathe," said Gardner to himself, "Breathe." And the hubbub of people circling the scene began to fade.

The paramedic team arrived. They carefully turned the man face up and Gardner saw that he had opened his eyes. "Yes!" he said excitedly with a profound sense of relief. "I didn't kill him, he's alive. I didn't kill him." Only then did he ask himself where was Genevieve. He turned back, half expecting not to see her, but there she was; eyes closed, head reclined, looking as beautiful as ever.

Gardner had liked her, maybe even loved her, but better let her go back to her Arab prince. For all he knew it hadn't been an Arab prince at all. Maybe she was in with the retinue of nurses that had attended to Colonel Gaddafi in his waning days. It didn't matter anymore. It was over.

Some loose ends would have to be tied up, though, and costly ones. The man he had struck was an out of work actor whose last job, about a year before, had been a lead part in a new play that had made it to Off Broadway. Since then, though, he had not fared well. Drinking had been part of it. The blow Gardner had landed stunned the man but no more. If the man had not been intoxicated, he would have taken the hit and given Gardner a good whooping, since he was the stronger one. The man suffered no fractures and the blood that oozed out was only from the bruised nose. Gardner, however, had broken his hand and wrist, something he didn't discover until he was sitting in the tank at the police station waiting for the bondsman.

The matter was settled out of court. Genevieve's testimony was helpful and the fact that Gardner's level of alcohol was under the limit – he was so glad he hadn't taken that last drink – led to a more favorable outcome.

But it was still expensive. The attorneys asked for a cool 100 grand and the actor got 150, so he could go away, as the saying went. Gardner was out of work for over two months, what with the legal proceedings and tending to his broken hand and wrist which required an operation. He ran out of cash and was forced to borrow against the equity in his small condo.

When the incident occurred, Gardner had had a small private practice, a solo affair where he made a modest living, but he had time to spend with his patients and time to spend with his daughter. Sometimes, though, the spirit of adventure would seize him and he would travel for months at a time. Maybe he was more of a wanderer, he thought. An old friend had once told him that he was a man of uncertain vocation and there was some truth to it. But no matter how much he traveled, how far he strayed, he had always returned to his profession.

He had pretty much settled on the notion that that would be his life's pattern, a life without a sharp focus, when one day, while casually reading a medical newspaper, he came across a statement from a fellow psychiatrist, a lady somewhere in New Mexico whose name he could not recall. She had said that if a person can heal, he should do nothing else. And it occurred to him that maybe he did have a little gift after all, a little gift that allowed him to help a fallen man to get up on his feet.

As he looked about for new pastures, he heard that prisons where hiring psychiatrists. He would give it a try. More wandering, he thought. But seven years on, he was still glad he had made the move.

27

Though Paytrell, in cell 127, was ostensibly doing well, nurse Turner had observed that, of late, he had begun to skip doses. Remembering how quickly he could regress, she had called Gardner to let him know. Paytrell, however, refused to see him and then waved him off when he came by for a cell door visit.

Legrand had taken notice.

As far as Paytrell was concerned, Leroy and Hyena had become the devil incarnate. The night of the assault he had awakened with the ruckus and seen the two men shoot out of his neighbors' cell and up the stairs to safety while Legrand staggered to the stairway followed by a dazed and battered Joey. Shaken up by the incident and fearing that the assault would be repeated, Paytrell had concluded that reducing his medication would increase his level of alertness – just in case his assistance would be needed. So far, the wild dogs had not returned.

Legrand was not going to wait.

"Paytrell…" said Legrand, speaking through the vent, "…these people are not devils at all, just ignorant. They thought they were going to score some points with the rest of the ignorant people… and maybe they did, but it's got nothing to do with you."

Paytrell would have none of it. Up by his vent, too, he said, "Look LB, you can tell me that till you're blue in the face but I know these devils, and I have to be ready for them because you're my friend and I have to help out when they come back to get you."

"That's very kind of you, brother, and I appreciate it. But if you really want to help, get back to your meds. If you don't, then before long, you'll be working the toilet again and driving me insane. I need to stay alert."

Paytrell stood quietly as he thought about Legrand's words, then, "Look, man, I have to do something…"

"Take the medicine, bro, you're worrying me," insisted Legrand, "and think of your lady, too. She's waiting for you to get paroled with a clear mind."

Silence followed.

"LB?"

"Yes?"

"Why are you protecting the chomo?"

"I'm not protecting him. He does his own thing. But he's become a friend and I will stand up for a friend in trouble. But I know what you're getting to and I have an answer. The courts gave him a sentence. Why should I give him one of my own?"

"I know but… that's the way we do things around here."

"So? Should you be like everybody else or be yourself?"

"But the things they did…"

"They had their day in court."

Paytrell lowered his head.

"Would you stick a chomo?" pressed Legrand.

"I never have."

"Good. Anything you do to harm another person jeopardizes your freedom. You and I are here because we made poor choices, so why make things worse?"

"Something happens to our minds… we give up," said Paytrell.

"But not everybody does. You haven't. Butterfly hasn't, and he's got life, like me."

Paytrell thought about Legrand's predicament. No exit date. He would die in prison. "LB… you've been in a long time… how do you do it? I think I'd go crazy if I didn't have a date."

"Maybe the law will change… or something else will happen. Maybe they'll let me out when I'm 90. That's another 40 years from now. The families of the victims may want to meet me and see how I've changed. I don't lose hope. I want to get out. I want to get out so I can go to France, you hear me, because that's where my family came from. I want to go to Paris so I can walk along the river Seine and stop at a café and order a chocolate croissant. Even if I have no teeth left, I'll gum the damn thing. Does that answer your question?"

Paytrell nodded in silence. "LB… you're not angry at me, are you?"

"No, man, you're my friend. Just keep taking your medicine."

"I will."

"And stop the pot."

That one was a tough one for Paytrell.

That evening, Rivers and Morelos were on duty and they both went up to visit with Johnson. He was looking much better.

"No telling what a little sunshine and some exercise can do for a man," said Rivers to Morelos in a lighthearted mood as they stood outside his door.

Johnson grinned broadly. "My son's going to talk to a lawyer to see if we can introduce new evidence."

"You're on your way," said Morelos.

"And I heard from my brother, too. When I get out he'll help me get into rehab."

"Wonderful," said Rivers.

"And I can go to his place straight from here. You know, that's what the nightmares were about. I served time for it but that didn't get rid of the dreams."

Morelos and Rivers stared back at him.

"I was intoxicated when I crashed into a truck on the freeway. My nephew, my brother's son, he was in the passenger seat, up front. A beautiful kid. I didn't put him in back, in a safety seat."

Morelos and Rivers glanced at each other.

"I've never said anything to anybody in here."

"Not to your doctor?"

He shook his head. "Too ashamed. But my brother says he's forgiven me. I'm getting a fresh start."

"That's a lot of love, right there," said Morelos.

Johnson looked off. "Do you know when the lab results will be back?"

"I'm sure the doctor will have them for you soon."

"I appreciate your help," he said. "You're the best."

"The doc started you on the antidepressant. Keep taking it, okay?" said Morelos.

"Oh, yeah. I know I have to."

"Why don't you go see him in his office?"

"I don't know. I think I'm more comfortable talking to you guys."

"One step at a time, Johnson, you'll get there," said Rivers, "We'll see you later, okay?" and the two officers marched off.

On the way down the stairs, Rivers confided to Morelos that she was worried about the inmate in 118, who went by the moniker Double X and was fairly new to the unit. He was serving life without parole for a homicide. Some inmates had told Rivers about his open threats to Butterfly and they thought he had been sent in to finish the job. Rivers had checked the records but there was no evidence tying him to the assault on Butterfly a year before. Meanwhile, Butterfly declined to say he had any enemies on the unit.

"Let's just keep an eye on him," said Morelos.

It was one week later, on a Wednesday morning, that Gardner got to see the lab results for Johnson. He had turned up positive for both Hepatitis C and HIV. Johnson had tested negative two years before so he had got infected in prison. Gardner called for him and got to see him early that afternoon. It would be the first time that Johnson had consented to come to the office.

"You look so much better," said Gardner in greeting as Johnson took a seat across from him.

Johnson looked back, unsmiling, and said, "Just give it to me straight."

Gardner did and he saw Johnson's expression turned somber. "Internal Medicine will be calling so treatment can be started."

"What for?" said Johnson, slumping forward and hanging his head. "It was the sharing of the needles. I knew it. I could've done something about it but didn't." A renewed sense of defeat was overwhelming him. What could he do? As he pondered his future he told Gardner about his young nephew and how he had died. "He would be alive if it hadn't been for me. I crashed the car and didn't even get a scratch." He looked up at Gardner. "Does God have a plan for me?"

"I'm not a religious person…" said Gardner, "but if he did it wouldn't be for you to be doing drugs."

Johnson looked off. There was always that seemingly unshakable sadness right under the surface of him. "I used drugs because I wanted to forget... but more than that... I used drugs because I wanted to punish myself." He paused as he closed his eyes and pinched the bridge of his nose. "In the back of my mind I knew I would get the infections... I knew it... and did it anyway."

They paused momentarily.

"Did you enjoy the effects of the drug?"

Johnson hesitated. "I suppose I did."

"Then it wasn't all about self punishing."

Johnson snapped. "I didn't say it was. I told you I wanted to forget. You don't know me, do you? I have nightmares, too. And the drugs helped."

"How?"

"They kept me from killing myself."

Gardner sat back and bowed his head. The loss of the nephew had happened more than 20 years ago and maybe he had underestimated its lingering impact, the slow corrosion of Johnson's sense of worth.

"You know," started Johnson, "all of you should spend a week in a cell just so you can get a taste of what it is to live in those conditions. Just so you can develop a little empathy. I've been in one for 13 years." He looked at Gardner in the eye. "And before that it was 8... 6 months in between."

"I agree that it's easy to lose sight of the effects of confinement," replied Gardner, "more so when there are so few things for you to do, so few program activities."

Johnson nodded.

"What were the nightmares about?"

"Guilt. They still are."

"Could you have reached out?"

"To whom?" asked Johnson.

"Us... mental health," said Gardner.

"I could have... and I didn't. That's on me... my own prejudice. And then I chose to put myself at risk of getting the infections. Get it over with."

Silence fell between them.

"We all have our failings, Johnson. I have mine."

Johnson gazed at Gardner, curious. "You've been hooked?"

"No. But I've had other demons."

They peered at each other for a moment.

"But we can't give up the fight..." said Gardner.

"The fight for what?" asked Johnson.

"To be productive with our energies... to transcend ourselves."

"I don't know how to do that," said Johnson. His guilt had hemmed him in and he had not found a way of breaking through.

"I can teach you," replied the doc.

Johnson smiled sadly.

"You don't believe me, do you?" asked Gardner.

"It's not that... it's... why now... after all this time?" said Johnson, ruefully.

Gardner shrugged. "We hadn't met."

And Johnson lowered his eyes pensively. "How do we go about it?"

"It starts with opening up your heart."

"Open up my heart?" said Johnson, doubtfully.

"That's right. Just a little at first... and start to talk about your life... your emotions... your regrets... your aspirations... and as you do... strength will come to you."

"The strength to go beyond?"

"Exactly."

Johnson remained skeptical. "Will it bring back my nephew?"

Gardner smiled. "You're a religions man, right?"

"Yes."

"You believe in the spirit?"

"Yes."

"Then you just might bring him back."

"You got my attention," said Johnson.

"With the strength you find you will piece together your story. Piece together your story and you will have a gift for whoever is ready to receive it, and those who listen will hear what mistakes you have made, and they will know not to make them for you have made the mistakes for them, and their lives will be brighter because your story will have steered them away from recklessness... and meaninglessness."

Johnson closed his eyes and sighed softly.

"And you will have done so in the name of your nephew."

Johnson opened his eyes and there was a sparkle in them. Now he really wanted to believe Gardner. And he felt that a glow of hope had shone in his heart. "Maybe God has a plan for me, after all."

28

Joey felt the brrr of the January chill as he walked out of Bravo Three on the way to Dr Jeffries' office: the possibility of snow loomed ahead. He had an appointment at 9 am and as he crossed the yard he overheard a passing guard say to another that the temperature was in the low 20s and not expected to rise much. He glanced up at the sky and there was a gray overcast as far as the eye could see. He fastened the top button in his jacket and quickened the pace.

Once inside the mental health building it turned comfortable. On the rack in the corner of her office, the doctor had hung her long coat. She wore a pale yellow shirt under a soft brown leather jacket and draped around her neck was a white silk scarf with loosely hanging threads at each end.

It took a minute to warm up to the subject.

"Darla, the older sister – began Joey - she was pretty but cold. I think she faked her orgasms. She needed drugs to feel something, anything…"

"Or not to feel," put in Dr Jeffries.

Joey narrowed his eyes but continued. "Once, while we were having sex, she asked me to choke her…"

Dr Jeffries arched her brow.

"I said forget it. I don't even know why I was with her. But she had come to the theatre with her sister and that's how I met Melanie. At the end of the show they came up and asked that I autograph the playbill. Melanie didn't seem that interested, just tagging along, but she caught my eye. Something about her smile, something kind. She wore a little black round hat and a flowery print dress, plucked right out of a teen fashion magazine, and she had cute little dimples on her cheeks too." Joey shook his head lightly, a glimmer of disbelief in his eyes. "I knew she was young… but she was lovely."

"How young did you think she was?"

"Fifteen…sixteen…" He said it and just as he did he realized he was nearing owning up to his guilt. A sense of apprehension came over him. "I didn't know what I was doing."

"So you knew she was underage…" said Dr Jeffries, gently, as she brought her hands together, the fingertips in the one hand touching the fingertips in the other.

Joey was as close as he had ever been to telling the truth but it felt to him that doing so would be akin to surrender and he resisted. "It's not just about me confessing, you know," he said as he raised himself in his seat.

"What's it about, then?"

"It's about what I felt for her… it was something special… you can't leave that out."

"Let's leave nothing out."

"Society may arbitrarily draw a line at age 18 but… there was something very strong between the two of us… something beautiful… I never forced her to do anything… she did it because she wanted to… because she liked me."

Dr Jeffries looked him in the eye. "That was just the second meeting, wasn't it?"

"Yes."

"Did you ask her about her feelings?"

"No."

"But you thought there was something very strong between the two of you…"

"I know it seems difficult to believe but I just felt it. The minute I saw her again, after that night in the theatre, I felt my heart flutter. I thought I was in love."

"And she too?"

He lowered his gaze. He remembered the young girl in her flowery innocence, her enchanting serenity, and couldn't help but imagine what she would look like now, three years later, all grown up at sixteen, surely stunningly attractive, going to school and having fun with her friends, maybe even having sex, but with nothing to worry about, just the sheer, carefree enjoyment of it all.

He looked off and crossed his arms. Two more years and Melanie would be 18, he only 25, and it would have been perfectly legal to be with her, but he would still be in prison.

"Want to share any of that?" asked Dr Jeffries interrupting his reverie.

"I was just thinking of how impulsive I was."

Dr Jeffries nodded.

"Just that one act… and here I am, talking to you, in Lancaster, California."

She said nothing.

"Not a pretty sight, is it?"

Joey felt the weight of regret, of the lost possibilities, the botched life, even a wave of self pity washing over him. But he was where he was and there was no turning back. He had to move forward. He thought of brave Legrand, how he had shielded him from what could have been a deadly blow, and what more proof did he need that he was worthy of claiming his own life.

He looked up at Dr Jeffries.

"You want to tell me what happened?" said she.

He rubbed his face slowly, taking his time, as the memories streamed back. "She had come to spend the night and stayed in the sofa, in her pajamas. She was just a nice, beautiful girl. She was half asleep when I went by. I didn't have a shirt on but was wearing my pants. I lied to you the other time when I said I was naked."

"Why?"

"I don't know. Maybe I just wanted to give you a juicy story…"

"Why?"

"I suppose it's a way of distracting you."

"But it's not a juicy story at all… it's very sad."

"That's what Legrand said, too, and he scolded me." Joey had half expected a rebuke from her, too, but none came, just her inquisitive gaze.

A shadow of sorrow settled on his expression.

Dr Jeffries sat back without a word.

"Do you mind if I tell you the rest?"

"Please."

"The TV was still on and I sat next to her. She woke up and didn't look upset at all at seeing me there. She said hello and I said hello back.

I think I told you I thought she had a crush on me, the way she stared… but maybe I was lying to myself. I reached over and touched her hair… I touched her ears…"

Joey paused.

Dr Jeffries waited.

He shrugged. "I'm just remembering that she looked lonely… a little down maybe. Darla had told me that their mother was not well and had gone off with a man she had met just two weeks before."

"Where was her father?"

"Not around." And Joey thought that even knowing all of that, that Melanie's relationships with her parents were tenuous at best, that she was drifting and vulnerable, even knowing all of it, had not stopped him from going forward. He had seen the opportunity and pounced.

A sense of shame and regret filled him and made him think of stopping the session, of running back to his cell.

"Please go on," prompted Dr Jeffries.

Joey vacillated. He met her gaze. Her expression reassured him. Right there, directly across from him, was a mind seeking to understand, and to do so for his benefit… and he yielded. "Melanie took my hand in hers and brought it to her lips… and I knew she would be mine."

"Heady feeling."

Joey assented. "Lust… and power."

"Did you ask her how old she was?"

"I did… and she didn't answer."

"What did that tell you?"

"I know."

Joey raised his hands together, palm against palm, and rested his face on them.

"Had it happened before…?" asked Dr Jeffries.

"Never." He averted her gaze.

"Did she feel like a child?"

He looked down at the ground. "Yes…" And in his mind the word he'd just uttered appeared to linger in mid air… and if he wanted to he could still reach out and capture it… take it back… but there it stood… suspended… still in transit… not yet in Dr Jeffries's possession… but not in his either… and he thought that he was quietly going to where he had not gone before, and the word he had just spoken was taking him there, and that once it arrived in Dr Jeffries... once it settled in her ears... if she didn't push him away... if she didn't spit on him... if she didn't vomit her scorn upon him... why then... then he would be filled with a great sense of relief.

Joey took a deep breath. "Yes... she was a child... drawing me to her." He had leaned forward, head bowed, but then he looked up at Dr Jeffries. He needed to search her expression... find something... not forgiveness... he wasn't asking for that... but something... he didn't know what... and then he saw it... in her eyes, in her face, in her total expression... and he felt immensely grateful. It was compassion.

His eyes had moistened and he rubbed them dry. "I knew she was young... and innocent... and that I was seducing her... and I didn't stop."

Dr Jeffries just looked at him.

"I could have stopped but did not..." continued Joey.

"You had intercourse with her?"

"No... but I did go inside of her with my fingers."

She dropped her hands to her lap and tilted her head slightly to one side as she weighed his confession. He was charged with one count of oral copulation, nothing more.

"How are you feeling?"

"Sad."

He drew back as he fiddled with the buttons on the cuff of his shirt. "Are you sad, too?"

"Yes, I am," she replied.

"Thank you."

Joey looked at the flower on her desk. "Odd, isn't it?" he continued, "That it's taken all this time to connect up with the real thing."

A guard walked by and glanced inside the office.

"I've fought this moment for so long..."

"How were you caught?"

"Darla stepped out. I had forgotten completely about her. I thought she was still trapped in her madness, intoxicated with the meth she had snorted."

"What did she see?"

"Melanie with her head resting on my lap. We were both naked. Darla came up... I didn't notice till I heard the camera in her phone click."

Joey paused.

"It could've been worse," he continued.

"How so?"

"She could've seen it all... but Melanie never said a word about the rest."

Dr Jeffries turned to the computer screen and scrolled down to the page with the list of charges. There it was, only one instance of Oral Copulation. That was all.

"Sometimes I feel vile... but not always... and sometimes I feel more sorry for myself than for her. It's the predator in me, isn't it?"

"We have to explore... avoid labels..." said Dr Jeffries.

"I worry that this is just the beginning... that I'll do it again, that I'll go on to rape, to murder or some other ghastly crime." He closed his eyes and rubbed his brow slowly. "Not all the time but it's there. It comes mixed with other things... like feeling that I'm a complete failure in life... unable to find my way. Everybody else is out there, dancing and loving, working and creating, joining in the feast of life, making something of themselves... and I, here, staring at the four walls, with nowhere to go... playing out my self destruction."

She nodded lightly.

"I wonder, too, if I'm even capable of feeling guilt... that maybe it's all an act on my part. But then I think of the times when I've put myself deliberately in harm's way, and maybe that's really guilt... because I could've died. The two times I got stabbed in Salinas, I could've avoided the knifings. People had told me to not go out to yard, that they'd be waiting for me, but I went anyway. And when I was in the middle of it and I realized I might die, at the last minute, some survival instinct kicked in and I fought with all I had. But I could've avoided it. Was that guilt that made me go out even though I knew I would be getting it?"

"It looks that way... you were reckless, and often unconscious guilt is at the root of it."

"A lot of people, whites and Hispanics, think I deserve to die. Some Blacks do, too, but some don't. That's why I hang with them, even though I'm mixed white and Hispanic."

"Makes sense."

"Do you think I deserve to die?"

"No," replied Dr Jeffries.

"Thank you."

The doc believed in healing, reflected Joey, she believed in redemption. He crossed his legs and ran his fingers down the crease of his pants. He liked to keep a natty look about him, his hair cleanly cut and parted meticulously on the left.

"It's complicated, isn't it?" he said.

"It is."

"See, I've had a troubled youth, but I don't think I was born a predator. Something happened to me. There must be a reason I didn't grow up right."

"What reason would that be?" asked Dr Jeffries.

"I don't know. I seem to have difficulty remembering some things in my past…"

"You haven't spoken about your father."

"I know. I suppose I've been avoiding it."

"Why?"

"He was good. I loved him. But the beginning was better than the end."

"How so?"

"He was kind, playful, then things changed. He's human, right?"

"Yes…?"

Joey folded his arms on his chest. "I'm not sure I want to bring him in to all of this."

Dr Jeffries sat back.

"For sure, I was never able to talk to him like I do with you."

"What work does he do?"

"He's a custody officer."

"Ah," said Dr Jeffries.

"See, I knew you'd react that way."

"Which way?"

"Like that, Ah! Like if we had opened a can of worms and it didn't smell so good."

"I couldn't help it," said Dr Jeffries. "You're in for a sexual offense and given the prejudice against it, of course it sets up a huge conflict. There may or may not be bad smells coming out of that can of worms but, if there are, they ought to be dealt with."

She had leaned forward on the edge of her desk as she finished her sentence.

Joey liked her assurance. It seemed to him that to her, anything could be dealt with.

"I wish he could have a session with you."

"Why?"

"Once I got charged, they spent a lot of money on my defense, they even mortgaged the house, but my father and I haven't talked for years.'

"How many years?"

"A lot."

"Beginning when?" pressed Jeffries.

"I think he sees it as a reflection on him, like he had something to do with creating the problem."

"Do you think he did?"

"No. It's my responsibility. All of it. Neither of my parents had anything to do with it."

"Well, then, there may be no smelly worms in the can."

"Maybe one or two," he added with a smile.

"So, then, we should be able to talk about it freely."

"No, because if we begin, then I know you're going to find something."

"But that is my job, to find things, to suggest connections. But they won't have any value unless they resonate with you."

"What do you mean, resonate?"

'Whatever connections I make, I'll present to you, then you decide whether they make sense or not. You'll be making your own connections as well, of course. I'm not here to force anything on you, but to reflect on what you present. You may be ready to run with what is offered, accept some things, or not."

Joey clasped his hands. "This is going to take longer than I thought."

"It doesn't happen overnight, but neither did your difficulties develop overnight. A process took place culminating with the offense. And the same thing can be said of every inmate that we have in here, every single one. Some disconnect occurred on the way to the offense. Our task, in mental health, properly understood, is to find those disconnects and repair them."

"Doc, judging by the people we have in the units, you haven't even started your work."

"You're right. Allow me to add that our task is not to judge the inmate; our role is not to punish. The courts do that. Our function is to first, accept the inmate as a human being, regardless of the offense, second, to help him understand his behavior, and third, to assist him in the arduous task of change, of reshaping his existence so he will not harm again and have another shot at life. We ought to be, from the beginning, all about adult development. Lamentably, too many of our practitioners miss the point."

Joey was struck by the verve and conviction with which Dr Jeffries spoke and felt fortunate to have her in his corner. But there was something that he was curious about.

"Doc, do you see other patients, every week, for as long as you see me?"

"No. I should've brought up that earlier and I'm glad you're doing it now. Look, here in general population, we're only required to see inmates in our caseloads for 15 minutes every three months, and that's if you're in mental health, unless there's an emergency, of course. But since many people have no interest at all in being seen, given that they're too afraid to delve into their pasts, some of us take from Peter to give to Paul."

"But you see me almost every week for 50 minutes. Are you going to get in trouble because of it?"

"No. But that's for me to handle."

"I still feel that I've become someone special in your work."

"And you have."

"I feel privileged."

She nodded. "You're beginning to do the work that needs to be done."

29

Sergeant Krause had scheduled to meet with officer Grisholt but had to postpone it. There was some background information she needed to gather for the occasion but now she was ready. She gave him notice the day before and the meeting took place in the office of Internal Investigations. Dressed in an all-black uniform, she stood ramrod behind her small desk that had a single light brown folder lying on it. In her mid-forties, tall, African American and all business, the military bearing about her was clear.

The room was tidy, sparsely furnished, and on top of a corner book case to her left stood a desktop flagstaff with the Stars and Stripes. She bid Grisholt to have a seat.

"We haven't met but I know of you," she began. Her tone was official and curt, no niceties wasted.

"I hope it's good," said Grisholt, a hint of scorn in his eye.

"Everything all right?" she said, softening her tone.

"Just fine. Listen, that thing that happened the other day, it was a mistake. You know all the stress we're under dealing with these hoodlums, your nerves get shot. Stuff happens. I accidentally pushed the wrong button. Won't happen again, I guarantee."

Krause said nothing. Instead, she moved to the book case and felt the cloth of the small flag with the back of her hand. Slowly. She then picked up the small flag and placed it on the center of the book case.

Grisholt shifted his weight in the stiff wooden chair and heard it creak.

Then she turned. "Were you in Corcoran four years ago?" It seemed like an innocent enough question, a conversation opener, for she surely knew the answer, but Grisholt flinched.

"Yes. I was there for a bit."

"About two years or so?"

"Three."

Krause crossed to the other corner of the room. She had a long stride and her black boots sparkled with polish. She turned to face him, "You were having marital problems?"

"What's that got to do with anything?" said Grisholt, annoyed.

"It can have an impact on an officer's work, wouldn't you say?"

"I went through a divorce. It's over now."

"You remember an officer, Buck Wilson?"

Grisholt squirmed. It was a quick thrust that caught him by surprise.

"Buck…?" he began, as if he hadn't heard from the man in a long time, needing to search his memory for a clue to his existence, "Maybe… yeah… oh yeah, old buckaroo… yep, had a house in the prairie. We weren't friends or anything like that. I might've gone to one of his barbeques, knocked back a beer or two. Is he all right?"

"Perhaps. We're investigating him."

"No kidding?" That wasn't news; Buck's life seemed to be under constant investigation.

"Some irregularities…"

"Been around for a while," said Grisholt, not liking the direction the questions were headed.

Krause pulled out her chair and sat at the desk. "So, it's been seven years for you?"

"Long enough to know right from wrong," he said, trying to lighten the mood.

She looked directly at him and he held her gaze.

"It was a mistake, like I said, sergeant. You give them an inch and… heck, they just don't care."

Krause leaned her elbows on the desk. "See… it's not whether they care or not, *you* have to care."

That got a smile out of Grisholt. "Hold on, now, let's get one thing clear. I am a custody officer. I'm not here to hold these guys' hands. That's for the mental health folks to do. Cop, Cuckoo, two different breeds." He had managed to sound amused when he spoke and the tone irked the sergeant.

"You were being paid to ensure the safety of the inmate and you didn't do your job," she pressed.

Grisholt slid his chair back an inch and gripped the armrests. "Why do I get the impression you didn't invite me over to work with me?"

"Because I don't have to work with you."

Grisholt smirked. "Then what's the point of calling me in?"

"Excellent question. You might say, I want to be able to document your… undoing?"

Grisholt snorted. When he thought back on this moment, after he had left the office, he realized that he had not properly considered the seriousness of the situation. Sorely unprepared, he had assumed the sergeant would be more tolerant. Didn't this have to do with a child molester? What was the big deal? But no, the woman seemed to have a bug up her tush. He felt like he was in a free fall with nothing to grab on to.

"See, this is not the first time this happens, is it?" continued Krause, "There were a few of these incidents in Corcoran and you were given warnings…" Her style was piercing and forceful.

"I don't know what you're talking about." His hands had started to sweat.

Krause reached for the folder on the desk and opened it. "You want to read about them?"

Grisholt glanced nervously at the folder but didn't move. Did he want to revisit that painful chapter in his life, the reason he had come down to Lancaster and get a fresh start? "You know what?" he said, feeling a surging, reckless, desire to blast back at the sergeant and go toe to toe with her, "I'm going to plead the fifth on this one." And leaning forward he added, "And I don't like the way you're coming at me. I'll just have to tell my rep that you called me in to threaten me. That way we're all on the same page, how about that?"

Krause was relishing having the advantage and acted like it. She had clear green eyes and Grisholt thought she looked like a vicious cat thirsting to pounce on him. In fact, she was already sticking her fangs in him.

But she spoke calmly, instead. "They won't cover for you, Grisholt. It's a new ballgame. You just can't see it. Let me run it by you so you get the picture. Prison work is going through a transition - a culture change - and there's no stopping it. This is just the beginning. We either get on board or we're going to be left behind. Now, it so happens, that we have excellent officers, thoughtful, intelligent people, with sound interpersonal skills. Others, however, are a little slow to catch on. That's you."

"You're selling me down the river, aren't you?" said Grisholt. He just couldn't shut up.

Krause knew she had this puppy locked in, so she could be graceful. "As custody officers we're given a measure of power, power to contain these inmates whose lives have been warped by circumstances; wounded men, overwhelmingly from the lower classes, but still our fellow citizens…"

"You sure about that?" said Grisholt, defiantly, unable to hold back the urge to mock her.

But she ignored him. "We are *not* given the power to abuse them, Officer Grisholt. Does that make sense? Does it ring a bell?"

"I must be hard of hearing."

"And so it falls to us," she continued with practiced poise, even pausing to tug at the sleeve of her shirt, her words oozing with benevolent understanding which rankled Grisholt to no end, "it falls to us, sir... to clean up our act... and believe me, we are doing it, which is why I am here today."

It was too much for Eddie Grisholt. "You write your own speeches?"

"You can't stop yourself, can you?" said Krause, calmly. "But I'm in a good mood today and I'm not going to cite you for disrespect. I know you're confused and overwhelmed or just don't have it and ought to try the car dealership down the road. There's a place for all of us in this world."

Grisholt glared back.

"I'll just add one more thing. We, in custody, are not the only ones who have to adapt to the culture change so we can advance the cause of prison reform. Mental health, too, has to clean up its act, and that means getting rid of the folks who don't listen to the inmates, either because they don't give a damn or can't handle the problems. That is all. You are dismissed."

She said it as casually as if flicking off a speck of lint from her jacket. And Grisholt could not resist taking a parting shot. "A real global perspective, sergeant," he said as he stood up to leave. "I thank you from the bottom of my heart. Let me know when you kick off your campaign for warden. I'll send you my five bucks." He turned and walked out.

Krause smiled to herself. Krause 1, Grisholt 0.

Her take on him had been correct. Some people know they are self-destroying and cannot stop it. Grisholt was one of them. She would now move to dismiss him from the job. The other question was, were there grounds for a criminal charge? She relished the thought.

Grisholt had been right in one respect, thought Krause: she really wanted to be warden. Was it that obvious? It didn't matter. If she needed to string up a few wayward officers to make her case that she stood for a new, enlightened, custody corps, she would do it without hesitation.

Grisholt left the meeting chafing at the bit, certain that he had screwed up. He was not a stupid man but had behaved like one. He resented that Krause was a woman calling him on a man's business but she had the power and he would have to figure out a way of dealing with her. As to Buck, he was through with him. That last-minute phone call of his, right before the assault, was him trying to call it off. He was certain of that. But Buck should've known better than to let the inmate up in Corcoran knock him down three times before he stepped in to halt the fight. No real friend would allow that.

Grisholt sat in his truck in the parking lot for a while. He leaned his head back and closed his eyes. He had to be back at work at 10 that night. He let his mind wander. Maybe it was time to walk away from the job. He had been at it 7 years. He thought of Buck again, those first days in Corcoran, when he was just getting started. He thought of how he had looked up to him, how he had wanted to be like him. And it came back to Grisholt, slowly, that part of the reason he had challenged the inmate was that he had wanted to impress his old mentor. Grisholt smiled at the memory. He had heard that old Buck had swung a mean fist in his day, and he had wanted to show him that he could, too. Maybe it was time for him to go.

30

*I*t was early evening and Grisholt was in his kitchen preparing his food for his shift when Buck called. Grisholt thought twice about answering. He had decided to be done with Buck but now he wavered. He picked up the phone.

"Hi"

"Hi"

In the silence that followed Grisholt stood perfectly still, the knife he was using to slice the peach on the counter suspended in mid air.

"Why didn't you answer my call?" asked Buck.

Grisholt had expected the question. "I had turned off the cell right after we hung up. I needed to focus, I was about to rack open the door for the guys to go in. Just a minute before, my ex had texted me cursing me out because I hadn't loaned her some money."

Buck said nothing.

Grisholt congratulated himself on sounding convincing. "He's all right, don't worry. He just got roughed up a bit. Nothing serious. And with that right there, no one will think you're covering up for him."

"I know what happened," said Buck. "I have the nurse's report in my hand."

A chill went through Grisholt. How the hell did Buck get the nurse's report? Or was he bluffing?

"Someone stabbed Legrand in the neck," pressed Buck.

Grisholt felt the blood drain from his face. He needed to sit down so he crossed quickly to a chair in the dining room. His hands had turned pale.

"You're a punk," said Buck.

Grisholt could not find the words for a reply.

"Why didn't you answer my call?"

Grisholt's throat had dried up. He still could not come up with anything.

"I went over what we had talked that night," continued Buck, "everything I said, every answer you gave. I was having doubts... and you knew it... and what does a friend do when he hears his friend having trouble with something?"

"Buck... I'm sorry."

"He talks to him. A real friend asks questions... but not you... you found it easier to just go along with me, didn't you? If I had said, God forbid, 'kill the little prick,' you would've gone along, wouldn't you?"

"Buck... believe it or not, I did think of saying something to you... because it's so odd, the whole thing..."

"And what were you waiting for?"

"It's not easy for me... it just isn't, I don't know why..." Saying the words had somehow lifted some pressure off him – as if Buck had taken his boot off his throat - and Grisholt could draw a full breath.

"The shank that Legrand got was meant for Joey," said Buck.

"You can't say that," said Grisholt, his breath cut short again, that boot of Buck's pushing down on him.

"Yes, I can. You said they wouldn't have weapons, didn't you?"

"I did say that."

"So you had no control over those assholes, did you?"

"Buck... I really thought I did..." The seemingly small admission brought him a bit of relief. He was desperate for it. His skin had turned cold and he saw that his T-shirt was drenched in sweat.

"Why didn't you say anything?"

"Buck… I…" His head was swimming. He wanted to muster the courage to speak the truth but he couldn't come up with it.

"Go ahead and say it…" Buck pressed, his anger mounting, but still Grisholt couldn't come forth.

"Say it, goddamn it! I'm going to get you to say it even if I have to go over there right now and beat the crap out of you. Now, say it!"

And Grisholt felt that Buck had given him an opening, barely a slit but an opening, and that's all he needed. "Because…."

"Say it!"

"Because I've been pissed off at you all this time!" he said finally, bursting out, jumping to his feet and pacing frantically in his living room as he spoke. "God damn you, Buck Wilson! God damn you for not sticking up for me. God damn you for letting the fight go on and letting the bastard whoop my ass. Three times he knocked me down, and only then did you step in. Couldn't you see that all the time I had just wanted to impress you, that all I wanted was to show you that I could be like you? So fuck you, you blind sonofabitch. Fuck you!"

And at the other end, Buck did not feel offended by the words but instead felt engulfed by a deep sadness. He was still sitting down on the crate in his garage as the long pause fell between them. They heard each other's breathing and nothing else for a few moments.

Grisholt now regretted what he had done. Had he been able to stand up to Buck and speak his part he would not have gone ahead with the assault. He was sure of that. Now. After the fact.

Buck remained seated on the crate in his garage. Was that true, that Grisholt had wanted to impress him? Surely there were other reasons for fighting the inmate, but was the desire to gain his recognition a part of it? If so, he hadn't seen it. But it could have been true because Grisholt looked up to him. And it had happened with Joey, too. Yes, Buck had sensed that his son had wanted his forgiveness but he had not yielded. Little Joey had not put it into words but it had been there in his demeanor, the plea to be embraced again, the plea to have his father back.

Buck felt very alone in his garage, sitting there on the old crate, holding the phone, staring down at the still broken floor that he had hammered into dust the night of the assault. He muttered thoughts to himself, old thoughts, new thoughts, thoughts that he needed to learn to put out, thoughts he needed to understand. Was it not a simple measure of courage that was needed? Just for starters?

He looked up and there was Janice at the door. Again.

He gazed at her for a long minute and then shook his head.

He got up and went inside.

He didn't drink that night. He got in bed, slipped the cell phone under his pillow and lay still. It would be half an hour before Janice joined him. He was looking away from her, eyes closed, but she knew he was awake. She didn't say a thing for a long time, then she asked, "Is Joey okay?"

"Yes."

And he fell asleep.

31

Buck Wilson was a broad shouldered, square jawed man, 6 ft 3 in, whose boyish face led some people to underestimate him. He loved eating and long ago had gone beyond the pale, which had earned him a permanent ample girth and yet, somehow, had managed to remain agile. He was a few months older than Janice but looked younger. He had had trouble with drinking and smoking but had given up both, the smoking completely, the alcohol almost so. He had drunk in binges, one of which had nearly cost him his life, but he had finally stopped and done it all on his own. Occasionally, though, under heavy stress, he did break the rules. But it was seldom.

It had been a magnificent stroke of resolve. "I'm through!" he had cried out after a drunken spree in Las Vegas that numbed his brain to the point that he had wandered aimlessly out of a casino only to be rolled by some hoodlums who fleeced him out of the thousand dollars he still had in his wallet. His two drinking buddies had been equally incapacitated but they had stayed in the lobby. Janice had gone to a late night show with the other wives. The men, by themselves, had just lost it.

Buck had made his dramatic declaration of independence from

alcohol as he lay on a bed in an emergency room not far from the spot where he had been assaulted. The doctor was sewing together an ugly gash he had on his forehead. He had already repaired the jagged cut on top of his skull where he had been struck hard with some object. Tests had shown no underlying damage.

"It could've been worse," said the doctor, a rail thin young man from Iran who was in residency to become a plastic surgeon. "Why do you drink?" The doctor's hands seemed to do a ballet over the wound, his fingers gracefully intertwining with the fine suture that brought the edges together.

"Why do I drink?" repeated Buck, still in a half stupor from the bashing. His hands at his side, he kept counting his fingers as he opposed the tips to his thumb, 1 for the pinky then 2-3-4 and back again, a simple task that he found reassuring since he had not been able to do it when he had first arrived in the emergency room. He was coming out of it, though slowly. His entire head throbbed with a dull ache and he found the doctor's question irritating, but he was pleased he was being looked after. "Good question. I suppose the answer is that I like it," he slurred out.

"But you have no control."

"That's right. I don't. You're right about that, doc." Buck clenched his jaw, which made the headache worse. How the hell had he got so intoxicated? He ran his tongue over his teeth but felt that something was wrong. Only now was he becoming aware of it. "Doc, I don't know if you've noticed… but there seems to be something wrong with my mouth…"

"One of your front teeth is missing."

And Buck let out a howl that made the doctor back off for an instant. How did he let that happen? He was so proud of having kept all his teeth, after all the fights he'd been in. The bastards, how dare they? But it was his own damned fault, wasn't it? He had asked for it. Heavily intoxicated, he had straggled off in search of fresh air and vaguely recalled stepping into an alley to relieve himself when a man accosted him and asked for his wallet. And he had refused. Then two others sprang from the dark and jumped him. That's all he remembered. Three against one, and the one was drunk. Not a fair fight. That explained it. Otherwise he would have kicked ass like he was used to; licked them fair and square or given them the fight of their lives. Instead, two hours later, they had found him bleeding and sprawled on the ground at three in the morning, nearly unconscious, under a heap of refuse.

When Janice and the other wives returned to the hotel there was no trace of Buck. The two other husbands were zonked out and snoring in the lobby. Janice contacted the police immediately and they had made the discovery. But the waiting had been agonizing and she vowed to do whatever was needed to stop him from bingeing again.

"You know, I work in a prison… so they're going to get it when I get back," said Buck.

"Get it?" asked the surgeon.

"Yep. I'm going to kick butt when I get back."

"But why? You don't know who it was."

"I do know. It was a member of the criminal class. That's good enough for me."

"You are embarrassed, but why should you punish without knowing who it was?"

Buck tried mulling that over but he was too drunk. It seemed like it was too much work to try. And as he thought about it, he drifted back into stupor.

"You will have no scar on your forehead or your skull," said the doctor, "I have done an excellent job for you." But Buck didn't hear it. He was gone. Janice came in from the waiting room and thanked the surgeon. Buck was kept under observation for a day and then went home. And he had now been free from bingeing for the last 12 consecutive years.

Buck had also quit smoking, but that story was quite different. He had done it under duress. Janice had acquired strong views about the addiction while working briefly at a medical clinic before starting up on her real estate career. In that short span she had seen all manner of smoking related disabilities parade before her eyes: vascular problems, heart conditions, emphysema, premature aging. What else did you need?

She loved Buck and had been very patient. She had commended him on his remaining binge free and argued that quitting the smoking was not a question of willpower - he had it - he just needed to make up his mind. But he did not. So she decided she would not let him continue to self-destroy or let him drag her down with him.

Janice started by first asking that he only smoke outside the house, which he did, though not without a fair amount of grumbling. Next she refused to kiss him in the mouth. That really got his goat and they didn't speak to each other for about a week. But still he smoked. Then one day, while showing a house to a customer, the lady asked Janice, "Do you smoke?" Janice was stunned. How would she know that? Janice replied that she didn't but then added, "my husband does." And in that brief interaction she realized that no matter what distance she put between she and Buck, so long as he smoked, it would still cling to her.

She picked up dinner that night and they ate it in the living room. Their daughter Margaret had started college and Joey had been in county jail for six months, fighting his case. The legal fees were mounting and money was tight. Janice was working extra hard to give her son the most she could afford but the struggle ahead promised to be long and arduous and she didn't want to do it alone. Buck was already overweight and it concerned her. The smoking had to go.

As soon as she finished her meal she related the interaction she'd had with the lady customer. He nodded slowly and averted her gaze. Then she pinned him down. "You have to give it up, Buck."

He gave a little shrug.

"You're harming me, too."

Buck said nothing.

Janice waited.

"I'll get going on it," he said, anything to buy him a little extra time, but that was not enough for her. She had come to the end of the road.

"If you don't… I'll go somewhere else until you do."

And it stunned Buck. They sat quietly, staring at each other. She had said it without inflection, a straight, in your face delivery, one word right after the other. He had known all along that it upset her and that he'd been pushing it and that he needed to make up his mind but the abruptness of it all sent a jolt through him.

"Smoking is such a risk factor, and if you add to it the extra weight… I just don't want you to have a heart attack and die on me."

He thought of replying 'But you're willing to walk out and let me die on my own,' but he held back and instead said, "I wondered how long it was going to take for you to say that."

Buck had grown up in San Diego, on a little hill from where he could see the ships below. His father had been in the navy and his mother, who had come from Minnesota and was of German ancestry, had run a taco stand for as long as he could remember. At age 14, Buck was already 5 foot 11, lean and strong. The coaches at school snapped him up and he dove into athletics with relish. He tried everything and was good at all of it, but he liked boxing most of all. Dad, on the other hand, thought he should aim for football. Mom stayed out of it but when Buck helped her out at the taco stand after school and on weekends, he talked to her about the fighters he admired and she listened and smiled.

Dad's affection was very important to Buck. The old man had spent a life at sea but had trouble showing the warmth his son yearned for. But it occurred to Buck that maybe he could pull it out of him. And so Buck chose to play football to please his father. For a while at least. Afterwards he would do what he liked the most. He was so young he could afford it.

Soon after he took up football he became the star of the team. He was good in all positions but he was an outstanding lineman with a keen sense of position and able to quickly squash his opponent.

On the sly, though, he began to go over to a gym run by Nino Caputo, a former heavy weight contender and transplanted New Yorker, where he spent time watching young men learn the sport. Buck was so assiduous in his attendance that one day, having noticed his physique, Nino Caputo himself came over, sat next to him and asked if he wanted to train.

"I want to but my dad won't let me."

Nino Caputo saw the excitement in his eyes.

"You want me to talk to him?"

Buck broke out into a wide grin. "Would you, Mr Caputo?"

And he did. But Mr Wilson would have none of it. Football required full attention, particularly if the boy had a chance of going the distance. That's what the elder Wilson told Mr Caputo. Maybe dad knew better, but Buck kept returning, if only to watch.

It was Buck's secret; his and his mom's. None of his peers at school knew of what he was doing. When he went to the gym he kept his eyes on the action in the ring and memorized all the instructions from the trainers. Then he would go back home, close his bedroom door, and practice in front of the mirror.

His first fight came when he was sixteen, and it happened with another boy from the football team. They were grumbling in the locker room after losing a game. The other boy, who was a receiver, loudly complained that Buck had not given their quarterback enough protection. Buck had ignored him. Then the boy, sneaking up behind his back, dumped a bucket of ice on Buck's head. Buck sprang from the bench, chased the boy across the room and grabbing him by the neck said to him, "You better apologize." The boy, about the same build and height as Buck, glared back in defiance. "Take your stinking hands off of me, taco boy!"

A hush went through the room.

"Okay," said Buck, releasing the boy and backing up as he took a boxing stance, "then fight me." The boy hesitated but there was no way out. It was fight or eat crow, and since he had no appetite for the bird he decided to square off with Buck. They sized each other for a moment, moving from side to side. Then Buck landed the first blow, a hard jab to the forehead that stunned the other boy snapping his head back. The boy, believing himself outgunned, thought of rushing Buck and wrestling him to the ground. Still, he hesitated, thinking he might land a punch himself. But Buck gave him no opening. He charged with one, two, three quick jabs and, as the boy backed up and ducked under the flurry, Buck moved in and let go with a vicious hook that caught the boy in the left ear. The boy's legs gave and he crumpled to the ground. The audience let out a gasp. They had never witnessed such a display of quick, coordinated, elegant brutality. Two of the fallen boy's friends rushed to his side. As they tried to revive him, one of them, with a look of awe and fear, said to Buck, "You're dangerous."

A word must be said as to how Buck developed his massive shoulders. He was fond of stating that he had not pumped iron as a youth. Instead, whenever he misbehaved, which was often, his mother, who loved him dearly otherwise, would ask him to stand in back of the taco stand, out of sight of the clientele, and hold up the trunk of a tree that had been sawed off for the occasion. Buck would hold the trunk up and over his shoulders until fatigue overcame him. He was free to walk about as he held it but hold it up he must. With practice, he had come to be able to hold the weight for up to a half hour at a time, but then his mother would have a larger size trunk sawed off. He was about 12 years old when mother had settled on this type of punishment and though he bellyached at first, he soon saw the benefits of it. As he grew stronger, he himself would ask for larger sections of a tree to hold up.

Buck kept playing football and father continued to rejoice in his performance on the field. The elder Wilson had even contacted the athletic department of several universities to alert them to the possibilities of his son. Scouts had come to see him play and had encouraging words; there were no doubts about the developing talent, they told him, but they had questions about Buck's interest in the game.

Father and son had a row over it and Buck promised to show more enthusiasm. But it was proving to be harder and harder.

In his schoolwork, Buck got passing grades, not because he couldn't do it but because he didn't find it exciting. He sensed, correctly, that he had to decide soon and confront his father, for youth meant everything in the serious pursuit of a sport.

Meanwhile, on the side, hiding it from dad but with mother's full consent, he had begun to train once a week with Nino Caputo. In back of the taco stand, whenever he didn't have football practice, he skipped rope and slugged away at the punching bag mom had bought for him.

Then, in his senior year, in one of the final games of the season, when all the boys were giving their best because the city championship was in sight, Buck suffered a serious injury. Near the line of scrimmage, as a play unfolded, an opposing player struck him hard in the knee. The leg swung out from under him, like a piece of rubber, and he fell flat on his back. As intense as the pain was, Buck lay very still on the ground. He felt like he had been sequestered into a bubble, unable to hear or respond to his teammates as they gathered round, while a jumble of thoughts raced through his mind. He thought of how crushed his father might be, the anguish he might be feeling, and how the hit he had just suffered might shatter all the expectations his dad had of him.

The moment the blow was struck and Buck hit the turf, dad had buried his face in his hands, wincing with pain, as if he himself had been hit. "Get up," muttered the elder Wilson, reflexively. "Get up," he said again. Then louder, "Get up!" as he rose to his feet. But there lay Buck, still on the ground in the middle of the field, surrounded by his teammates. He was being lifted off the ground by his fellow players and slowly carried off on their arms and shoulders, when the sight of Buck's leg wobbling under him ripped the breath out of Buck's dad. He turned pale from the fright.

From the stands, the elder Wilson thought he could see in Buck's eyes that he was calling it quits. He could bear it no more. He sprang down the stands nearly tripping on the last step as he cried out, "No! No!" and ran onto the field, heading straight for Buck and his teammates, "Get back in there, Buck, get back in there!" And Buck shook his head, tears streaming down his face as his father approached. The elder Wilson had never seen his son cry. "Don't cry you wimp!" Buck hadn't realized that he was doing so. "It's over, dad, it's over!" he said, pleadingly, and the elder Wilson lunged at Buck, tearing at his jersey, poking him in the chest, waving his fist in his face, "Get back in there!", and had to be restrained by the players.

Buck had fractured the lower portion of his femur and cracked the kneecap in half. He had surgery and took a while to recover but he had been able to graduate with his fellow students. He showed up for the ceremony in crutches to thunderous applause. He had given so many exciting moments to the school and to his father. But dad was not there. The elder Wilson had spoken to the surgeon who had said that there was hope: with rehabilitation all was possible, but it would be up to Buck.

The elder Wilson told Buck what the doctor had said. He could be up on his feet and playing again if he worked hard. Buck answered that he would do it, but not for football. "I played for you, dad, but I don't want it anymore. It's not in me. I want to be a boxer." And his father had glared at him, face flushed with rage, and then slapped him across. "What about me? What about all the work I've done? What about the scouts that came to see you?"

"I'm sorry," said Buck.

The old man felt lost, the reality of his broken dream finally breaking through to him. He stood before Buck in silence, head bowed, a man spent, emptied of his dearest longings. When he looked up again at Buck, for one last time, Buck peered back, his eyes asking of his dad… do you have something for me?

Dad turned around and walked out.

The slap across the face had brought much pain to Buck: the wasted effort, the unrequited love, but it also had put an end to his efforts to please his father. In fact, the matter could not so readily be put to rest but that would take some years to acknowledge. Still, a sense of freedom had come to him and he devoted his energies to his passion for boxing. The only question mark was the knee. Would it hold up? He had seen lots of boxers in action and had concluded that if you could pack a punch you were okay. You didn't have to be the swiftest on your legs. Anyway, a boxing adversary would not be aiming at his knees like the son of a bitch that had injured him. True, he wouldn't be able to float like a butterfly and sting like a bee, like Muhammad Ali in his heyday, but his forte was his punch. He just had to be strong enough to stand up and slug away. His fists, not his legs, would do the talking.

He got a job with the city working in sanitation, moved out on his own and put all his efforts into rehabbing and training to be a boxer. He would train every night after work and on weekends too, but he always set time aside to help his mom with the taco stand. His fellow boxers would commend him on his dedication and grit. Then Nino Caputo approached him one day. Sitting next to him he said, "You've done very well. Let's go ahead and set up something for you so you can get started. But keep in mind, these knee injuries are tricky, it's hard to say how they're going to behave. Keep doing those exercises they gave you." Buck was thrilled. Mr Caputo patted him on the back and added, "You have fast hands and a high tolerance for pain." Buck beamed with pride.

A year and a half after the knee injury, he went up on the ring for his first amateur bout. Mom came to see him. His adversary was Troy Ling, a heavy-footed Asian American, about his age and build, both being heavyweights at 210 pounds. Buck agreed to the fight, in part, because the fellow didn't have a lot of speed. It was billed as the Battle of the Bruisers and bruising there was, plenty of it. At the start Buck used his left jab, scoring repeatedly. But then Troy Ling rushed in with a flurry that backed him into the ropes. Buck covered up well and managed to pull away but as he did he thought, 'Wow, I got out of that because of my legs. I'm going to need those legs.'

Returning to the center of the ring the two men went toe to toe for the rest of the round, both landing and taking punches.

The second round was another slugfest and by the end of it, the judges had Buck up on points but not by much. Back in his corner his assistant said to him, "Use your strength. You're stronger than him, bully him, you want to be a boxer, right?" And at the sound of the bell for the third and final round, Buck came out rushing to the center of the ring. Buck went at Troy Ling with both his cannons and he overwhelmed him. About a minute into the round, as they clinched, Buck caught Troy Ling with a right uppercut to the chin. A quick cross with a left hook followed and Troy Ling was flat on his back looking up at the headlights. Where had that come from? Buck could not believe it. He stood over the fallen man, just in case he chose to get up, while the referee kept signaling for him to move away. But Buck, overjoyed, launched into an impersonation of Muhammad Ali, lecturing to Troy Ling, who could not hear a word he was saying, until Buck's assistant rushed to his side, grabbed him by the arm and took him to his corner. "You're too green for that kinda crap," he said to him.

As he stood by, waiting for the referee's announcement, exulting in the applause, smiling back at the crowd, Buck caught sight of his mother jumping up and down in the seats below. She was ecstatic.

Buck fought 16 amateur fights and won them all, 15 by knockout, and Mom was there for every single one. Then, just before he turned 21, he went pro.

His first bout was against a Tijuana man, 4 years older than him. It was set for 5 rounds. Buck needed only 3. He made five hundred dollars. After 6 more victories, he was invited to fight in Mexico City, Puerto Rico, Venezuela. He won every time. He got paid five thousand and expenses for the one in Caracas, his purse a little better each time he won. He was living his dream.

After the bout in Venezuela, where he had got a unanimous decision – the other guy just wouldn't go down – a reporter asked him, "Why do you fight?" and Buck replied, "I've always liked it… I'm an athlete." "You like to hit people?" the reporter pressed him. The others laughed. He hadn't thought about it that way but there it was. That was the reason, wasn't it? Why else become a boxer? No, he thought, there's more to it, and he said to the reporters, "I'm good at it, and I enjoy being good at something."

His knee, meanwhile, had begun to show signs of strain. His manager observed that he wasn't as fleet of foot as he had been although he had got away with it. Buck brushed him off. He had kept up with the exercises the doctor had ordered. Whatever strain there was it was temporary.

As soon as he had returned to San Diego the call from Miami came in. A young fellow, 20 years old, calling himself The Miami Kid, was making his way up the ladder fast and needed some good adversaries.

They had heard of Buck. He fit the bill. Neither had lost a fight. Buck would have 8 weeks to prepare. Was he game?

Nino Caputo got hold of a film of the Kid's last fight and they reviewed it. The Miami Kid was not quite as strong as Buck but had stopped his last 7 rivals, not one going past the third round. And he had impressive speed. The money was good. Buck would get ten grand. And then there was the exposure. He would be on TV. But did Buck want to wait, give the knee a break, then go back?

Buck was confident he could take the Kid, he had momentum going for him. He consulted with his mother. He thought that eight weeks of rest was all he needed. "But you won't be really resting it, Buck, you'll be training. That takes a toll, too." He agreed but said that, in training, he could pace himself. "You're doing very well, you don't have to rush things, it's okay to wait," she said. Buck took it all in and then made his decision. The fight was on.

It was a Saturday night in Miami and the arena was sold out. The audience was festive, noisy, the beer flowing freely. Latin music blared and pretty girls in hot pants sold food and beverages and even went up on the ring to strut their stuff. An overhead video replayed the highlights of the three previous fights, all of which had ended in knockouts. The folks came to the arena to watch knockouts and the promoters carefully chose the fighters so the audience could get what they wanted.

Buck's fight was next, just before the main attraction, a rematch between two former middleweight Olympic medalists, Silver and Bronze, from Argentina and Panama. Buck had got a ticket for his mom five rows out and had flown her in. "You won't have any money left, after all that," she'd complained but he had insisted. He needed her there and she didn't want to miss it either. Buck had trained hard, maybe a little too hard, conscious of all that was riding on the fight. For the last couple of days he had felt twinges of pain in the left knee but he had made light of it. He wanted the fight badly. He'd rest afterwards.

When Buck made his entrance he was greeted with a wave of boos. It was, after all, the Miami Kid's home turf. Buck was wearing his new, shiny, white robe with his name emblazoned in back. The moment he stepped into the ring he raised his arms in triumph and did a little dance which only increased the booing. But he also gave a little flinch, barely noticeable, but spotted by his manager and corner man who were watching him closely. Buck felt giddy in the glow of the lights and the booming music and the pretty girls up on the ring doing circles, carrying advertising cards for local businesses, and flirting with him also. He saw the cameramen with their equipment hovering just outside the ring, getting ready to film him. It was show time!

He glanced at his mom and blew her a kiss with his glove. Buck was beside himself; he couldn't believe he would be on TV, even if only for local broadcast, but Miami was a big city and if the fight was good the networks might pick it up for a late-night replay nationwide.

Then it was the Miami Kid's turn to enter and the house went wild. He came in with an entourage of handlers. He had even adopted a theme song that thundered out of the speakers. Feeling gracious, he came over to Buck's corner to say hello. The crowd loved it.

A moment later they were at center ring huddled with the referee. They touched their gloves, went back to their corners for the final blessings and the bell rang.

They both went quickly up to the center of the ring. The Kid landed the first jab. Buck jabbed back. The Kid then began to move in a circle and Buck found himself in the center, moving just enough to stay facing the Kid. There was no question of the difference in foot speed, but as they exchanged blows Buck thought he had just as much hand speed so he wasn't worrying about it. The Kid came back with a one-two combination that caught Buck in the jaw. He had a strong jaw but he felt it. The Kid had power, all right, but Buck had a longer reach and was two inches taller. The Kid came back in with a combination but left just enough daylight and Pow! Buck tagged him with a short right. The Kid stepped back. 'Got the message, didn't you, sucker,' thought Buck. But the Kid was back in again, crouching, feinting, doing a little dance around Buck, dazzling the audience with his agility. He was very good. He worked as a dancer when not boxing. In and out he went, unsettling Buck, circling, Buck planted in the center, the knee… what the hell did he get into? The Kid once more, the quick feint, two fast jabs with both hands, stinging each time. Buck knew he packed a cannon but the Kid out jabbed him. The Kid putting on the pressure, darting in, dancing out, then one, two, three successive blows and the audience went up in a roar. Buck was strong but he felt it. The Kid was piling up the points and it was only the first round. A trickle of blood came down from

Buck's nose. He got me, thought Buck as he brushed back the blood. The din in his ears, the crowd thundering, clamoring for more, "Deck 'im!" "Stomp on 'im!" And Buck concentrating, watching closely. He was being outgunned. A few more of those combinations might be trouble. The Kid was fast. The damned knee. 'I have to finish this off soon,' Buck said to himself. The Kid's shoulders were like butter, that's how smooth were his movements. Buck saw that the Kid had a little smirk on his face as he circled, ready for the kill, in control, and Buck was the prey. He had never felt that way and it was happening right there, in Miami, his mom watching, and on TV. The Kid crouching in, sticking his head out a little, teasing, the smirk on his face, playing to the audience... and Buck unloaded. It was a devastating right hand which caught the Kid on the left temple, just above the ear. And the pride and joy of Miami dropped to the canvas. The audience gasped. All became instantly mum. And then came the slow, very slow count of the clearly partisan referee as the crowd stood breathless. The Kid, flat on his back, didn't stir. He was done for, out cold.

After the referee finished counting him out, which took about 17 seconds instead of the regulation 10, all of which was later confirmed by a video cameraman, his handlers rushed to his side and tried to rouse him. It took another minute before the Kid came to and was helped to his corner. With the audience still stunned, the referee called Buck to the center of the ring and grabbed his arm to raise it. Buck leaned in and whispered in his ear, "Call me the San Diego Bomber," and the referee, a bit ashamed that he had taken all that time counting out his opponent, did just that. "And the winner is – he bellowed into the mike - by knockout in the first round...Buuuck Wilson!! The San Diego Bomber!!" The crowd let out a long and rancorous boo and then proceeded to cut loose and rain upon the ring a thousand cups filled with beer, soda and other unnamed fluids. It was a most unhappy crowd, having to contend with the notion that their hero would have to stick to dancing instead. But it had been an unforgettable night.

When Buck got back to San Diego he went straight to see his doctor. He was given tests and all the necessary examinations. The results were not good. The knee had to be operated on again. There were no assurances as to the outcome. Even if he came out okay, chances were that he would not be able to have the agility needed to continue his boxing career. Buck was devastated. He was just beginning to live the life he longed for and there it was being snatched away from him. He hadn't lost a fight and he had to give it up. His mother was at his side when he got the news. She comforted him as best she could but the infinite pain of the loss was Buck's alone to bear.

And so it was that Buck Wilson, the newly minted San Diego Bomber, grudgingly relinquished his dream.

32

Joey had continued to attend his sessions with Dr Jeffries and looked forward to them. When he pondered this, he remembered how reluctant he had been at first and how, if it hadn't been for her gentle persistence, he might have cheated himself out of something precious. He hadn't thanked her for it but one day he would.

It was the middle of February and winter had a bite. His small slit of a window had frosted overnight and the ground outside looked icy and hard; by midmorning, though, the temperature had risen to the low forties.

Joey had discovered he liked winter. He thought that when he got out, he would want to go live for a while in a place where the seasons were marked. The changes in foliage, the colors, all of it gave him a keen sense that change was inevitable, that it was built into his body, that it was the law of life and that his mind would be the wiser if he accepted it. He and Legrand talked of such things: human transformation, the seasons of man. They had become good friends and would go out for walks when they had yard in the middle of the day.

Joey also felt he was maturing, that the time in prison was not being entirely wasted, and how lucky he had been to have a cellmate like Legrand. He probably wouldn't even be alive if it hadn't been for him. He didn't ask for it, but the fact that Legrand had extended his friendship had granted him a protective mantle. Nonetheless, he would take nothing for granted; things could turn on a dime.

Dr Jeffries was sitting at her desk, writing in a notebook, when Joey came up to the door and stood by waiting for her acknowledgement. She nodded him in and he stepped forward and took a seat. She was wearing a mauve turtleneck sweater with matching earrings. He liked her taste in clothes, the grace of her movements, the manner in which she tilted her head; everything about her. He had concluded that he was in love and yet, well, there were those boundaries to observe as she had stated at the outset, and if those boundaries were not observed the work could not continue. He sighed.

She continued writing for a few moments before she put the pen down and closed the notebook. "Where did we leave off?" she asked.

"I'm glad to be here."

Folding her hands, she placed them on the edge of her desk and sat back.

He was conscious of the fact that he simply wanted to enjoy the silence with her. Aware of his breathing it occurred to him that he could inhale her, if nothing else, and the thought made him smile.

"Whatever's on your mind," Dr Jeffries prompted.

"Nothing, really."

"You were smiling…"

"I know. I thought if I could just breathe you in…"

She laughed.

"That way I could take you with me everywhere."

"But you do, don't you?"

"I do. And I talk to you, too."

"About what?"

"About aggressive and erotic feelings I sometimes have."

"Like what?"

"Like I'd like to have you."

They were looking at each other and Joey saw that she remained serene and unruffled, as always. "But I know that's all grist for the mill and I have to try and understand it… because that's what the work is about."

She nodded. "What else comes to mind when you have the aggressive and erotic feelings?"

"Melanie."

"What about her?"

"She couldn't defend herself like you can… and I knew it… and still I did what I did. I don't like that about myself."

"Had it happened before?"

"No… not with anyone underage… but you could say I was precocious… what I mean is… I was playing with girls my age… just feeling them up… pinching… beginning when I was 8 or 9… maybe earlier… older girls, too. Got slapped a few times, but sooner or later one would welcome the advance."

"What was that about?"

"I thought it was the cool thing to do."

"And the slapping didn't deter you?"

"Nope."

"In any of those instances… did word get back to your parents?"

"A few times. Mom dismissed it and dad… he didn't seem to mind, either."

Joey leaned forward, elbows on his knees. "But that's all in the past. I know I was wrong."

"It's pertinent, given your offense… so I think it should be explored."

But Joey didn't want to dwell on the subject, not just then. Instead, he straightened up in his chair and said, "I think I'm getting better… but I'm a little worried about that, too."

"How so?"

"I think you'll stop calling me out."

"When the time comes that would be a good thing, wouldn't it? You'd be ready for new challenges."

That was not what he had wanted to hear.

"There's a lot more work to do," she added.

At least that was soothing. He would just have to keep coming up with more issues so he could keep seeing her. It could last forever, he mused.

"I know you've never asked me this but I know you're wondering about it…"

He met her eyes.

"Have I ever had a satisfying relationship with a woman my age?"

"Good question."

"I haven't."

"Why's that?"

"I didn't know how. It seemed to me like I was growing up physically but not emotionally. I can say that in hindsight, but back then, all I knew was there was something off with me. I wasn't getting something right. Like the girls, they were maturing faster and I thought they could see right through me and see what a fake I was. Not with Melanie, though. With her I felt secure, I felt strong. With her I felt I could have a relationship."

"A sexual relationship with a child," said Dr Jeffries.

He winced in irritation. "I don't like the way you put that." He crossed his arms, hands to his shoulders and sat back. "I know you're not intending to be critical of me, but I still don't like that you said it."

She didn't stir, just gazed back at him.

"A little angry, too," continued Joey, "like you're pulling away the covers I've been hiding under. Maybe I should be grateful." His breathing had become deeper and he paused for a moment. "You don't have anything to say?"

"Stay with the feeling…" she said, calmly.

He trusted her and knew he could go forward. "Maybe if I'd… if I'd learned to put words to what I felt… maybe if I'd done that… isn't that right there at the beginning of thinking… the dialogue with your emotions?"

"Stay with the feeling…" she prompted, gently.

"Calling shame by its name… not letting it beat you down… standing up and facing it…"

"Accepting it…" said she.

"…Wrestling with it… understanding… my father." And Joey halted. "I don't know where that came from."

Dr Jeffries arched her brow.

He pushed back his chair and stared back at her. "Can't you say something?"

"You're doing just fine," she said.

"Why the heck couldn't we talk in our home? Why couldn't we tell each other what we felt, instead pretending that all was well…" His eyes had moistened and he shook his head lightly. He remained quiet for a moment. "I just want you to know I'm not blaming anybody."

She nodded lightly.

"You're impossible, you know that?" said Joey.

Just then the guard passed by and peaked in through the glass in the door.

"Mom…" continued Joey, a hint of irony in his smile. "She was great, though, always there. Busy, busy, but always there, a phone call away."

"How so?"

"It was true, she really would answer when I called. She's worked since I can remember. She was a good mom… she just wasn't into physical affection. It just wasn't her. My father, on the other hand… at the start… before everything turned around…"

And he paused.

"Was he warm to you?"

"Yes."

"Whatever happened… before everything turned around?" asked Dr Jeffries.

Joey looked off for a moment, the expression strained, as if struggling with an uneasy feeling. Then he peered into her eyes. "I stabbed him in the back."

Dr Jeffries tilted her head slightly, "Literally?"

He nodded. "I don't want to talk about it now. Obviously, he survived, but I was very angry. I can see now that I was wrong… but back then… I thought he was turning me into a girl."

Dr Jeffries picked up her pen. It was a blue pen. She liked blue. "How do you think he was doing that?"

"Dad… he had a problem at work. Big. There was a threat of a lawsuit and they were getting ready to let him go. He had been suspended without pay while they did an investigation and he had turned to drinking. There were arguments all the time. Nasty ones. Mother never told me the details but it had to do with his temper. You have to be pretty together to deal with us inmates; we're all damaged goods. Money was getting tight and it looked like we were heading for disaster when mom stepped up and saved the day."

"What did she do?"

"She knew the warden. She pleaded with him and he took him back. He gave him a job where he had little contact with inmates, but the arguments at home continued and one day things came to a head and she left."

"Left…?"

"Left."

Dr Jeffries put down the pen. "Who'd you stay with?"

"Him. It was just him and me. Mom took Margaret with her. But she hired some baby sitters so dad could go to work."

"What was that like?"

"Terrible. Dad couldn't pull himself together, he couldn't handle whatever was going on between them."

"How old were you?"

"Six. Margaret was four. I was really angry that mom had left me behind, but when the baby sitter came in I fell in love with her right away and that made me feel better. She must have been about 14 or 15. I couldn't tell at that time."

"A pretty normal thing for a child."

"Her name was Penny."

"But how was it, then, that you thought your dad was turning you into a girl?"

"I thought he was."

"How?"

"Well... he'd be kissing me all the time. He'd hug and kiss me and cry like a baby."

"This is after she left?"

"Yes."

"He must've been very sad that your mom was gone..."

"I'm sure that's what it was but I was too young to put two and two together. All I knew was all that kissing made me feel very weird. I didn't see the other kids my age being kissed so often. I didn't like it."

"You didn't tell him?"

"I was afraid. I thought there was something wrong with him. My mom was gone. I wasn't sure she was coming back."

"What did your dad say?"

"He shut down, kept everything stuffed inside. If anything even began to get out, he'd wash it down with whisky. Of course, I didn't know back then that's what he was doing."

Joey dropped his eyes.

"How're you feeling?"

"As I talk, things that I'd forgotten come to mind... like I'm recovering lost parts of myself."

"Integrating," she remarked.

"Is that what it's called?" He shook his head in rueful disquiet. "This place is not built to integrate anything… I mean… those units… you have to keep a tight lid on your emotions … for your safety." He looked at her wistfully. "But we're still expected to turn things around and fix ourselves. I'm one of the lucky ones."

Dr Jeffries had her view on the subject and did not hesitate to express it. "Society's main concern is that you be properly warehoused, with a lukewarm commitment to mental health since prisons became mental hospitals."

Joey pulled up closer to the desk and rested his folded arms. "I wish I would've been able to help him."

"Your dad?"

"Yes."

"You were too young for that, don't you think?"

"True."

He glanced at the single flower on Dr Jeffries' desk. "You changed the color, last week it was yellow, the carnation. A new beginning…?"

"Renewal…" she nodded.

"I want a new beginning, too."

"You could have one."

He smiled. "You know… when Penny took care of us at night, when dad worked late…"

"The baby sitter…?"

"Yes. I'd sit in the sofa next to her and lean my head against her shoulder. It felt so peaceful. Then, one night, I don't know what got into me, I reached across and put my hand on her breast." Joey looked at Dr Jeffries, uncertainly.

"Why did you stop?"

"The memory of Penny aroused me…"

"And?"

"I guess I thought I'd get punished for it…"

"That I'd punish you?"

"Yes."

"Why?"

"It's sexual"

"Which is at the heart of the matter."

He nodded.

"What did the baby sitter do?" continued Dr Jeffries, "after you put your hand on her breast?"

"She took it and put it down, told me not to do it again."

"Did you feel like she was punishing you?"

"No... but it was very clear she was putting me in my place."

"Which is what she needed to do."

"Yes."

"You were talking of your father kissing you a lot and crying like a baby... making you feel weird and you not being able to tell him to stop. Then you thought of Penny, the attraction you had for her and touching her breast. What about that transition?"

Joey pondered for a moment. "I wanted to run away from that weird feeling I had with dad... I wanted to feel like a boy again."

"Did that bring you peace?"

"Yes... some... it made sense to me."

"Feeling confused you made a choice... an affirmation on your part, inappropriate but an affirmation nonetheless."

Joey nodded. He felt he was integrating.

"You may think this is strange... but someone slipped a copy of 'Lolita' under my door, Nabokov's novel about a man obsessed with a young girl. He's a brilliant writer but I'm not like his main character." Joey scrutinized Dr Jeffries expression. "I don't know why I thought about that."

Dr Jeffries said nothing.

"I mean, I admit Melanie excited me but I was never obsessed. Do you think I was obsessed?"

"I don't."

"Have you read the book?"

"I have."

"What did you think of it?"

"This is not Nabokov's session, it's yours."

"Okay, you got me, I was trying to get out from under your microscope."

"Not just my microscope but yours and mine. This is a joint venture."

"Thank you for that."

"Any idea who slipped in the copy of the book?"

"Paytrell, our neighbor, was near his window and saw him. It was officer Tanpuro."

"Don't believe I know him. Why would he do that?"

"Everybody in the world knows I'm a child molester," returned Joey. "Sometimes it feels like a life sentence, that my mug shot is all over the internet, that I will never be rid of that label, and I'm only 23 years old. No parole for me."

Dr Jeffries reflected for a moment, then said, "That is the law as it stands today, but allow me to remind you that there's a bigger picture here. So long as you continue to strive to advance your development as a human being, other men and women will not see you through the narrow lens of the law, but through the broader one of your accomplishments."

"I want to believe you," he said, touched by her support.

She nodded and then looked at her watch; they had a few minutes left. "Before we stop, I'd like to do an exercise. I'd like for you to imagine Melanie, sitting right here to my left."

Joey was surprised.

"Why?"

"Bear with me. Can you see her?"

Joey shifted his weight in and looked into the empty space next to Dr Jeffries. He readily conjured Melanie's image. "I see her."

"Describe, please."

"She's older. She's sixteen. She's blossoming."

"What would you like to tell her?"

Joey shrugged, a bit dejected, "That I'm very sorry for what I did."

"Just tell her directly," said Dr Jeffries.

"You know, I've done this before, on my own," said Joey.

"Good. Do it with me now. Keep your eyes on her, let her affect you… imagine her skin, her hair, her expression."

Joey focused on the imaginary Melanie seated right in front and began, "I was wrong for what I did to you. Even if you felt attracted to me… I was in the wrong because I took advantage of you. I did not think of the fact that your mind had not matured enough to make sound choices. Had you been of consenting age, you may not have picked me as a partner, but someone else more to your liking. So please forgive me." And he thought he really would have liked to say those words in person to Melanie. Then he turned to Dr Jeffries and added, "There was something else I wanted to say to her… or maybe it is for you."

"What was that?"

"It's something I've been meaning to say for a while." He paused momentarily, then continued, "That I know that society has devised rules to protect the young and I knowingly did not observe them… and that society does so to preserve the species and the diversity that makes us rich."

Dr Jeffries nodded.

"I still love her."

"What if she told you that it's best that you forgot her?"

"I would do it. But is she really saying that?"

"We don't know, do we, but for you, for your healing and hers, it is best that you surrender your longing for her. We will work on this as we go along and address the grief. For now, say goodbye to her."

And he did.

33

*L*ater that day, while working second watch in Bravo Three, officer Tanpuro, going off a tip from another inmate, had gone into cell 218 and confiscated a cell phone. The inmate, Zambrano, had been out of his cell attending classes toward his G.E.D. When he returned and saw the shambles his cell had been reduced to, he was stupefied. Everything he had lay in tatters; the pictures of his family he had glued to the wall; a detailed drawing of himself riding freely in a motorcycle; photos of landscapes he had hoped to visit when released; all had been ripped up and left on the floor. Zambrano fell to his knees in anguish.

Zambrano knew he was violating the rules by having a phone in his cell, so he would have to deal with the consequences. He had borrowed it from a friend so now he would have to pay it back, which meant hours and hours of writing letters and poems for other inmates to send to their girlfriends and relatives, which is how he made his money. But what reason was there to destroy his personal possessions? It was sheer spite.

"Why? Why?" he muttered angrily to himself, rocking to and fro as he knelt on the floor, face pressed hard against his fists. Then he stopped, leapt to his feet and banged on the door. "Who did this to me! Who did it!?"

His neighbor had witnessed the ransacking and let him in on it.

"Tanpuroooo!" screamed out Zambrano. "Come here! Don't hide from me!"

Down below, in his office, Tanpuro was calmly eating his burrito. He had the door cracked open but now he closed it; the door banging interfered with his digestion.

A half hour went by and Zambrano had not let up. Finally, Tanpuro wiped off his mouth, threw away the meal's wrappings in the trash and stepped into the day room.

Walking with even pace, holding up high in his hand the confiscated cell phone, Tanpuro crossed to the staircase, climbed up unto the second tier, and turned in the direction of Zambrano's cell.

Seeing him approach, Zambrano stopped banging on the door.

"See this," said Tanpuro, waving the cell phone as he stood in front of 218 facing Zambrano. "Are you supposed to have this?"

"Why did you have to tear up the pictures of my family?"

"Answer me. Are you supposed to have this?"

Zambrano was managing to keep a measure of composure. "Okay, I'm guilty, but why did you have to tear up the pictures of my family?"

"You're not supposed to have this, comprende, chamaco? "I'm writing you up, you hear?"

"Answer my question, man."

Tanpuro leaned in so as not to be overheard. "You answer me first. Who's bringing them in?"

"I don't know, I was just borrowing it."

Tanpuro got closer to the crack on the side of the door and whispered, "Just tell me. We'll keep it between you and me and your buddy that let you borrow it… who's bringing them in?"

Zambrano grew quiet. He was trembling with anger and thought of spitting in Tanpuro's face. But no, he would not give him that satisfaction. His family visited often and his mother brought him his kids. That was the most important thing in the world for him: seeing them, embracing them, hearing them talk about their school, their friends, putting his arms around his mom who had stuck by him through all of it. All of that rushed into his mind to remind him to hold back and not let Tanpuro push his buttons. He could replace the photos but not his freedom. Then Tanpuro leaned in once more and whispered even softer. "See, if you tell me who's running the scam, I'll even drop the charge. You do something for me, I do something for you, they call that quid pro quo, you dumb ass."

"I told you, man, I borrowed it," said Zambrano.

"Isn't there a phone down there you can use?" said Tanpuro, pointing to the day room.

"It's too expensive, you know that."

"Welcome to Prison USA, buster. Now listen to me good. I know you're running drugs… and unless you give up your connects, I'm going to write you up so we can get the DA to press new charges and you know how those cats love to keep the prison business going, right? It's a living, isn't it? Just as it is for me."

Zambrano didn't reply.

"But what do you care, right? You've got three squares and a cot and you've managed to smuggle all your kin into the country."

Zambrano let Tanpuro run his mouth. Tanpuro might be an old hand like he said he was but he seemed to know nothing about the workings of the unit. Every inmate knew where the drugs were coming from and some officers might be on it, too, though he had no proof, but Tanpuro was definitely out of the loop. No one trusted him, not even the snitches. Zambrano shook his head and turned away.

"Well?"

"Well what?"

"How'd you get the phone?"

Zambrano waved him off.

"I know I can get to you… but I like you and want to give you a chance," pressed Tanpuro.

"Do what you have to do," said Zambrano in resignation. Then he sat on the floor, his back to the officer, and began to pick up the pieces of his torn-up photos and drawings.

Tanpuro cursed under his breath as he remained at the cell door. Screw the little prick. He had been needing a win, he reminded himself. He had failed to make an impression on his fellow officers and had even got a slew of complaints from inmates for improper behavior. The captain had called him into his office after the incident with Poncho Sterling, and had issued a warning. So he had started to seriously wonder about his job security when he came upon the idea that if he uncovered a drug ring or a cell phone racket, why then the brass would look upon him favorably. Brownie points. Ah, what the hell.

That Zambrano was now completely ignoring him sent a wave of rage and contempt through him. "Come back here, I've got something to tell you," he commanded.

Zambrano was determined to stay centered and resist the provocation. He still had five years left on his sentence for domestic violence but he knew he was going to get through. Even if his wife chose to move on, there were his kids waiting for him. He had vowed to keep his nose clean and get out of the rat hole and, except for the phone affair, he had been able to stick with the plan.

"Come back just a second," insisted Tanpuro, now in a softer, entreating tone.

And Zambrano returned to the door.

"See, you need protection…"

"Protection from what?" asked Zambrano.

"From me."

A cold shudder went through Zambrano. And Tanpuro, giving him a devilish smile, got ready to land the nasty blow. "See, if you don't give me something, I have to make it up. For instance, I could say that you told me that your mother had stuck the phone up her pussy to bring it in to you, so next time she comes in we'll have to search her… properly."

Zambrano just stared back. And it occurred to him that Tanpuro might, in fact, be deranged, but then he thought that if he could see it so could his coworkers, so it might be better to leave him alone so the man would unravel on his own.

"Heck, maybe I should do the inspection myself…"
continued Tanpuro.

And Zambrano, very calmly, leaned into the crack of the door and whispered softly in Tanpuro's ear, "You're crazy." Then turned away from the door and went back to picking up the pieces.

"Fuck you, goddamned wetback. Fuck you and all your brown cousins."

Tanpuro bit his lip and began marching back to his office. Okay, he thought to himself, I couldn't put the squeeze on that one but another one will cooperate. He needed to find himself a weaker one.

34

Joey had become a chronic runaway at 13. At first he stayed with friends in their backyards or garages, then, after a year or so, he was taken in by Caprice, a lonely divorced woman in her late thirties who lived on the other side of town. Janice had thought of calling the police but Buck had stopped her. "What are they going to do? Pry into our business? Send him to a state facility to be with other maladjusted kids?" She thought of this and gave it some weight but what had helped dissuade her was that, since settling in with Caprice, Joey appeared to be content. He would call often, at least weekly, and the conversations soothed Janice. Sometimes he would even ask to speak to his father but Buck always refused.

Now and then, Joey met with Janice. Caprice was helping with his homework and he helped her with her small farm business: raising pigs and chicken that she took to market. "I like her, mom." And Janice had no reason to doubt him: he appeared healthy and strong. "Are you happy?" she dared ask, and Joey said yes.

For his part, Buck had his reason for feeling satisfied with the unexpected turn of events. He had worried that Joey's closeness with mom had affected his sexual identity, though there was nothing outwardly feminine about him. Buck had fretted that the strain between them – they hadn't had a conversation since Joey had plunged the sharp kitchen knife into his back at age 6 – had had an irreparable effect on the young man. But if Joey remained a boy, well, that was enough for Buck. So when he heard that a divorced woman had given him shelter, and all that went with it, he breathed a sigh of relief. At least he was being educated in the ways of being a man.

Of late, Buck's craving for a cigarette had returned. It had been at least two and a half years since Buck had last lit up, after Janice had pushed him to it. So he thought he was due for a break. After all, some famous people had smoked all their lives and that didn't keep them from doing great things. Take Winston Churchill for example. The man smoked and drank his entire life. And so, believing he had plenty of historical support, Buck decided to defy Janice and get himself a pack.

He knew that if he smoked Janice would find out, he was sure of that - the woman had special sensors - but he was so eager for a moment of clarity, so uncomfortable at having to do it all on his own, that the thought of lighting up became impossible to resist. And it wasn't that he didn't put up a fight, either. When the cravings mounted anew, he fought them bravely, going off for quick walks or finding things to do around the house, anything to withstand the pressure to yield. But after two, three, four days of fierce resistance, his resolve crumbled.

It was a bittersweet moment. He went to the back of the house after Janice left for work, sat on the stoop, took the pack out of his pocket and stared at it. It was only then that he noticed that he had not bought his old brand and that, inadvertently, he had purchased the same exact brand his father had smoked all his life. Was there any significance to that? He rarely thought about his father anymore but when he did he felt immensely sad. Not because the old man had never forgiven him, not because he had driven off a cliff while intoxicated a few months after his mother had died of a stroke – Buck was convinced it had not been accidental – but because if the old man had not been so stubborn and had heard him out and supported his dream of becoming a boxer, Buck would not have played football just to please him, and he would not have injured his knee and yes, like Brando had said in "On The Waterfront," he "could've been a contender". The simple thought of it brought tears to his eyes. He could have had a boxing career. Imagine that, "The San Diego Bomber". Wow. What a difference a man can have in another's life. Mind boggling. And Buck looked down and he had already torn off the wrapping and the sweet aroma of the rich tobacco was wafting up luxuriously into his brain. He lingered, pressing the pack to his nostrils, hoping perhaps that he could inhale the cigarette without having to light it.

So what about the significance of choosing the same brand his father had smoked, after all those years? He lamented that his father had not had a dream of his own because, if he had, he would not have pressured him the way he did. Had Buck known that back then, he would've said to his father, "Get a dream of your own, dammit!" But he had been too young to know that.

Did bringing his father into his worries about Joey have any significance? Buck's father had been too involved in his choices but he, in turn, had done the opposite and not been involved at all in Joey's. But wait, no, at first he had, yes, he did, and everything changed only after the incident. Buck wished that he and his dad had been able to talk. And after his mom's death from the stroke, when they were both grieving, if they would have talked instead, maybe dad would not have turned to drinking and then gone off the cliff.

But they had been too angry at each other. His mom, bless her heart, he loved her so much, had not been able to facilitate that dialogue, and maybe she had not because she did not think it was possible. And Buck acknowledged that, after the knee injury, he had thought he could break up with dad, once and for all, not realizing that things were not that simple between parents and children. Like it or not, they lived in each other forever and keeping a dialogue was the only way of learning to not make the same mistakes again - the only road to acceptance - regardless of what had happened. He wasn't talking about forgiveness but about something more basic: simple acceptance, serene acceptance. No judgment attached. So now, by lighting up his father's brand, was Buck bringing the old man back into the conversation?

Thinking his thoughts had distracted him from the cravings but now they came back, stronger than ever, demanding full surrender. Buck tapped out the little devil, held it between his fingers and admired the power such small roll of dried tobacco leaves had over him. He put it between his lips. Maybe he could just eat it instead... you could do that with marijuana and get an effect... and he struck the match... and he took the loooong and deeeep drag... ahhh... what ravishing delight.

But it was brief. In the next moment, a feeling of nausea rose, unforgiving and accusing, and a swell of disgust swept over him. He felt dizzy and wanted to throw up. He thought of lying down on the grass but instead leaned against the doorjamb. Maybe it was the anger at himself coming through that made things worse. He still held the pack in his hand. He looked at it, cursed it... and then crushed it in his powerful hand and flung it violently to the far end of the yard where it bounced off the back wooden fence onto the grass. "Damn cancer sticks!" he bellowed. Cold sweat oozed onto his temples and heavy jowls. He wiped it off with his hands. "This must be what a junkie goes through," he muttered to himself. "Heck, no, what am I saying? I am a junkie. Just look at me, look at how this crap has brought me to my knees."

But the dizziness had started to ebb. He breathed easier. "No, it's not so bad. I can deal with it." And he got up, the knees faltering slightly, but managing still, then turned to go back into the house. Then he stopped. He was steady on his feet, feeling a little better. And he glanced over his shoulder and let his eyes wander to see if he could find where the crumpled pack of cigarettes lay in the yard. He spotted it. And the damned craving rose again. Harder this time. Buck closed his eyes... one last fight? No. He strode over to the crumpled pack, picked it up, opened it, took out what was usable and lit up again. He inhaled deeply once more... ahh... he could feel it coming back... the slight nausea... yes... but the pleasure... oh, the pleasure it gave him. Yes! Yes! Where have you been all this time, my dear? Oh, the peace that tobacco brought him. "Hell, you've got to die of something," he said to himself. He walked back to the steps of the porch and sat down. Yes. Now he could think, now he could endure the misery. "Bring it on, goddammit! How did all this crap we're in get started, anyway?" And he smoked three more of the bent, crooked, torn, salvaged cigarettes, one after the other, as he tried gamely to answer the question.

Feeling invigorated by the smokes, the savory toxins he had inhaled, though a little numbed by it all, he jumped into the exercise bike he had neglected for months and cycled away for half an hour. The energy was coming back. He hopped off, popped into the shower and then zipped to the market to get some healthy food to prepare for dinner. Salmon was a dish they both enjoyed. Janice would be pleased. Of course, a fruit salad to begin and then, for dessert, a little nonfat yogurt with a serving of chocolate mousse. Heck, Janice might be so pleased that she might just ignore the scent the cigarettes left in him. Nevertheless, he took pains to deodorize the house. He emptied an entire can of rose fragrance spray in the bedroom and living room and rinsed his mouth at least ten times with a special mouthwash for smokers. He tidied up a bit throughout the house, so that the spraying could be seen as part of the overall cleaning. He put some Johnny Mathis music on – Janice had had a crush on him when she was a youngster - and let it suffuse the living room with the romantic melodies. He sat on the sofa to wait. He had put on a dash of perfume, also.

Half an hour passed. A last minute client might have delayed Janice. He called but she didn't answer. Then the thoughts returned. After all the smoking, he had the sense that he really hadn't made any headway in figuring out how the whole problem with Joey had got so entangled and confusing. He was back at the same spot, feeling racked again by the fear of being discovered as the man who spawned a child molester, and still unable to think clearly and get some answers. Worst of all, he felt he could not muster the courage to speak to Janice about his anguish. Oh, how he needed her. And he remembered how painful the separation had been, how he had begged little Joey to try and understand the pain he was going through, and that little Joey didn't quite get it. Why had his pain been so wrenching? Why did Janice mean so much to him? And why did he not tell her all that had been going on at the prison? And Buck remembered how much he had loved his little Joey, and how he wanted his son to grow up to be strong, like him... no, stronger than him... and how he wished he had been Joey... yes, sometimes he wished he had been his own son... free from an overbearing father... free to do what he wanted... and when he hugged and kissed his little Joey... it was like he was kissing himself... nurturing a second chance to be what he had wanted to be.

Buck thought of taking a drink; he had replaced the bottle of whiskey he had nearly emptied after the garage meltdown when he tore up the cement floor with the hammer. But this time he hadn't hid it. He had placed it on the high shelf of the closet and not bothered to stick it in the shoebox. What Buck did keep hidden, though, in the same closet, in the pockets of an old winter coat he no longer used, were the letters from the warden in Salinas. The letters addressed to Mr and Mrs Wilson. The letters that told of what injuries Joey had suffered and that Janice had never read.

Janice was a little flustered when she stepped in an hour later. Another vehicle in the parking lot at the office had backed up against her luxury car and put a small dent in her front bumper, minor stuff but enough to bug you for a while.

Buck had welcomed her with an embrace. "Don't worry. It'll be all right. He's good for it, yes?"

"Of course, he's a client of the office, I have his information; social security and everything."

He took her purse and laid it on the sofa. Only then did the whole preparation Buck had gone through strike Janice. She looked around and smiled: she smelled the spray, took in the music, the tidying up.

"You've been busy, honey."

"I have."

"How sweet of you."

They kissed on the lips. She said nothing. Phew! Passed that test.

"You hungry?"

"I am. Cooked something, didn't you?"

"Yup, for my cutie pie."

"I'll be right out," she said and headed for the bedroom.

After dinner, Buck and Janice went out for a walk. They held hands and climbed up a little hill from where they could see the freeway in the distance. He put his arm around her, pulled her close and felt her relax. Then Joey came up.

"You think he'll be safe?" she asked.

He had lied to her before. He had told her that he had spoken to fellow guards he knew, to watch over Joey, but had never done so. He had set up a secret P.O. Box so that all official correspondence about Joey was sent to him directly. And he had convinced her not to make inquiries herself, for fear she might reveal something inadvertently that could be traced back to him.

Janice had asked Joey about his safety but the conversations had always stopped short. And it worried her. On two occasions he had shown bruises in his face but he had made light of them, reassuring her that they were unimportant. He was strong and could take care of himself, that's what mattered, and so he would be just fine.

"You think he'll be safe?" asked Janice again.

And Buck lied again. "I've talked to some old friends of mine, Driscoll and Putnam; I didn't know they were still there. It's been awhile. They can watch over him without it being an issue."

"Where do you know them from?"

"Corcoran; they moved up in the ranks, they're both captains now. Back in the day, when he was starting, Driscoll and I would go out and get a bite to eat. Putnam is more of the stuck-up sort but he's all right. But please don't call them – he added with haste - I'm checking in with them." What made matters worse was that the officers he had mentioned were not even his friends. In fact, years back, Putnam had reported him to the warden for getting into a fight with an inmate, having heard that bets had been placed and that it would give the CDCR a black mark.

When Buck spoke to Janice he had looked her in the eye, at close range, and it was then that Janice caught the fullness of his breath. And it smelled of cigarettes. How could he? And it struck her that if he was lying about the cigarettes he was lying also about the protection she so dearly wished for her son.

Janice removed Buck's arm from her shoulders and walked off a few paces. The setting sun was vanishing and the sinking orange cusp pulled the day to a close. She turned to face him. "You've been lying to me." A gleam of fire shone in her eyes.

"Lying?" said Buck, warily. "I admit, I did sneak a cigarette." But Buck knew it was not about the smokes.

"You've been lying to me about Joey."

"I've told you I don't want him in my life... I don't want anything to do with him."

"And I accepted that," said Janice, "God knows why, because I accepted it without really questioning why a father would reject his son the way you have. But that's on me. I should have confronted you then but I am confronting you now. You are a liar and a fraud."

Janice stood there on the little hill, all 5 feet 2 inches of her, feeling tall and full of fury as she laid into her burly and muscular husband, the conviction that she was in the right giving her the extraordinary sense that she could take on a man his size.

"What are you talking about?" returned Buck. "It was you who walked out and left me to comfort and console Joey, knowing as you did that I am clumsy with affection, knowing as you did that it would tear me apart and overwhelm me... and you were gone for two months."

"Six weeks."

"Two months, Janice. Two months of tears and anger and confusion and god knows what..."

"You touched my son, didn't you?"

The words burnt through him and he was speechless. "What?"

"Why would he want to kill you?"

Buck was stunned. "I don't know…" he began, as he searched for words, "You're accusing me of molesting my son?"

"Why would a son want to kill his father?"

He shook his head slowly in disbelief, "I don't know, Janice… to this day… I don't know why Joey wanted to kill me. And I should've asked him but never did… and did you ever ask him?"

Janice said nothing.

"Then we both failed… not just me… and because we both failed he left when he was thirteen."

Buck was surprised at how controlled his response had been, but Janice's words had wounded him deeply.

"I thought he was all I had left…" he continued, "and maybe I kissed him too many times… maybe I was too affectionate… and that scared him… maybe I wasn't thinking of his feelings and only of mine… but I never touched him the wrong way."

Buck had faced Janice as he spoke, the memories of those fateful days stumbling into his awareness.

"When you were gone, sometimes Joey would soil his pants and I would clean him up, wash his bottom. He would come and ask me to clean him up… and he had tears in his eyes when he asked… and I washed his bottom like a father is supposed to for a son, a son who soils his pants because he's scared his mom is not coming back."

Yes, he had failed to parent, but no, he was not guilty of that ghastly transgression.

"He was six years old," pressed Janice.

"Would you have said, 'Go wash yourself?'"

The anger in Janice would not be appeased. She turned and walked off.

Buck looked after her. A sense of relief had come over him. And it occurred to him that maybe one day he and Joey should have the same conversation, and if they ever did, why then Joey would tell him his side of the story… and maybe… maybe… they could embrace as father and son.

Twilight was fading. Buck sat on a log on the hill and gazed out at the traffic on the freeway beyond. He felt the light breeze of the springtime evening and he wondered if their troubles would ever be solved. He was

56 and feeling every bit of it. He discovered tears on his face; tears of pain, of regret, tears he hadn't felt since that time, seventeen years before, when Janice had walked out on him.

A light rain had fallen earlier and the earth under his shoes turned muddy. He took a small stick that lay near and scraped it off. If he had got help earlier, how different would it all now be? It would not have been the end of the world to ask for help. He had seen some of his peers go through marital problems, get counseling and pull through. True, he had thought them weak at first, but then he had discovered that he secretly admired that they had had the courage. But it was hard for him.

A sparrow landed on the ground a few feet away. The little bird pecked at the leaves and sprigs around him. The bird was light and he was free: if he could only be a sparrow, thought Buck.

His mind took him back to his parents and he remembered that they never talked to each other. They reacted to each other but there was never any open discussion of anything. He had seen his father explode and walk out; he had seen his mother listen quietly and then do what she wanted; but he had never witnessed an effort to compromise, to air out a matter and see it to its end, with both people making efforts to control their tempers to not hurt each other. And then Buck thought that if he had been open from the start, all the burden the family was now bearing, why even the whole affair with Joey, might never have happened. If he had not been so closed minded... he would even have embraced his son after the knifing... held him in a big bear hug until the child had poured out all his rage.

And why did he not confront Janice when he felt that she was doting on Joey and keeping him from him? Oh, the nagging question. Did he think then that he had too little to offer? Did he believe that not having done what he had really wanted with his life, forever branded him as flawed and barred him from being a proper parent to his son?

He stood on the hill for about an hour and then slowly made his way back down to their home. He opened the door. Janice was tearing up the house.

She was frantically looking for something and as soon as she heard that he had come in she went to him. "Stay out until I'm through!"

"What are you doing?"

"Stay out until I'm through," she repeated sharply, angrily.

There was nothing he could do. Struggling with her would have made things worse, so Buck went outside and sat on the swing by the porch. He didn't want to fight anymore. She would find the letters he had hidden, and that would be the end of their relationship. She would ask him to move out and he would. How would his daughter Margaret react? Margaret, too, was more attached to her mother than to him. If Margaret saw the letters that would be the end of that relationship, also, and he would be all alone again, like he felt at the start, after his mother had died.

Could he bear it this time and not fall apart like he had 17 years before? Could he stand the pain of the rejection? He thought of the inmates back at the prison, the complaint of those whose relatives didn't write or visit. The loneliness. The suicides. His father's older brother had done it. The eccentric one: uncle Harold, the one with the ostrich farm; the one with the cold, battering wife; the one who one day had gone to the barn at the other end of the farm, got on his knees, stuck a shotgun in his mouth and pulled the trigger. Double barrel.

Buck never heard the whole story about his demise, only that uncle Harold worked very hard, was often depressed and rarely talked. Maybe I have uncle Harold's genes, thought Buck. His mother would tell him that he needed only worry about his father's side of the family, that's where the problems were, not her side. On mother's side, kin were bright and talkative, sometimes crazy, too, but happy crazy, not gloomy and dour like on his father's side. And Buck had asked, 'then why did you marry dad?' And mom had said, 'A moment of weakness, son… a moment of weakness can change your life.'

Janice came out the house and sat on the swing next to Buck. She didn't look at him at first. She was winded and sweaty from all the searching.

"Where's the ladder?"

"What ladder?"

"The one we had in the garage. It's not there, I need it."

"It should be there."

"It's not."

Janice had not found the letters. But she did not need a ladder.

"What is it that you're looking for?" he asked softly, innocently.

"Something from the prison." She shook her head with a mixture of disbelief and self-disgust. "I can't believe I've been so naïve, relying on you for information about Joey when I've known all along you didn't give a damn."

Buck said nothing.

"Have we had letters from the prison?" she asked firmly, fixing her gaze upon him.

Buck leaned forward in the swing. He rubbed his hands. He turned to her and looked her in the eye. She asked the question again. He just stared at her and thought of his mother, what she had said to him that day. 'A moment of weakness can change your life.' And he thought again of uncle Harold.

"Answer me," cried out Janice in exasperation, trying to break through to him. But Buck didn't budge. Instead he kept staring back. He thought of what he had said at the top of the hill an hour before, how all of it was true, that he had nothing to hide, and that the only thing that hiding the letters had done was make matters worse. He had made one mistake after another, starting 17 years ago, but he was going to find a way out because he had done nothing wrong to Joey. Not then, anyway. He had done some terrible things afterwards, that was true… but Joey was still alive.

"Answer me!" cried Janice again, this time striking him violently in the arm with her fist.

Buck did not flinch. Then he said calmly, "There are some letters…."

"I knew it!"

"…And I will give them to you."

That moment on the hill had been a turning point for Buck. The quiet intensity with which he spoke had reconnected him to something dear to him. He had reconnected to the fighter in him. And although he knew this brawl was different than the others and called for every ounce of his honesty, he thought he had a chance. And he was going for it.

Buck got up, went to the closet, found the letters in his old winter coat, and brought them to Janice who was still sitting on the swing in the porch. He sat back down. She read the letters. They told of the two stabbings Joey had suffered. Short sentences, to the point. Tears rolled down her face as she read. When she was finished, she didn't look at Buck. She just sobbed at his side.

Buck sat without a sound, his expression peaceful.

"This is the end, isn't it?" she said softly through her tears, and Buck nodded slowly in reply.

Janice stayed in the living room, curled up in the sofa, but she couldn't sleep, and half way through the night she got up and went into their bedroom. She slipped under the covers, her back to his. She wanted to talk. Buck was awake, too. "Why Buck?"

"I've been thinking about that. I think he scares me," said Buck.

"Why?"

"Something wild about him… something free. I've been envious of him all my life."

Janice was quiet for a moment, then said, "He loves you… loves you and loves me."

Buck turned on his back. He felt grateful that Janice had said this. Maybe she had believed him after all when he said what he did up on the hill. And he felt again the deep love he had had for her all his life.

"Thank you," said Buck, and he reached over for Janice's hand and took it in his. "Thank you for that."

"I wasn't a great mother…"

"Why do you say that?"

Janice was on her side, her eyes open, her back to him. "I pushed you away."

Buck thought he'd never hear those words. "That you did."

Janice squeezed his hand. "I'm so sorry."

Words would not be able to grasp the depth of his sorrow, but now he knew he could endure it.

"I didn't try to figure him out," said Janice, "You know, like that lady he's working with in prison. I'm jealous of her. Envious too."

She turned to face him. Buck did the same.

"When I first realized it," continued Janice, "I thought, how dare she get to know my son better than me…"

Buck caressed her hand.

"… and that woman that took him in when he was thirteen…"

"Fourteen," said Buck

"I'm sure they had sex. I never asked him."

"He was a boy… boys that age like older women."

Janice narrowed her eyes. "She was molesting him… did you think about that?"

"I suppose. I didn't dwell on it."

"You think that might have contributed to what he did to the girl?"

Buck thought that was the first time he had heard Janice acknowledge Joey's guilt.

"It could have."

Janice reached over and slowly felt Buck's face with the back of her hand. It felt smooth. "You shaved for me."

"I did."

"I think we've done a better job with Margaret," said Janice.

"She takes to you more than she does to me."

"I'm her mom."

"I'm just letting you know, I'm going to reach out to her more."

"Sure."

The howl of a pack of coyotes went up in the distance. It was a celebratory sound. A feast was on. The intensity would die down a bit, then rise again.

"The fuckers," said Janice.

Someone's cat or small dog was being served for dinner.

"I hate them."

"Joey's stronger than I am," said Buck.

"Why do you say that?"

"Not a word has come out of him… even though he's been slashed and stabbed."

Janice recoiled at the thought and turned away from him. That Buck had withheld the letters, that he had willingly chosen not to protect her Joey, was that not an unpardonable sin? She was quiet for a moment. There he lay next to her… talking about it… they had shared a life. "He always says… at the end of our visits, that you have nothing to worry about."

"I lied to you about talking to the officers." It was the first full admission to his wife.

And yet Joey had survived. He hadn't needed Buck's help after all. But there was the betrayal.

"You need help, Buck… more than I can give you. It's complicated. It's the culture you work in… it's been with you all this time."

"Nobody put a gun to my head. I found it easier to join in the prejudice than stand against it. That's on me."

"I'm angry," said Janice.

"You have a right to be."

She turned to face him. "Will you visit him one day? He'd really like that."

"I'm working on it."

"How?"

"I'm doing it now, talking to you."

She took his hand in hers.

"Buck…?"

He gazed into her eyes.

"Did you ever think of having him killed?"

Buck was hesitant for a moment, then said, "It crossed my mind." His expression did not change when he said it. If there had been any feeling to it, Buck had kept it well hidden.

Janice had suspected it. What could she say in reply to his confession: I'm leaving you? You're a monster? She had done her share of muddying up the waters. Those first years with Joey, when she had striven to monopolize his attention, she knew Buck had resented it. She knew Buck had become needy of her and had been reluctant to go up against her, and she had taken advantage.

"I was scared…" said Buck, "scared about what other guards would say. I'm not anymore."

"Have you thought of quitting?"

The question had been raised many times before. Buck had been a guard for nearly thirty years, a career filled with ups and downs, but there was something left in him. "I'd like to get really good at it before I give it up," he said.

He was stubborn all right, thought Janice, had been all his life.

And then he added, "Besides, I'm finally learning to communicate."

She remembered the old saying, hope springs eternal.

"Give me a day or two to find a place," he said, "I'll move out."

Her lips moved like she was trying to say something but nothing came out.

Buck slept well that night, like he had not in a very long time. A new beginning loomed ahead in the relationship with Joey and he felt very good about that. And that night he dreamt of that glorious day in the ring when, at 21, in the fullness of his physical powers, in front of a full house and the television cameras in Miami Beach, he had decked the Miami Kid in the first round. And he had seen his mother jumping up and down in unrestrained joy, all by herself, because everyone else around her was rooting for the man he had just laid out.

35

*I*nmate Zambrano spoke to officer Rivers about the incident with Tanpuro – the cell phone and the attempt at intimidation. Rivers, in turn, spoke to Poncho Sterling. It was one man's word against another but Zambrano was known to be a straight shooter whereas Tanpuro was not.

"Anything in the cellphone?" asked Poncho Sterling.

"He borrowed it," said Rivers. Zambrano used it to talk to his kids."

Poncho decided to confront Tanpuro but wanted to have a witness, so he approached his friend Bull's Eye. Bull's Eye had been a guard for over 15 years and before that had worked as a psych aide in a mental hospital in Oregon. He worked mostly Bravo Two but now and then covered in Bravo Three and knew of Tanpuro's problems.

The next day Poncho Sterling and Bull's Eye came through the gate at 5:15 am, a little earlier than usual. They stood around waiting for Tanpuro. He was a little late but when he did come in he seemed to be in a good mood. They greeted him and the three started up the road to B yard.

"You weren't waiting for me, were you?" asked Tanpuro.

"No. Just standing around enjoying the cold," said Bull's Eye. A cold snap had come in overnight and it had been 20 degrees when they had arrived.

Tanpuro found himself flanked by Sterling on the left and Bull's Eye on the right.

"How've you been, man?" started Poncho.

"Everything's great." Tanpuro felt a puff of unease with Poncho's new friendliness.

"Family all right?"

"Oh, yeah. My oldest was asked to be captain of the basketball team next year. Found out last night."

"Congratulations," said Poncho.

"How's the acting career?" asked Tanpuro.

"Slow. Haven't got any calls lately."

"I wanted to be an actor when I was a kid," said Tanpuro.

"Who didn't?" put in Bull's Eye.

They kept walking. Poncho was now unsure whether to proceed, but how could he forget that Tanpuro had tried to blame him for the incident between Joey and Hyena? The man could lie. Poncho pushed on.

"You know Zambrano in 218?"

Tanpuro flinched but went with it. "Beautiful man."

"We got word you were trying to squeeze him," pressed Poncho.

Tanpuro stopped. "That piece of shit... I've bent over backwards to help him out, how dare the bastard?"

Nothing wrong with appearing deeply offended, thought Poncho, in fact, not a bad acting job. Poncho looked him in the eye. "Look, man, I've already had a problem with you and caught you in a lie. Now, in all the time Zambrano's been here, no one that I know has had a problem with him." Poncho turned to Bull's Eye, "Have you?"

Bull's Eye shook his head slowly. "Have known Z for a while. Used to be in my unit."

Tanpuro was about to walk off when Poncho said, "So here's the deal, we've got to protect our name..."

"Hold up, now," snapped Tanpuro, "What the hell you think you're doing? It's an inmate's word against mine."

"For your word to mean anything, you've got to earn it," said Bull's Eye.

Tanpuro was incensed. "You hear a two-bit inmate slander me and you find me guilty? I can't fucking believe it."

"Watch your language," said Bull's Eye.

"Look, Tanpuro, we're here to help, not to intimidate," said Poncho. "We're doing this on our own, no one sent us, no one else knows about it. We want to simply remind you that your behavior is not accepted, that you have to improve. That's all. Think about what you do. It'll protect your job and your family." Poncho turned to Bull's Eye. "Got anything to add?"

"Oh, yeah," began Bull's Eye, "if Z had a cell phone, that's wrong, he gets written up for it. But you don't tear up the drawings and family photos he had on the wall. He showed me the pieces. That's not cool, a grown man like you."

"He's a fucking idiot, a gangster, that's what, and he's got a drug thing going. I'm working on it."

Poncho was surprised. "Bull, does Z have a drug thing going?"

"Never heard of it."

"I'm telling you, he does," insisted Tanpuro, "and I'm going to break up that ring."

Poncho and Bull's Eye glanced at each other. The man had a plan.

"Brother Tanpuro," said Bull's Eye, "they may be inmates but they've got feelings."

Bull's Eye had deliberately lit up and rolled out that firecracker just to see if Tanpuro picked it up. He did.

"What?" Tanpuro said, irately. "I'm a cop, you hear me. A cop! I'm not being paid to pamper these scumbags, but to give them what they got coming, and if you think…"

"Shush," said Bull's Eye, raising his finger to his lips, "No need to raise your voice. I have very sensitive ears."

Tanpuro was seething but held back. The sight of Bull's Eye intimidated him.

"We actually like you, bro," continued Bull's Eye, "but you need to chill out. With a little work, you could become one of us. And don't think about ratting because it's two against one. And we know those guys, the Sergeant, the Lieutenant, the Captain… we play golf with them."

Tanpuro let out a laugh. "Driscoll doesn't even play golf."

"How'd you know, you invite him?" asked Bull's Eye with a frown.

Tanpuro glared back.

"Of course he's going to tell you he doesn't. You just got in, you've got to earn it. You're not trying to brown nose your way in, are you?"

Tanpuro grunted, spit on the ground and strode off.

Poncho and Bull's Eye looked after him, then Bull's Eye said, "He'll think it over, he's not stupid. But we should do this more often. It's good for us."

"Next time you're the lead guy," said Poncho.

"No. I work best as second banana. But I came up with a name for us…"

"What's that?"

"Operation Reboot."

"I like it."

They started back on their way to their unit.

"Does Driscoll play golf?" asked Poncho Sterling.

"Heck if I know," said Bull's Eye.

Poncho chuckled.

36

*I*t took four weeks for Leroy Cadenas to finally put in a request to see Gardner. The Doc had sent for him a few times following the stabbing of Legrand, but Leroy had always declined. Now, hands in back, as regulations called for, he walked the shiny hallway towards Gardner's office. Gardner was sitting behind his desk, reading some notes he held in his lap, when Leroy showed up at the door. Gardner glanced up and waved him in. Leroy took a seat.

"We have some unfinished business," said Leroy.

"We certainly do."

"I spent a few days in Ad Seg. They did an investigation and couldn't find a weapon. No referral to the DA. Returned to my same cell, too."

Gardner was incredulous.

Leroy looked down at the ground.

"There was a deep wound in Legrand's neck," began Gardner, but he stopped. He was angry and had to temper his reaction. "I had him here in my office, sitting right where you are, aching from his wound, the hospital report showing a puncture of his chest wall and a collapsed lung… who's to blame, then?"

Leroy shrugged lazily. "An investigation was done. It could've been the sharp edge of the bookshelf that got him."

Gardner was quiet as he weighed the facts.

"Did he say I did it?" said Leroy.

"Of course not," returned Gardner.

Good, thought Leroy with relief. "It's none of your business, anyway, it's a legal matter now."

Gardner leaned forward on the desk. He had to be calm, he reminded himself. "So you think you can put this matter aside, stuff it in your legal folder, so to speak, then stroll in, 'Good morning, let's open my mental health folder today', the two to be kept neatly separate?"

"Who said that I had to tell you everything?" countered Leroy with irritation, "You're just the psychiatrist - the medication man - and you know what, I just want to talk about that."

"Medication? What medication? You hadn't wanted any."

"Now I want it," demanded Leroy, imperiously.

Gardner didn't want his anger to twist his words. He clasped his hands together and said, gently, "Medication for what, may I ask?"

"For my impulsivity."

Gardner stared at Leroy.

Leroy sat back, the expression surly.

"What you did..." began Gardner, "...was deliberate, planned, obviously with assistance from staff. That you got rid of the weapon, that the reports have been falsified, that you have had help to make it go away, all of it, has become all too clear to me."

"I just want my medication," deadpanned Leroy.

Gardner nodded slowly. He rubbed his chin.

"They need to have video cameras," said Leroy.

The cheek, thought Gardner.

"And it's okay to be angry at me," Leroy added.

"I am angry," said Gardner, "... you're right... and terribly disappointed."

The two men locked eyes.

"Go ahead, lash out at me," said Leroy.

"No. That is not what you need from me. I am angry, yes, but this is not about my anger but yours, because you're the one who is willfully self-destructing, and you are not going to get anywhere unless you own up to it, unless you put it on the table and start working through it," said Gardner, firmly.

"And I'll put it on the table when I'm good and ready, okay?" shot back Leroy, infuriated.

"What are you waiting for? You almost killed Legrand. Who else do you have to harm before you come to your senses?"

Leroy drew back, startled.

"In your madness, in your blindness," pressed Gardner, "you didn't even see that I was here, right here." Gardner shook his head in frustration. He swiveled in his chair and stared up at an abstract painting that hung on the side wall, a jumble of geometrical forms that a manic patient had given him when he was in private practice.

"Are you going to give me the medication or not?" said Leroy.

"We have to talk… and yes I will give you the medication, because it may help keep you from completely wrecking your life, but that is not enough… we have to talk," insisted Gardner.

A part of Leroy wanted to bolt out the door and not return, be rid forever of this pushy, meddlesome doctor, but then he thought that the pushy, meddlesome doctor might know something that he didn't, that maybe the doc could see through the fog that had encircled his mind. Leroy looked off, eyes drifting toward the small window and the blue sky outside. Would he ever stop making the horrible choices he'd made?

"Was Legrand the target?"

"He was not. He got in the way."

A simple statement, thought Gardner, and Legrand's life had been nearly snuffed; Legrand, who had made a lifelong effort to atone for his guilt; Legrand, who had committed his life to remaking himself.

"Did you want to kill Joey Wilson?"

"I didn't want to kill anybody, just scare them."

"And I was here all along… right here," said Gardner, as he weighed the senselessness of Leroy's actions.

A guard passed by the door and glanced in through the window.

"I lost something… a long time ago…" began Leroy, putting his palms together, as if in prayer, the tips of his joined fingers touching his lips. He had thought of Tiara, his girl up in Philadelphia. "I'm serving life for all those things I did, but I never killed a man, not even tried, and yet, in here, I've come close to. It's getting worse." He closed his eyes for a moment. "I've trapped myself… built a wall of anger around me… anger at the world… at myself… and I've been doing it all my life."

Leroy sat back. He had grown calmer. "That assault and battery on a security guard up in Sacramento, on my way down from Philly... I was angry that I couldn't have Tiara... that I didn't find my mother... and all piled up inside and I didn't sort it out. It got the best of me. I didn't have to react the way I did... it was not the guard's fault... but I blamed him... like I blamed Legrand... like I blamed Joey."

Leroy looked at Gardner. "I knew you were here... so it's on me."

They were silent for a moment.

"If you don't start working on yourself you will sink to the bottom... and take others with you," said Gardner.

"I've done enough of that already."

Gardner opened a drawer in his desk and pulled out a book. He handed it to Leroy. It was Pinocchio, by Carlo Collodi.

Leroy's face lit up. "You remembered."

"It's been waiting for you," said Gardner.

37

Janice was one of the first to arrive in the visiting area in Lancaster. She had risen at 4 am for the trip up from Pomona and had left Buck asleep. In her handbag she carried the letters from the warden, although she was still debating whether to show them to Joey.

She sat and waited.

She looked around, examined the faces of other visitors, of the guards that processed their entry, some familiar by now. There were mothers, fathers, siblings, wives and children, girlfriends. There didn't seem to be anyone getting married that day but it was hard to say. She thought she could discern in all those faces, the patient expectation that the loved one would show up, that no last minute glitch would keep him from the visit. Janice thought, too, that she could see a veil of resignation, the sense that there was nothing that could be done but to accept their circumstances – accept and wait.

The moment Joey came in through the door he flashed her a big smile. He walked confidently, looking strong and handsome, everything

Janice had desired for him, and she felt a profound sense of relief. He came up to her and gave her a warm embrace and they held each other for a moment. They looked into each other's eyes and said nothing. She took his hand in hers and they sat down. "How are you?"

"Great. Everything is okay."

"You look luminous," said Janice.

"Luminous?"

"Yes, luminous. Came across that word the other day, thought I'd try it out."

Joey chuckled. "Never heard anyone say that to me." He reached over and kissed her on the forehead. "Thanks, mom, for seeing light in me. How's dad?"

"He's fine… coming along."

"Coming along?"

"Yes. We've had some talks. I think he's getting closer to you."

Joey reacted with surprise.

"I know," said Janice. "You didn't think that would ever happen. Neither did I."

"How did it?"

"We've had some moments… difficult moments…" She squeezed his hand. "But I see hope. The truth is coming out, Joey… finally the truth."

He looked at her, "The truth…?"

"The truth about all of us, him and I, you and me, everything."

Joey nodded. "That's a lot."

"I know it is." She put her other hand on his shoulder and rubbed it.

"I say that because I know how hard it's been for me to get to it, working with Dr Jeffries," said Joey.

"You don't tell her everything about me and Buck, do you?"

Joey pulled back a little, cocking his head, "Mom, I have to. How else am I going to figure things out?"

Janice frowned. "Once we get everything out in the open, you may not have to talk to her anymore. Once we do that, there will be no need."

This was new, thought Joey, this investing herself with analytical powers. He leaned forward, hands clasped, and said calmly, "Mom, I think it's great that you and dad are talking and that you feel the truth is coming out, but I have a life separate from yours and dad's, and to sort things out I have to keep talking to Dr Jeffries."

Janice reached into her handbag and put the bundle of letters from the warden on the table.

"What's this?" asked Joey.

"Read them. Your father finally gave them to me." There, thought she, lay unquestionable evidence of her determination to get to the bottom of things.

Joey picked up the first letter and read it. He showed no expression as he did. There were no details of the incident leading to the injuries, only a technical, summary description of the medical care he had received. He pursed his lips as he came to the end of the missive, then folded it, put it back in the envelope and replaced it on top of the bundle. He did not read the rest. He slid the bundle back to Janice with the back of his hand.

Janice looked at him. "Your father kept them from me"

Joey stayed quiet for a moment. "Let it go, mom."

"He had told me he would protect you."

Joey turned to meet her eyes, a spark of amused curiosity.

"He had told me," continued Janice, "that he would talk to the guards so that they would look out for you."

"How could he do that?" said Joey, lowering his voice. "He's a guard… imagine the shame he'd feel? No. And I would've rejected the help."

Janice glanced nervously at the neighboring tables, concerned that the conversation might be overheard. Drawing near to him, she whispered, "First of all, you're not a child molester. That… thing you got involved with, that was not a child at all. She was a tart, a wicked tart, that's what she was; a wicked little bitch of a tart, both she and her sister."

And Joey turned instantly on Janice. Seizing her by the arms, he spoke firmly to her in a low voice. "I molested that girl. I did. I am finally acknowledging it. And I resent you trying to sugar coat things for me. So, please, do not interfere with what I have to do. And there's one other thing, don't you go calling her a wicked tart because I loved that girl. I loved her then and I still do."

Janie took the letters from the table and put them back in her purse. But she wasn't through. Leaning in again she said, "Did your father touch your bottom?"

The question jolted him. "What?"

"Answer me, son. I've been reading up on these things."

"You think dad molested me?"

Janice narrowed her eyes. "He never touched your bottom… or your other part?"

"No," he replied, clearly annoyed.

"Never?"

Joey glared at her. "Yes, he did!" he shot back.

"Shush!" warned Janice again. "Keep your voice down!"

"Yes, he did, mom, and he had to because I kept soiling my pants."

"You couldn't clean yourself? I had taught you how to do it."

"I don't know, mom," said he, his voice growing with exasperation, "But maybe I was depressed and didn't know it. Maybe I was depressed and couldn't put it into words because I was 6 years old and all I knew to do was shit in my pants. And maybe, mom, I just wanted you to come back."

Janice had not taken her eyes off Joey and now placed her hand on his shoulder, rubbing it gently. "There, you feel better?"

But it only infuriated Joey even more. "What are you doing?"

"What?"

"Are you trying to be a therapist?"

Janice pulled back slightly, "Joey, I just want you to be happy…"

He drew a breath and looked off. There was a new strength in her, that much was clear; something he hadn't seen before, in fact, something he welcomed. But the new found strength was so novel that perhaps she was simply borrowing it from someone else. But wasn't he borrowing, too? He, borrowing from Dr Jeffries, mom borrowing from her through him, maybe dad plugging in also into the grid. Maybe that was how things worked, like an electrical current flowing from post to post, for there was Janice daring to delve into an issue she had long avoided, and standing firm, too.

Joey smiled inwardly. "Then you don't have to worry anymore", he said, "Because I am happy. I may be in prison but I am happy, bizarre as that may seem. And I am happy because I am working on myself. Happy, because I am thinking on my own for once in my life."

38

*I*t was an average day in Bravo Three in early April. Two porters were out mopping the floor and wiping off the day room's steel tables; another was going cell to cell on the upper tier handing out request forms for canteen; the barber/inmate was cutting hair down by the benches and officer Rivers was going door to door passing out the mail.

Joey and Leblanc were both in their bunks in cell 128. Joey was reading a tattered copy of Boris Pasternak's "Doctor Zhivago" and Legrand was writing on his journal.

Rivers knocked on the door. "Mail for you, LB," said she. Legrand rose and crossed to the door. Rivers was holding up a slender envelope from a corner and letting it dangle, teasingly, in front of him.

"Have some fancy friends," said Rivers, smilingly.

"What do you mean?"

"Mail from Europe."

"Got to be from Danny, for sure. About time, too, the rascal."

But Rivers shook her head. "No. Not Danny. I know his handwriting. Looks like it's from a lady."

Legrand was suddenly very curious. "Let me see." He pushed out the cover on the port hole to make enough space for the thin envelope to slide through the crack. He pulled it in and looked at the name of the sender: "Lilly Tambin," from a P.O. Box in Paris, France. Legrand felt an indescribable flood of emotion as he held the letter in his hands. He thanked Rivers and returned to his bunk. He could feel his heart beating. He sat down and examined the envelope in detail. What was this? The handwriting was elegant and feminine. The name Lilly brought back a rush of memories. Although he had never met her, he had learned from his father of his grandmother's name, Lilly Deschamps. Was there a relationship or was it mere coincidence? Legrand's hands trembled as he held the envelope in both hands, afraid to look yet dying to do so.

From the bunk above, Joey glanced down and said casually, "Having trouble reading it, aren't you, LB?"

"I think so." Legrand held it up against the light. The envelope itself was made of fine stationery, something he had never received before.

What did it all mean? There was no mistaking the addressee: Mr Lebeau Legrand, Los Angeles County State Prison, Lancaster, California, USA. He slowly caressed the envelope; he smelled it; there was no perfume on it but he liked the scent of the paper. After all, it was coming from another continent, it had traveled far and wide, had breathed the Paris air and now there it was, sitting in his hands. Legrand lay back on his bed, resting the letter on his chest. He kept wondering whom it might be from. A long, lost relative in France? Someone his old cellmate, Danny, knew? He let out a long breath.

The envelope was open, of course, like all correspondence the inmates received. How long was he going to wait before he pulled out the letter? He sat up, smelled it once more and, holding his breath, his fingers trembling anew, he pulled out the single folded sheet. Not much had been written on it, just a single paragraph. "Dear Sir," it began, in the same refined handwriting as in the cover, "I am looking for my father…" Legrand let out a cry. He felt his body jerk forward and tears welled up instantly in his eyes. Joey looked down from his bunk. "If you are approximately 50 years old and my first name means something to you, please write me back and tell me the names of your grandparents. You may be my father. If you are, I would very much like to meet you. Please reply at your earliest convenience. Sincerely, Lilly Tambin." Leblanc sprang to his feet and, with tears streaming down his cheeks, choking on his words, he said to Joey. "I knew she was out there, I knew it!" He could not contain his emotion. He went to the door and leaned his head against it, sobbing, his chest heaving, all the while holding the precious letter in his hand.

"Who's out there?" asked Joey, swinging his legs off his bunk.

"My daughter! She's out there and she's in Paris!"

Joey jumped off the upper bunk and hugged his friend. "I'm so glad for you, LB, so glad."

"Thank you. Thank you. I've been waiting for this for a lifetime."

His face flush, his body bursting with energy, Leblanc paced his tiny cell back and forth. He read and reread the letter. He cradled it in his hands and treated it like the most valuable possession in the world. Nothing like this had ever happened to him. He had despaired in his solitude, lived in darkness and sorrow, lashed himself with the whip of self-contempt but he had never crumbled. And here was the reward, at last.

It took a while for Legrand to settle down and Joey had witnessed it all in silence from his bunk. Fully aware of how precious this moment was for his good friend, he had not dared break the spell. He waited until Legrand chose to share the moment with him.

"If I write the letter today it will go out in a week, don't you think?"

"I think so," said Joey now raising himself up on his elbows.

"I'm going to answer her now." His tee shirt was still damp with sweat. He smiled broadly at Joey. "I just don't know what to say."

Joey had never seen a man so happy. "She told you in the letter."

"I'm afraid my writing won't be as neat as hers, and I'm trembling still, see?" He held up his hand for Joey.

"It doesn't matter how neat or shaky the words come out, she wants to hear from you, LB."

"Yes." And the big man sat down on the edge of his bunk to write a reply to the daughter he had never seen.

Leblanc shared the news with everyone he knew and that night, on her rounds to give out medication, Ms Turner smiled. It was a rare occasion, indeed.

39

Sergeant Krause sent for Leroy Cadenas. A guard walked up to his cell and told him he was to be escorted to a meeting with an investigative officer. Nothing else was said. He was given a few minutes to dress. Half hour later, when he arrived at the Office of Internal Investigations, the escorting officer led him in and then left the room.

Sergeant Krause sat at her desk as she reviewed some notes. She did not look up at him. Leroy had never seen the woman so he simply stood there, handcuffed in back, shackled at the ankles, taking in the spare room while waiting for her to acknowledge him.

She was dressed in the black uniform, the chevrons on her shoulders a crisp gold, her hair neatly combed, the desk carefully arranged with not a thing out of place. Obsessive, thought Leroy. He had had cellmates like that and had grown to distrust them. Life was messy, he mused, and too much freaking organizing was unnatural.

When Krause finally spoke she did so without raising her eyes. "Now and then there's a rotten apple in the crate and we have to do our best to get rid of it," she said as she placed her notes in a drawer.

"What's that got to do with me?" returned Leroy, nonchalantly.

Krause pushed back on her high back swivel chair and looked him in the eye.

"Officer Grisholt pulled some strings to get an assault charge dropped. The DA could have easily picked it up but, instead, for some obscure reason, it was reduced to mutual combat and then, miraculously dropped. You were named as the leader of the assault."

She was coming at him with both barrels and he would have to watch every word.

"It's done, isn't it?"

"I have the power the review the case and change the outcome."

The words cut right through him. He had dealt with threats before and yet something about this woman gave him the creeps. Power could be very capricious.

"If the DA picks up the case and you go to trial you're looking at another 15 to 20 years for attempted murder - at least - and I assure you we can make it stick. You're already serving 25 to life and have 19 years before you go to board. Do the math and it doesn't look pretty."

Leroy felt an itch in the back of his right ear but, being cuffed, he couldn't scratch it. He raised his right shoulder to see if he might but could not. He tilted his head forward. In his silence, he had become aware of his breathing. What did the Sergeant want from him? He looked at her again. Her face was attractive. She hadn't stood up yet but she looked like she had a body to match, and he couldn't help but think what would drive a woman like her to get into this line of work. She, too, must have her demons.

"Would you like to sit down?" the sergeant offered.

Leroy shuffled to the side and did so. The chair had a soft bottom. Was she there to negotiate?

"Comfortable?"

What did she care, thought Leroy, "So you want me to snitch?"

"More like cooperate." She had picked up a pencil and was slowly twirling it by the ends. "If you do, I can use my influence to dismiss the case and, here's the best part – she leaned in slightly - push some levers to take some years off your sentence. For good behavior."

Leroy chuckled derisively. "What good behavior? All I do is screw up."

"True, but you've started to see Dr Gardner and that's a step in the right direction. If you take the deal I can make it work. I have reviewed your strikes and consulted with an attorney and there's the possibility of removing one. We could recommend that… say… 10 years be lopped off your current sentence, so that you'd have only 9 years to serve before you went to board. And with a good recommendation, well, you could be out on parole that first time."

What the world was coming to, mused Leroy.

"We have the ear of some judges," continued Krause with a cocky air.

"Really?"

They were all in bed together, thought Leroy, and just as corrupt. Everything was possible, dish out a cruelly long sentence one day and find some technicality to reverse it the next. If you played the game.

"Did you talk to Dr Gardner about me?"

"No. That's between the two of you."

The thought was comforting.

"You must want this guy real bad," said Leroy.

"We have access to state of the art technology and can monitor private cell phone calls. We have a strong case. Still, your testimony would be helpful."

"Just so I am clear, who're we talking about, testimony against whom?"

"Grisholt."

So they had been on his scent for a while, thought Leroy. "How do you know I have anything to say?"

Krause smiled. "You've enjoyed a cozy relationship with him."

Leroy wasn't surprised. He had suspected there were informants on the unit, ever watchful, ever striving for advantage. But here was this sergeant wanting something from him and willing to offer a deal. He was 28 now; add another 9 and he could be out at 37. Sweet. And all he had to do was turn in a dirty guard. How could you beat that? Of course, all that assumed he wouldn't be double-crossed somewhere along the way.

"Will I have to testify in court?"

"Maybe. Maybe not."

Leroy nodded pensively. "If I do testify, I won't have a chance when I get back."

Krause swiveled to her left, to where the American flag stood on top of the book case.

Leroy couldn't help but notice her elegant facial profile.

"You won't come back here," she said. "You'll be going to a new unit we have created especially for informants. While there you'll have a TV, access to remedial education, vocational training, college courses if you like and conjugal visits, if you have such interest. We will even arrange for a new identity as well." Krause folded her hands. "It's all part of a State initiative to clear out the bugs in the system."

"What assurances do I have you'll keep your word?"

"It is policy to not put anything in writing… but, if we didn't stick to our commitment, word would get out and we wouldn't be able to do business anymore. And we rely on informants like you to keep the system from falling into the hands of corrupt officers."

Informants like him? Where had she got that from? He had never informed on anyone. But he had something on Grisholt and that might get him out sooner. Still, it would be a gamble. The idea of a special unit sweetened things and yet, could he live with himself? He thought of talking to Gardner to get his opinion.

The sound of Krause's fingers tapping on the desk brought Leroy back to the moment. "Let me think about it, okay?"

"I can ship you out immediately so you can start working with our legal team. The more you talk, the more I do for you."

"I need a week, at least, maybe two."

And Krause looked him in the eye and laid it out, "We don't have that kind of time."

"I'm sorry, but don't the wheels of justice move slowly?" returned Leroy.

Krause let out a smirk. An insolent twit is what he was… but she needed something from him.

"The longer you take, the more likely I will get what I need from another source."

"You do what you have to do, sergeant. I need to think about it," and he stood up to leave.

"There's always Hyena," said Krause, her face growing long as she arched her brow.

Hyena an informant? No, you could call Hyena anything but not an informant. Krause was trying to play with his mind.

"There's always Hyena," returned Leroy without inflection. "Have a wonderful day."

40

Mary Jane Jeffries had called to ask Gardner to meet her at the club that following Saturday night. He was pleasantly surprised and readily accepted.

The place was filled when he arrived at around 10 pm, but there was a small empty table near the entrance to the kitchen with a great view of the performer. He began to wend his way to the spot when the headwaiter noticed him and beckoned. Yes, the table was open. The man held the chair out for him. He was feeling lucky, thought Gardner, to have landed such a good table, but then he saw Mary Jane flash him a smile and he understood that she had arranged for him to have it. He sent back a silent thank you.

She looked splendid. A black satin dress showed her angular, feminine shoulders and enticed the eye to wander to her cleavage, her delicate chest rising and falling gently as she effortlessly took in air and delivered her nuanced melodies. Her lips sparkled in the light.

The applause grew louder with each tune as the show drew to a close and then the time came for the last song. She took a moment to thank the audience, speaking as she riffed on the keyboard. They had had a wonderful time, too, they had replied, and then she paused, pulled the mike closer, glanced at Gardner, and started up on a rendition of "Stormy Weather." Gardner blew her a kiss.

After the show, they took their separate vehicles and drove to a small restaurant they both knew in Eagle Rock. She had performed there once, she reminded him. It was near midnight but the owner himself, a portly man with a big round face and a curly head of hair, greeted and escorted them to a table by the piano at the end of the main room.

"I remember you," he said to her with his heavy Italian accent.

"I remember *you*," she replied.

"Why you not come back?"

"Probably had another offer," she answered courteously.

"You always welcome here," and waving expansively to the grand piano behind him, he added, "you can play if you like."

"Thank you. But not today."

"If you change your mind, it is there." He bowed gallantly and ambled off.

Mary Beth leaned over and said to Gardner. "Nice place but I would have been working for tips only."

Gardner laughed.

"Glad you could make it," she said.

"I wasn't expecting the invite."

"We barely get a chance to talk at work and I wanted to catch up with you."

"I would have asked myself but I thought you were going out with someone."

"I was," she said.

"My instincts served me well, this time."

The waiter showed up and asked if they wanted anything to drink. They ordered Merlot.

"It's over now."

"I'm glad."

She chuckled.

"Otherwise we wouldn't be sharing this precious moment," said he. "How was it?"

"Up and down. He wasn't for me."

"Where you in love?" Might as well get to the bottom of it.

"No. For a while I thought so."

He felt relieved.

"How about you?" She lifted her chin slightly and her large, red and blue earrings clinked like chimes in a gentle breeze.

"The earrings, they're not too heavy for you?"

"Oh no. But now that you mention it…" She snapped them off and put them in her purse. "You were saying?"

"It's been a while for me."

She looked at him with her gorgeous light brown eyes and her partly opened mouth and
he felt his heart give a thump and had to resist the impulse to reach over and lick the gloss off her sultry lips. And he would have taken his sweet time, too.

"I need someone more cerebral," she said softly, gazing into his eyes. "I miss that."

It occurred to Gardner that there was something clearly inviting in her manner but he was famous for misreading women's cues. Tonight, though, he was feeling bold.

"That is exactly what I need also." And he reached over and took her hand in his. She was taken by surprise but didn't flinch. She squeezed back, instead, and a feeling of delight welled up in him.

The waiter returned and served the wine.

"You make some decisions in the glare of the lights and then regret them," continued Mary Jane.

He nodded, aware that he didn't feel an iota of compassion for the man she'd just dumped.

"I'm glad you could come."

Wasn't that the second time she'd said so? He felt his heart smile broadly. A woman like Mary Jane didn't waste words so he just might have a shot.

"I am, too," he said.

"How long have we known each other?"

"Three, four years?"

"About. You were there already when I came in," said she.

"I was."

He slid his hand gently up to the crook of her arm, and she placed hers on his.

"Ready to order?" said the waiter, reappearing to break the spell.

How rude of him, thought Gardner.

"Actually… I wasn't thinking of dining," said Mary Jane, "unless you…" she turned to Gardner.

"Not either. The wine is great."

The waiter nodded, cocked his head in the manner of polite regret, and walked off.

Gardner could wait no more. He leaned over and kissed her on the lips. It was a soft, lingering, breathy kiss. He touched the side of her face, lightly, caressingly, then continuing to the back of her neck nudged her to him. She balked.

"Not here," she said.

Her lips were right there, next to his, and the urge to possess them was raging through, the compelling lust to nibble at them tenderly, the lower one, mainly, the one that pouted a little when she spoke: that one. She was looking at his mouth, too, relishing at the way he hungered for her, then raising a finger to his lips repeated in a hushed tone, "Not here."

They drove to her apartment in Hancock Park and spent the night. After what seemed like an endless trance of ravenous agitation, they finally fell asleep and didn't wake up until past ten the next morning.

He whispered "G'morning" in her ear as she lay nestled in his arms, her back to him. It had been glorious for him and he told her so. She kissed his arm. Sheer delight, he said to himself, that's what he was feeling. And he felt glued to her and didn't want to be unglued. Ah, the joys of carnal pleasure. He was older than Mary Jane and no longer the driving buck of his youth so he relished every moment. He smelled her hair, the enticing fragrance of it; he let his hands wander curiously over every inch of her slender body, as if wanting to own it so it would always be there for him; and he kissed, kissed and kissed again, stamping her with his desire, imprinting her with his lust, nearly desperate to leave an indelible impression.

After feeling sated to the point of exhaustion, they made breakfast together and then drove down Wilshire to the La Brea tar pits by the Museum of Art. They found a bench in the shadow of a tree and sat back to take in the scene. Other couples and families sat on the grass, picnicking or chatting, the pleasant afternoon soothing their worries. A group of small children ran by giggling as they chased a red balloon, and a line moved slowly forward at the pretzel and soda stand.

Mary Jane had always liked Gardner but something or another had always got in the way. They had had dinner on several occasions but there had never been anything more. Some things took longer to gel, she mused.

"What does prison work do for you, Byron?"

"In every thief, crook, murderer, lies a human being trapped. My task is to free him."

"Wasn't there a famous sculptor who said something similar as he looked at a block of marble?" said she with a mischievous grin.

He winked at her. "Michelangelo, I believe."

"The work gives you a sense of purpose?"

"For the time being."

"Not your final destination?"

"I like to reshuffle my cards as I go along."

"I do, too. Good for the soul," said she.

She laid her head back on his shoulder, her eyes closed as she faced the sun. She had not slept much but the night had been memorable. She had even had a dream: a vast field of flowers wafting in a light wind with her daughter, Gracie Kim, running across joyously, feeling free and fulfilled. Gracie Kim was twenty-four and for the last couple of years had been working with an NGO in Bolivia.

Mary Jane turned toward him, touched his face, felt the stubble on it, glided her hand over it.

He kissed her.

She took the tip of her forefinger to the tip of his nose and pressed playfully.

"I feel I'm the luckiest man on earth."

"But you are," she said. "I am very picky, my dear." She slid her finger down to his mouth and let it trace softly the contours of his lips. "Have you ever had problems controlling your anger?" she asked.

"Interesting that you ask. I have."

"I have, too," returned Mary Beth. "I used to have a terrible temper. That's what led to the split of my marriage. When I hear the inmates' stories of uncontrolled aggression, they remind me of how much control I've developed."

"You tamed the beast."

"I did. Working with them has helped me do that. As I've given, I have received."

"That's the way it works," said Gardner. "You know you're highly valued as a therapist."

She smiled and closed her eyes. "Keep saying sweet things to me." She laid her hand on his chest and slipped her fingers through his shirt.

"I hear it all the time," he added.

"More, please."

"You sing like a goddess; you make love like I imagine Venus would."

"Venus. Yes. I've always wanted to have her charms," said she, enjoying the adoration. "Tell me what you'd like to do with the rest of your life."

"That's easy."

"Easy?" said Mary Jane, "I have a devil of a time with that one."

"I'd like to love and problem solve, all the way to the end… develop to my fullest. What would you like to do with the rest of your life?"

"Kiss me, first," she commanded. He did so, tenderly.

"Again."

He did once more, lingering, ever so slightly.

"One more time."

"I think you're dodging the question," said Gardner.

"No. Just gathering the strength to give you an answer."

He kissed her again and then she drew back a little. "Sometimes I dream of just going away somewhere and starting a new life; do something completely different."

"And the singing?"

"Maybe I'll keep singing, maybe I won't."

"Thought of doing it full time?"

"Not interested. Though I have the suspicion I'd starve."

He took her hand, caressing her fingers. "Can we love forever?"

"Works in the movies," she said.

"Yes, it does."

"I don't love my ex-husband anymore but I can't imagine not loving my daughter."

"I function better when I'm loving," said Gardner.

"Love as a fountain of energy," said she, "will you work till the end?"

"Probably. When I do it well, it gives me a sense of power. I have to, anyway. I'm not rich."

"I know that."

"How'd you know that?" he asked, amused.

"You wouldn't be working in prison."

He laughed.

"Are you searching for freedom?" she asked.

"Searching for it? I have freedom… but yes… I'd like to have more."

"You think you'd be giving it away if you loved someone?"

"There's that risk. If I need her too much then I'm not free, and neither would she."

"It would come at the expense of self-love?"

"I think so."

"Hmm. There's a method to your madness," said she.

"Something like that."

She smiled. "You're not going to ask me if that was original?"

"It crossed my mind."

She snuggled closer to him. "Freedom and loving. Freedom from envy, freedom to think, freedom to explore. And there's more in us than we have seen."

"Yes."

"I want to see it. That's why freedom is also very important to me."

They said nothing for a moment, becoming so quiet in fact that a small bird landed on the back of their bench, on Gardner's side.

"The adventure of life. The more we find in ourselves, the more we find in others," said she. "It's endless… it's love."

The small bird on the back of the bench glanced at them, curiously. And now another small bird, of the same stripe, alighted next to the first one.

Gardner noticed them. "Don't move, I think we have company."

"Who?"

"There's two small birds perched next to us."

"Maybe it's a sign."

"Do you believe in such things?"

"I do," she said.

"I do, too."

One of the birds chirped.

"I hear him, or her."

"I'd love to be a bird. We get stuck in the roles we play and, before we know it, life has slipped us by," said Mary Jane.

The two birds glanced at each other.

"If you have an imagination or anything you truly value, you'd better let it fly or you'll pay for it later," said Gardner.

Mary Jane turned slowly to look at Gardner's side and saw the two birds on the back of the bench. "How cute." She returned to Gardner's arm. "Are you letting your imagination fly?"

"I'm working on it," said Gardner. "What about you? Are you letting what you have fly?"

"Not to my satisfaction."

She glanced again at the two birds and they were not only still there, but had inched closer to each other.

"I think those two birds have something going on," said Mary Jane with a grin, feeling light in her heart.

Gardner chuckled. "They seem to, don't they?"

A light breeze came through and Mary Jane remembered the days when she lived in South America as a child and had learned to speak Spanish. Then the words of her dear father floated into her mind: when she left home for her first adventure, the trip to Japan with her first love, Norberto, her father had taken her aside and said, "When you're with others, cherish your freedom; it is the easiest thing to give up." She glanced at Gardner and smiled. She was feeling free with him at her side.

The two birds flew off.

41

*T*anpuro was still sulking from the confrontation he had had with Poncho Sterling and Bull's Eye. As far as he was concerned they were just a pair of nincompoops and he was not going to be intimidated by them. Not he, who had twenty-six years on the force and could fill a book with prison stories. How dare they choose to question his tactics, let alone attempt to put pressure on him. His pride had been hurt and thinking about it kept him awake at night. The more prudent choice, of course, would have been to let it go for a while, reflect on it, maybe even learn a thing or two from it, and if he still wanted revenge, plan it well. But prudence had never been one of Tanpuro's virtues.

He managed to get first watch filling in for Grisholt on a Saturday, and on that day, a little after 1 am, when the two officers on the floor were out on break, he came down from the control room and climbed up to Leroy's cell on the second tier.

Leroy was watching television when he heard the knock on his door. He was surprised by the late-night call and more so by seeing it was Tanpuro. The word was out that the man was a problem but he had stayed out of his hair so there was no bad blood. Tanpuro beckoned him to the window. Leroy stared back for a moment and then lazily stepped up to meet him.

"I'll let you out in a minute," said Tanpuro.

Leroy hesitated, wondering what it was all about, then said, "Okay."

Right after the meeting with Krause, thinking of the possibilities, Leroy had borrowed a compact digital recorder that a fellow inmate had smuggled in. He had tested it and the quality was excellent. Seeing the opportunity to put it to work, he turned it on and tucked it inside his pocket. Anything he could get on Tanpuro he might then use to improve his negotiating position with the sergeant.

A few minutes later Leroy was walking out of his cell and heading down to the rotunda. The door had been racked open. Tanpuro was waiting at the end.

Tanpuro was the first to speak. "You want a cellphone?" he said in a whisper.

Leroy had seen his share of quirky offers but this one seemed different. "Sure." Remembering the incident with Zambrano, he said, "Is that the one you took from Z?"

"No. I turned that one in."

Leroy didn't want to make any deal with Tanpuro but was eager to string him along. "What you got?"

"You send a confidential kite that Poncho Sterling sold it to you."

"Confidential?"

"Yes. Just whisper."

"Sterling? You mean Poncho Sterling?" Leroy had wanted to make sure the name was very clear in the recording.

"What's the matter with you, what other Sterling is there here?"

"Tanpuro, I don't have anything against that man."

"Whisper, please. No one would know anything, only the investigators."

"Interesting," said Leroy, not whispering. If he could reel him in a little more he would have more stuff to bargain with Krause.

"You want it or not?" pressed Tanpuro, impatiently.

"Tanpuro, why would Poncho Sterling sell me the phone?"

"Whisper, I can hear you," insisted Tanpuro, nervously, his wariness quickly mounting. Why had Leroy repeated his name? He glanced at Leroy's jacket and it occurred to him that it was a bit bulkier than usual. He was tempted to put his hand on Leroy's jacket, but then, how would Leroy react, and anyway, what was an inmate doing out in the rotunda at that time of night? Tanpuro felt he was stuck. "Make up something, maybe he wanted to give you a blow job," he said hastily.

Leroy nodded as he stared at him, "You know he's a damn good officer…"

Tanpuro flipped. Glaring at Leroy, he said angrily, "Get the fuck back to your cell, you motherfucker!"

But Leroy did not budge. Speaking clearly he said, "Tanpuro, you're trying to bribe me so that I lie on officer Sterling, a true gentleman, and you still tell me to f… myself, what's wrong with you?"

Tanpuro blushed with rage. He felt on the edge of striking Leroy but, unsure of the outcome, held back. He had set himself up. He turned away to go back into the control room when Leroy put in the last word, "There is something very wrong with you, officer Tanpuro, very wrong, to try and set up a fellow officer… your own kind." Tanpuro slammed the door behind him.

Leroy began to casually walk back into the day room, then across to the stairway to return to his tier. He was in no hurry.

Tanpuro was up in the control room, muttering curses at Leroy, when he saw him reach the top of the stairs but not turn in the direction of his cell. What?

Leroy walked a distance along the tier, then crouched by one cell for a moment, then rose and looked back at Tanpuro with a devilish grin.

"Get back to your cell!" shouted Tanpuro.

But Leroy went to the next cell and crouched by it, and then the next, and the next, his actions meant to confuse Tanpuro as to where he was dropping off whatever he had to drop off.

"You sonofabitch!" Tanpuro cried out. He could not contain himself. "You bastard!" Leroy could roam as much as he wanted, and what explanation would Tanpuro have for opening his door in the middle of the night?

Tanpuro felt defeated and confused. Fearing his fellow officers would be back any moment, and what embarrassment would that be, he then pleaded with Leroy, "Get back to your cell!" But Leroy went to the next cell instead. "I won't search you!" Tanpuro finally cried, the voice breaking, begging. "Please!" "I won't search you!"

And having heard the magic words, Leroy looked back at the officer, pressed his hands together and did a little bow with his head. He blew him a kiss. "Love you, baby."

And he returned to his cell, just in time for Tanpuro to close before the officers returned.

42

Grisholt had been doing some thinking. The conversation with Buck Wilson where he had burst out and confronted him had been a great relief. He was convinced he could now see things more clearly.

He didn't think he had a good card to play but doubted that Krause would take it all the way to the D.A. Buck had never explicitly said anything about having someone go in and hurt his son. He may have thought about it, danced around it, but had never spelled it out. If it were needed, he could state that on behalf of his old mentor.

It was he, Eddie Grisholt, who had engineered the whole affair knowing full well that the outcome could not be predicted and that his main motivation had been to get back at Buck. He cringed now that he thought about it. If Legrand hadn't duked it out with Leroy, who knows what could have happened. At least Leroy had had the good sense to get rid of the weapon.

Grisholt thought about all this and realized he needed to move forward. He had been a guard long enough. He was not a stupid man, he could go out in the world and make it. Prison had been good for him. He had saved a little money, divorced a woman who didn't love him and, in the process, learned a few things about himself. He could do it. He could man up. And it was in that spirit that he picked up the phone and made an appointment to meet with sergeant Krause.

Two days later, at exactly 12 o'clock, sergeant Krause flung open the door of her office in Internal Investigations and motioned for him to come in. As before, she was looking prim and natty in her starched-up uniform. Krause went behind her desk and sat down. Grisholt followed and took the seat in front.

"Yes?" She was all business, just like the time before.

"It was my fault," blurted out Grisholt.

They looked at each other for a moment.

"I put him up to it," he continued.

Krause tapped her fingers on the desk. "Is this a confession?"

"Yes."

"Why did you do it?"

"My own weakness… my own prejudice. I opened the door on purpose, so that Leroy and Hyena could beat up on Joey Wilson and teach him a lesson."

Was this too easy… or do I smell a rat, thought Krause. Her eyes danced around, searchingly. "Did you provide the knife?"

"No. They did that on their own."

"Do you know where the knife is?"

"No."

It came to Grisholt that Krause had not got anything out of Leroy and he felt justified in having taken the initiative. He didn't want to play catch up.

"Did you give him any inducement?"

"No." He had expected the question but had decided to lie since he thought it unlikely that Leroy would own up to it. He knew he was gambling.

"You didn't give them any drugs?"

"I did not." Grisholt knew they couldn't trace that back to him. The drugs would have been distributed quickly. Plus, as an extra precaution, he had used gloves when he handed out the bags. Just in case a set-up had been on from the start. He was cautious that way.

Krause looked him in the eye. "Buck Wilson put you up to it?"

"He did not." Grisholt felt good about making this statement. He was not an informer.

"You realize that we're dealing with the possible charge of conspiracy to commit murder, you being a coconspirator."

Grisholt said nothing and stared right back at her.

Krause was discovering that this was not the same Grisholt she had been able to pressure during the first interview. Something had changed.

"I have phone records," she added.

Grisholt looked off but remained quiet. He thought she was bluffing.

"Phone records that implicate you and him," she pressed.

Grisholt shifted his weight in his seat but didn't budge. He had expected the threats and knew to stand still. He doubted the prison system would have the sophisticated equipment needed to do that kind of surveillance.

Krause leaned on the desk and spoke softly. "What kind of father would want to attempt to kill his son?"

"I have no idea," said Grisholt, looking her in the eye.

Krause pulled back a little. She glanced at her fingernails. She was fussy with the nails, thought Grisholt. Surely she had a lover: he imagined her in a provocative sexual position and allowed that he had felt an attraction for her. For whatever reason, though, she didn't seem as intimidating today.

"He put the pressure on you and you let him," she said, almost casually. "You were a flunky of his when you were up in Corcoran."

The statement stung him and he felt himself recoil but he didn't let on. He had been a flunky, all right, but that was in the past. A man had a chance to a new beginning and he was taking it. And as far as the phone records of their conversations, he was now more certain that it was a ruse to get him to tell. But no, if the hunt was on for Buck Wilson, Eddie Grisholt was not going to be one of the hounds.

"Take you, for instance – continued Krause – you have some potential but are far from realizing it. Back in Corcoran, having Buck Wilson as a mentor might have saved you an embarrassment or two but then he became a liability and you wisely chose to come out here. It shows you have a brain."

Ah, the snake, thought Grisholt, there she was trying another tactic. Krause knew the back-story, that was plain, but that didn't mean she had all the facts on the case. Like the fight he had lost to the inmate. Maybe his fellow guards up in Corcoran, out of decency, had not blabbered on about it.

"You showed poor judgment in this instance but I would be willing to reconsider…"

"I won't," said Grisholt, emphatically, surprising himself with the strength with which he spoke and not even wanting to hear what it was she was willing to reconsider. It was over.

"What do you mean?" asked the sergeant.

"I stand by my story. And I will resign my post."

Krause snickered and seemed to relax. "Is that what you came here to tell me?"

"I came to tell you the truth. But it doesn't seem enough for you." Now he felt like he had seized the advantage. She sat up on her chair and he thought he saw a smile of disdain play on her lips.

"You've spent eight years in the system… want to give that up?"

Grisholt leaned forward in his chair and stared down at his shoes. He felt he was breathing easier. Yes, this was the moment. He could still stay but would have to play the game with no assurances that he would win, forever beholden in some way to Krause. Or he could just leave it all behind and start over. Walk away. Eight years, sure, but his conscience was more important. Prison had taught him a few things and he was young enough to put it to good use. And maybe, just maybe, Krause didn't have a thing on either of them and was just out to get an officer who had always been an easy target and step on him to move up the ladder.

Grisholt felt again the temptation to ask what Krause had to offer but stopped short. He didn't want to play the game anymore. He could tell she was a shark and he could end up getting hurt. Better to stick to his plan.

"All right, as you wish," began Krause, "but the fact that you're resigning doesn't mean I can't go after you in a court of law and charge you with conspiracy to commit murder."

Grisholt looked at her and saw the icy eyes, the cold, calculating look of someone determined to get her way. He didn't want her for her neighbor, never mind in the sack. His thing would melt. He then stood up and stared down at her with a sense of confidence that was new to him. He took a deep breath and said, "Have a good day." He turned around and stepped out.

Grisholt walked away feeling that a huge weight had been lifted off his shoulders. He had no idea where or when he would find a job or what he would be doing, but the sense of himself he had developed was his best reward in years. He had gone into the meeting with Krause not knowing what would happen, trusting only to his instincts, and they had come through for him. And that was precious. As to Buck, his old friend, he had his own troubles to sort out and Eddie Grisholt was not going to add to them by bad mouthing him. As far as the assault, Buck had done nothing wrong and his real battle was with his own conscience.

Grisholt kept walking back to the entrance. It was his day off. He filled his lungs and felt like a new man. His stride felt strong and determined. He thought of returning to his post to say goodbye but then changed his mind. He was out of there. He would not tell anyone, either, it was nobody's business but his. He would leave a message for his supervisor and that was it. He regretted what he had done and that a man had almost got killed because of him but it could have been worse and he thought he was one lucky son of a gun. Better quit when you're ahead.

At 12:43 pm., on a bright sunny day, he walked out of the prison feeling like a free man.

43

Krause sent for Leroy Cadenas. Like the first time, the officer who escorted him waited outside the office. Two weeks had passed since their first encounter and Leroy did not know what to expect. Had the sergeant lost interest? Had she been unable to build a case? Or was she slowly putting together one. Leroy was cuffed and shackled as before. Krause motioned for him to sit down but Leroy remained standing.

"Have anything for me?" began Krause.

"I might."

"I don't have time for any games, I already told you what I could do for you."

"Officer Tanpuro," said Leroy.

Krause paused, a look of sly amusement.

"Tanpuro?"

"I have him recorded."

Krause sat back and smiled. "Goodness. How'd you manage that?"

"I found a way."

"Ingenious."

"Leave it to an inmate," said Leroy.

She nodded gravely. Speaking with a measured tone she said, "But that's not who we talked about."

"Things change."

"Of course."

"When you least expect it," said Leroy with a glint of mischief. "But look at it this way, Tanpuro is better than nothing."

Krause laughed. "You must have some concern about the offer I made?"

"I'm most appreciative, I just need a little more time."

Krause was intrigued that Leroy would choose forgoing a deal that would cut down his sentence, even though in the end, the deal wouldn't be as attractive as initially presented. They never were. But still, he stood to get some sentence reduction: at least a few years. So why was Leroy blowing her off? "What do you have on him?"

"He wanted me to go after a certain officer, to set him up," said Leroy.

"Who?"

"Poncho Sterling."

"Never heard of him. "You have the recorder on you?"

Leroy gave a wide grin. "Why would I want to do that to you, sergeant?" He spoke with an air of cockiness that irked Krause.

"I'll have the officer check you."

"You're welcome to."

"When do I get the recorder?"

"When you make me an offer."

Krause sat back in her chair, swiveling a little to the left, toward where the small flag stood atop the bookcase. An officer setting up another officer. Not that infrequent. Desperate souls. But she didn't want to get distracted from her main objective. "I'll have to consult on that," she said, swiveling back and looking up at him with narrowed eyes.

"I know you're ambitious…" said Leroy.

She couldn't conceal a smile. "Really? How do you know that?"

"I can see it. And if you play fair with me there could be other things for you down the road."

"You could be my eyes and ears on the unit?"

"If you deliver… no telling what I could do." Leroy figured he could promise the sky and see what happened. Didn't politicians promise and renege all the time? He was learning from the best.

Krause pulled close to the desk and rested her chin on folded hands; the gall of this Leroy, she thought, not giving her what she wanted and an attitude on top of it. Yep, he had definitely got on her nerves.

"So, nothing on Grihsolt?" she pressed, wanting to give him one last chance.

"Still thinking about it."

"Okay. Tell you what I'm going to do with you. I'm going to send you to AdSeg for a while, just so you can think about it some more, and I'm going to search your cell and your entire tier for good measure. They'll love you for that."

"On what grounds?" asked Leroy, taken aback by the unexpected reaction.

"That you may be harboring information that could result in harm to an officer, and that you may be colluding with an officer to do so. We'll get to the bottom of it." She spoke calmly and almost sweetly, like a mother sending her child to do penance in the corner for 5 minutes, for his own good.

Leroy could tell Krause was used to having her way.

Krause picked up the phone, called the officer outside, ordered him to search Leroy in her presence and then escort him directly to AdSeg. She was already speaking to the officer in his unit when Leroy was led away.

Looking back from his cell in the hole that evening, Leroy thought he had missed a golden opportunity. He could have easily given the sergeant what she wanted and incriminated Grisholt, in exchange for whatever they decided upon in the way of compensation, but he had not been able to muster up the nerve to stab Grisholt in the back. They had had a good relationship and both had benefited, all their dealings being about drugs and cell phones, nothing else. Grisholt might be crooked, but he had never done Leroy a bad turn.

At Krause's request, Leroy's cell in Bravo Three was searched, plus the five adjacent on both sides, but they did not find anything other than a small stash of Marijuana in the room of a man who had been waiting for a space ship to land in the middle of the yard and fly him to freedom. He had been waiting 42 years.

44

A week later, Joey Wilson was coming out of Bravo Three when he crossed paths with Leroy just outside the entrance. Leroy had been reassigned to his old cell and was returning from the law library while Joey was heading out for his therapy session. The two men exchanged glances and moved past.

Soon after, Joey was sitting opposite Dr Jeffries.

"After I stabbed my dad I ran to the neighbors," said Joey. "He chased after me but I was faster than him. I felt sure that if he'd caught me he would've killed me. I got to my neighbors and they called my mom; they didn't know what was happening but I was really scared. I didn't tell them anything. When my mom came, I told her about the stabbing but didn't say anything about feeling like dad was turning me into a girl. I did tell her about the dream I'd had and that I'd felt I needed to do it. She was alarmed."

"What dream was that?"

"The one that I had the night… after…" He hesitated. He gazed at Dr Jeffries for reassurance. She nodded encouragingly. "Every morning, while mom was away, I'd wake up early and go to his bed… snuggle up against him. He'd put his arms around me and press me to him as he drifted back to sleep. Sometimes I'd hear him whimper, like he was thinking of mom… and I… I wanted to comfort him." Joey stopped, eyeing Dr Jeffries again, uncertain to proceed. "Then one day, when I was close to him and had my back to him… I felt like he had got aroused." Joey closed his eyes for a moment. "He pushed me away a little but still held on to me… but I had liked the warmth of his closeness."

Joey sighed. "I stayed for a while and then got up and went back to my bed. The next day I returned. He was still asleep… or half asleep… and he put his arms around me and pressed me to him… keeping his hips away… I remember that… but I pushed back… I pushed back against him… searching… looking to feel his manhood against my butt."

Joey paused, the expression anguished, the eyes moistened. There it was, he thought. He had said it.

He pressed his hands together between his legs and looked down at the ground. "If before I had not wanted the physical contact… now I searched for it. I suppose… looking back… that I had discovered that pleasure… and it made me feel like a girl."

Dr Jeffries looked at him with all the compassion she could muster.

Joey looked back, pleading for a word of relief.

"What else did you feel?" the doc asked gently.

"…Maybe that's how my mother felt…"

"Maybe… to ease your dad's sorrow… you wanted to be like her," offered Dr Jeffries.

"What got me was that I liked it," said Joey.

And Dr Jeffries thought of how unforgiving Joey was being with himself, and it pained her. "It's all mixed in," she began, "the need for safety… the wanting to comfort… the sexual pleasure… and you… six years old… not sure if your mom would come back… not sure that you'd see your sister again."

"Why did I have to ease his sorrow?"

"He was your father… deep in grief over the loss of his wife… and you could sense that."

He shook his head slightly. "I had sorrow too."

"Perhaps you thought that if you eased his… you wouldn't have felt so alone."

Dr Jeffries' words brought Joey some solace but still he could not forgive himself that he had felt pleasure. Wasn't he a boy?

"When I went to his bed and slipped into my mother's side… I felt her presence…"

"You were a child…'" said Dr Jeffries, delicately.

Joey dabbed his eyes with the sleeve of his shirt. "I liked being in her spot… I think you're right… it made me feel safe…"

"You were very scared…"

He shook his head. "I was a boy, I kept telling myself… how could I be a boy and my mother at the same time?"

"… boundaries can be fluid… and it's okay."

"What do you mean?"

"Six years old is a time of sexual ambiguity… of latency… still years away from puberty and the defining power of hormones… of which you knew nothing about."

Joey felt a vague sense of relief. He sat back, rubbed the back of his head. "I would scream at him that it was his fault that mother had left us. I began to skip meals and he didn't know what to do." He chuckled as he reminisced. "He'd go out and get me some ice cream. I would eat the whole container. Didn't give him anything. Refused to go to school, too."

"Who were you with when he was at work?"

"The baby sitter or with a lady who took care of other kids. I knew he was trying to console me but I ignored him."

"Didn't want to give him a chance…" said Dr Jeffries.

"One time I asked him to take me to see mom. My thought was, once I saw her, I would refuse to come back with him. I was prepared to kick and scream."

"What did he say?"

"He told me to stop acting like a baby, that mom didn't want anything to do with me or him and we might as well face it."

"What did you make of that?"

"I don't remember. I think I just blanked out," said Joey.

"It must've been terrifying to be pulled away from your mother…"

"He was giving up," interrupted Joey. "I didn't like that he was dragging me down with him. One moment he was angry, the next he was all sniffly… just like a baby. I cried in my bed, too, but I didn't let him see me." Joey looked at Dr Jeffries and then said with a grin, "Someone had to be the man of the house."

Dr Jeffries smiled. "How're you feeling?"

"Anxious."

She waited.

"I just remembered the dream I had the night after he refused to take me to go see mom. Funny how I remember it just now, after all these years."

"What was the dream?"

"You sure you want to hear it?"

"We have to look at everything, don't we?"

Joey ran his hands through his hair. He had grown calmer. "It began with mother taking me and my sister to the swimming pool. We had to take a busy road, full of trucks. As we drove, the car begins to sputter and mom pulls over to the side. She's not worried. She tells me to go for help, they would wait, but to be careful when I walk alongside the road and look out for traffic. My sister Margaret is in the back seat. I get out and ask her to come with me but she doesn't want to. So I run to go get help. But I had a feeling that something bad was about to happen. Then I hear a loud crash. I look back and a big truck had just rammed mom's car, and it's flipping over like a toy, end on end, bursting into flames. I'm so scared I turn and run as fast as I can to go get dad. I reach home and I'm feeling like I want to vomit but when I open the bathroom door I see my father on the potty with another woman, naked, sitting on his lap. That's when I wake up."

Joey had turned pale as he recalled the dream.

"Who was the woman?"

"I don't know, I'd never seen her, but I was furious and felt like killing him."

"What do you make of it?"

"I don't know. But I had just lost my mom and I get home and my dad is with another woman. Where did that leave me?" Joey rubbed his eyes and gazed at Dr Jeffries.

"How're you feeling?"

"Sad…"

"Strong dream," Dr Jeffries said.

"It was so real. I thought that, for sure, my dad was cheating on my mom. And I was angry at my sister, too, because she went with mother and left me behind." Joey paused momentarily. "She must've liked my sister more."

Dr Jeffries tilted her head, "But wasn't Margaret younger?"

"Yes."

"The family was going through a crisis and maybe your mother figured she should keep the child that needed her the most at the time. Or maybe your father had insisted you stay with him."

"I doubt it."

"Did you ever ask him?"

"No." And Joey thought that he had been too eager to punish his father. He folded his arms over his chest and looked off. "I know who was the woman in the bathroom… it just came to me. Or maybe she wasn't but she reminded me of someone."

"Who?"

"The neighbor's wife."

"The same neighbor you ran to?"

"No, the other one, on the other side. At first I didn't recognize her because she's a little different in the dream, but her shorts were on the floor, and that's what reminded me of her."

Joey shook his head lightly, smiling to himself. "One day we were out in the porch, sitting on the swing, my father and me, and this lady pulled into her driveway next door and began to unpack the groceries from the trunk. It was summer and she was wearing shorts. She waved at us. My dad waved back, then said to me, nudging me in the arm, 'That's a heck of a woman, right there. When you grow up, get yourself something like that.'"

"And your reaction?"

"I didn't like it. To me, she looked just like my mom. I didn't say anything, but it made me think that dad liked her more than my mom. Afterwards, I thought she might have been part of the reason my mother left but I doubt it, she never came up in the arguments they had. Not that I recall. Their arguments were more about dad having problems at work, getting written up because of his temper."

Dr Jeffries reflected on the burden of guilt that Joey had carried all his life: guilt about the rage he had felt when feeling abandoned; guilt and shame about the physical closeness he'd had with his father; guilt about his reaction to it all - the stabbing of his father. And she reflected, too, on how well Joey could recollect the dreams he had had, and how he was doing so in the service of healing.

"About the stabbing…" resumed Dr Jeffries, "it happened sometime after you'd asked your father to take you to see your mother and he had refused, right?"

"Yes," said Joey.

"And the night just before the stabbing, you had a different dream, one that had alarmed your mother."

"Yes. That dream happened the night after I had gone to dad's bed and pushed back against his manhood."

Joey stared down at the edge of the desk.

"When I did that... dad threw me out of his bed," said Joey.

"Threw you out?"

Joey nodded. "All I remember is I had cried... and still... as I lay in bed that night... I felt the desire to return to his side. Right then I knew I was turning into a girl. I fell asleep and had the dream. I was dressed like a girl. I walked to the kitchen, got a long knife, the longest I could find, and returned to my bedroom. I stood over my little sister... but she looked so innocent, like a little angel, that I didn't want to disturb her. So then I went to my father's room, right up to the side of his bed where he lay snoring... and I raised the knife... I had once seen my mother kill a pig in our backyard... I knew exactly what to do... then I woke up."

Joey looked directly at Dr Jeffries. "I stayed in bed for a while, thinking about the dream, then got up, went to the kitchen, just as in the dream, got the knife, a short one, for some reason, instead of the long one that was right next to it, and went to my father's bedroom. He didn't stir as I came in. I went to the side of his bed, watched him breathe in and out... lifted the knife aiming it straight for his neck... and thrust it into his back. At the last moment, I changed my mind."

Dr Jeffries, her face long and drawn, had remained attuned to Joey's every nuance.

A deep sense of shame welled up in Joey and he lowered his eyes. "You hate me," he said.

"Why do you say that?"

"I could've killed him."

"Yes... you could have... the anger you felt had overwhelmed you."

He had never shared what he had just recounted and now felt utterly vulnerable and exposed. Pressing his hands together and bringing them to his lips, he added, "What if my mother hadn't taken my sister with her?" The thought that he might have, in his torment, brought harm to his sister made him shudder.

"Perhaps," put in Dr Jeffries, "you might have felt protective of her. In the dream of the car you try to get her out and take her with you."

A subtle smile played on his lips. Maybe he was not a monster, after all.

"You don't think I'm crazy?"

"No… but you were a very disturbed child."

He nodded lightly.

"As the arguing between your mom and dad heated up, you ought to have been taken aside, reassured that you would've been taken care of, no matter what."

"My mother took me to the doctor right after it happened. There were a couple of people in the waiting room but we went in first because we were an emergency. She went in alone with him and left me in the waiting room with the receptionist. A few minutes later they both came out. The doctor smiled down at me and extended his hand. I thought he would be ready to scold me or something but no, he simply stood there, smiling and waiting for me to take his hand. I didn't but I did go inside. Mom stayed out. He started by asking some questions but I wouldn't answer so he said I could play with some toys he had on the floor. I didn't want to do that either. He had noticed that I had my little hands balled up into fists and he said that it was okay to open my hands, that I was safe there. I liked that. It told me that he paid attention. He asked me if I wanted to draw something for him. I said yes and he gave me some paper and crayons and said I could draw anything I wanted. I drew the picture of a man. I looked up at him; he looked back. He had big, round, kind eyes. He told me to continue. I drew a knife. When I was done, I clutched the crayon in my little hand but would not look at him. And he said that I would not be punished for anything I drew. So I took the red crayon and furiously scratched a mess of red color right over dad's crotch. It was just an impulse, but I felt so ashamed of myself that I ran to the corner of the room and covered my face. I was trembling I was so scared. What would he do now? Would he keep his word and not punish me? I peeked out through my little hands to see what he was going to do. He got up, came over and sat next to me, right there on the floor, leaning against the wall. He said nothing for a moment. I lowered my hands. Then he finally spoke and said that if we could just talk about things, they would be better; that maybe some things could not be fixed all together but they would be better. I didn't speak anymore, so after a short while he got up, went out and brought my mom back in. He told her that it would be best that I be hospitalized, at least for a few days, so he and I could chat about all that had happened. But mom would have none of it."

Joey paused.

"I wasn't scared anymore but maybe she was. I remember that she asked him to prescribe something for bad dreams but he said no, that was not what was needed. Mom didn't budge. She took me by the hand and we left."

Joey gazed at Dr Jeffries, a veil of sadness over his eyes. "A lot happened that day."

She nodded, sat back on her chair and folded her hands on her lap.

"Where did you go afterwards?"

"We drove straight to the place she was staying and I helped her pack her things. It was the best medicine I could've ever taken. Mom had decided, right then and there, that it was time to return home."

"Turned things around..." said Dr Jeffries.

"I was glad...and sad."

"Why sad?"

"I'd gotten back my mom but lost my dad."

Joey turned and looked out the small vertical window to the right of Dr Jeffries. He enjoyed seeing the blue of the sky over Lancaster. It made him dream of the freedom that he was fighting for. And, as he saw it, every session he had with the doc got him a little closer to that goal.

"Ever wonder what would've happened if you'd gone in the hospital instead, for a little while?" asked Dr Jeffries.

"I have. I might not have had the pleasure of meeting you."

Dr Jeffries smiled.

"You would not have come to prison?"

"That's right."

"Why?"

"Because the good doctor would've introduced me to the language of emotions... and, young as I was, I would've begun to develop an awareness of myself... and maybe my dad and I would've been able to make peace."

Dr Jeffries nodded.

"See, doc, I've always loved that man, my dad. I've just fought it. I miss him a lot... even though he's kind of a knucklehead, always getting into trouble at work. But I regret, deeply, that I didn't reach out to him after what happened. I suppose that to do that you have to have some clarity, some self-assurance. I didn't."

"Mom didn't help?"

"I don't think so but maybe she did. I don't remember all of it. I think I've blocked some things. But if he and I had been able to talk, it might've been better, maybe not perfect but better, and I would've found a way to apologize."

"Did you ever?"

"No." He joined his hands behind his neck, his expression distant. "I'm not proud of that. If he and I had been able to talk… just him getting to know me as a boy growing up… he could've used that to get along better with the prisoners."

"You would've been able to help him…"

Joey nodded, the sense of sadness surfacing again, "after all, we're all kids that had something gone missing in our lives and then went haywire."

Dr Jeffries wrote something on her notebook.

"When you were in the doctor's office and you were drawing, you scratched the red crayon over his crotch. What was that about?"

"I wanted to lop off his weenie."

"Why?"

"For what he'd done to me."

"But you said it wasn't his fault?"

"It wasn't. But I blamed him for everything." Joey leaned back in his chair and stared up at the ceiling. "On the way home after getting her things, mom told me it would be best if dad and I didn't talk for a while. Just hearing he was alive was a relief. I thought he'd gone back home after he'd chased after me and bled to death. But dad is a big man and the knife didn't go into the lung. And she told me that she had not told the psychiatrist the whole thing because she was afraid he might call the authorities and then the family would've been investigated and maybe I might've been taken to a group home and she had heard stories about that and would want to avoid it at all costs. When we got home dad was there, outside, waiting. I stayed in the car while she talked to him. After a while she returned and said everything was okay. Dad had gone to the doctor and they had patched him up. I had nothing to be afraid of, and dad had agreed to not speak to me for a while."

"And?"

"So I went in, holding on to her hand for dear life, afraid he might spring lose and trample me. He didn't even look at me. But I had trouble sleeping that night. I tossed and turned, afraid he'd come barreling through the door at any moment. It was past midnight when I got the courage to get up and go get mom. I went to their bedroom and stood outside for a moment. I was scared but I knocked on the door. I wasn't sure who was going to come out, mom or dad. She did. I told her I was having bad dreams, could she come and sleep with me."

Joey now held his hands in front of him, rested his forehead on them.

"And?"

"She did."

"Just that night?"

"No."

"How long?"

"A long time. But then I started feeling bad that I was taking his wife away from him. And I was."

"Were you still having bad dreams?" asked Dr Jeffries.

"I never did. I just told her that. But I said I still had them so she could stay with me."

Joey half chuckled. "Pretty deceptive, right?"

"Maybe. And maybe your mother knew that, too."

"But why would she stay then?"

"Aside from comforting you… perhaps she was angry at your father."

"I think I tricked her."

"Eager to see yourself in a particular light?"

"A little sociopath, perhaps? The beginning?" offered Joey, with a mischievous smile.

"I wonder if you're using that to punish yourself."

Joey thought about it as he shifted his weight in his seat and crossed his legs. An officer went by at that moment, glancing into the room.

"I was scared that first night, but not after."

He fiddled with the hem of his trouser leg while still pondering Dr Jeffries' question. Punishing himself? It had occurred to him before, in the context of his knowingly picking fights, daring other inmates to challenge him on the child molester jacket he carried. But that was not where he wanted to go at that moment.

"I had good dreams while my mom slept with me. In one I remember being king in this faraway land and my mom was queen. We decide to go for a walk and as we come out of our castle, a guard opens the door. The guard was my dad."

"So now you had replaced your dad."

"Yes."

"And?"

"I didn't like that, either. So I told my mom to go back to dad, that I was okay."

"And she did?"

"Yes."

"After how long?"

"I don't remember, but it was a long time. Weeks maybe."

"When did you and your father talk again?"

"We haven't. Not since that day."

Dr Jeffries drew back, surprised. "Not a word?"

"No. We kept our distance."

Dr Jeffries felt her credulity strained, "All this time?"

"It's hard to believe, isn't it?"

Dr Jeffries assented.

"Then, when I was fourteen, I left home." He looked at her directly. It was as if the grown-up part of Joey had suddenly kicked in.

Dr Jeffries said nothing, waiting for him to continue. Joey's mood remained pensive but he now seemed to be over the anguish of recalling the painful interaction with his dad.

"How long were you gone?"

"I've never been back."

Dr Jeffries frowned. "How'd you manage?"

"I was already a big boy at fourteen. I matured early, physically. I had been mowing lawns for a couple of years and had a notice up on the bulletin board of a local market. I had saved a little money and my mother let me keep it all. Then one day I got a call from a lady. It was a Saturday morning. She said she'd heard of me and was living in the outskirts of town and needed a piece of land cleared. Was I interested? The money was good and I had no customers that weekend so I said yes. She asked me to meet her at a certain corner. I began to describe myself when she cut me off. 'I know what you look like' she said, and I could feel her smile at the other end. Her voice sounded young. A couple of hours later I met her at the agreed corner. She pulled up in an old pickup truck and waved at me. I liked her right away. She was probably in her late thirties but looked very young and pretty. She lived alone in her property, except for a bunch of dogs to keep her company. She paid me well and kept asking me back to do more work. By then I had told her my life story, except for the part I shared with you today, and then she asked me if I'd like to stay and live with her. I would have a room to myself. I said yes."

Joey had a sheepish smile on his face as he looked up at Dr Jeffries. "She asked me if my parents would mind. I told her I'd ask them."

The recollection had brought him a sense of peace and contentment. "Her name was Caprice."

"Quite a story"

His eyes shone brightly.

"What did your mother have to say about it?"

"I told her it was better for me… and that I'd call her every week, which I did. And that Caprice would drop me off and pick me up from school so they didn't have to worry about my education."

"You became her lover…?"

"That came after… it took a while."

"And your father?"

"I don't know… like I said, we didn't talk."

"How long did it last?"

"Two and a half years. It was the happiest time of my life." Then Joey's sense of joy faded and he dropped his eyes.

"What happened?"

"She died in a car crash. She was coming home from work one night and was hit by a drunk driver who had swerved into her lane. She had just bought a small sports car."

Joey glanced up at Dr Jeffries. "She didn't have a chance. She had just called to tell me she was late but couldn't wait to get home and see me."

"I'm so sorry."

"For a while I thought it was my fault."

"Why?"

"In the police report it said she was speeding… speeding to come see me."

Silence fell upon them.

"Quite a loss…" said Dr Jeffries.

"My life changed just like that… like when I committed my crime."

The guard passed by the door, again, glimpsing inside.

"She had a sister in San Bernardino, older. I hadn't met her but Caprice had talked to her about me. She asked me if I wanted to stay in the property, take care of it. I was already 16 and a half and I knew everything that had to be done. Pearl was her name. So I stayed. I loved it, had the whole place to myself, but I missed Caprice."

"Did you tell your parents?"

"No. I just kept calling my mom every week, got together with her every couple of weeks."

"What did your friends say?"

"I minded my own business"

"How much longer did you stay?"

"Six months. I took my GED and left. It was a friendly parting. Pearl had started coming over on the weekends and staying the night." Joey looked up at Dr Jeffries. He didn't have to explain everything, did he? "But it wasn't the same."

Dr Jeffries nodded lightly.

"Pearl was older than Caprice, maybe 10 years, I couldn't tell. She gave me some money, I moved to L.A. and got an apartment. I started taking some courses in a community college and decided to try out acting. I got roles in a few student films. I didn't think college was for me so I took a job as a waiter instead. I wanted to travel, go to New York, try my luck there. I thought of hopping freights, like I'd seen in the movies, and I almost did, but I kept acting and began to do theatre. That's when I met Darla and Melanie."

45

Leroy was lying on his bunk, reading "The Brothers Karamazov," when Poncho Sterling showed up at the door.

"Leroy?"

"Yup?" He recognized the voice instantly and sprang to his feet.

"I'd appreciate if you would come out for a moment, I'd like to speak with you."

"What about?"

"It's private."

"Where?"

"Down in the day room."

Leroy had respect for Poncho so he did not put up any resistance to the request. Furthermore, he was intrigued. Had Poncho been contacted by Krause? Was that what the meeting was for? And what about Eddie Grisholt? He had not seen him in a bit so he was curious. Poncho signaled the tower to rack open the door and a moment later they were sitting across each other in the day room, in full view of the rest of the inmates, who were free to stare out of their windows and speculate on what was going on.

"About Tanpuro," began Poncho, speaking softly.

"Yes?"

"You met with him the other day, in the middle of the night…"

"That may or may not have happened," cut in Leroy with a mischievous smile.

"Several people saw you."

"We have eyes and ears in here, don't we?"

"Can't be avoided. What I wanted to ask you is this… if you have anything against him… give me a chance to work things out."

Leroy stared back. "It's an unusual request."

Poncho nodded slowly.

"I've never been asked by a C.O. to do that."

"So here it is now."

Leroy was hesitant. But doing a good turn for Poncho was like putting money in the bank, since he was known to be fair and square and willing to go to bat for an inmate if he thought the man had been treated unfairly.

"Why would you want to protect him?"

Poncho pulled himself up and rested both his arms on the table. "You know… just like you have some inmates that muck things up for everybody else, we get some officers that are a problem. Some of us would like to help before they lose their jobs. It's that simple; better for everybody."

Leroy chuckled and shook his head.

"You're under the gun on the Legrand - Wilson incident,"

pressed Poncho.

"Under the gun?"

"It was a pretty ugly thing, Leroy, you lost your marbles there."

"I haven't lost anything," returned Leroy, testily.

"You've met with Krause. Twice."

"You're up to date."

"All I'm asking is that you hold back on whatever it is that you got on Tanpuro."

Leroy looked off, weighing Poncho's words.

"Let me be clear," continued Poncho, "I'm not making a deal with you; I'm just asking on behalf of a coworker. If you can't because it doesn't fit with what you got working, so be it."

"Can you help me get a gig with the plumbing crew?" said Leroy, "I need some skills, man, I'm rotting sitting there in my cell."

"With what happened to Legrand, no one's going to be looking at you for a while."

And Leroy knew that. But what else did Poncho know? The question kept circling around in Leroy's mind. As far as he knew, inmate Venus still had the recorder with Tanpuro on it.

"That's all I have," put in Poncho as he started to get up. But then he stopped, leaned in and whispered to Leroy, "Grisholt quit his job."

"What?" The news jolted Leroy. "When?"

"Two weeks ago."

Not far from where they had sat, Double X, from 118, the man who had openly threatened Butterfly, slowly mopped the floor. He had been promoted to porter.

"Hey, Double?" called out an inmate.

"What's up?"

"Can you get me and extra roll of toilet paper?"

"We're short, but I'll check with the C.O."

"Double! Over here, 121," called another.

And Double X went to his cell.

Leroy had trouble falling asleep that night. With Grisholt gone he now felt completely exposed. But what was he thinking anyway, whatever Grisholt had done to get the assault reduced to a mutual combat had all become meaningless the moment Krause had got involved. She had blown the case open when she took control. Grisholt saw it and bolted.

But had he made a deal?

Leroy thought of Legrand. The day Legrand had received the letter from his daughter he had shared the news with a few people, but word quickly got out and most of his fellow inmates filed by to shake his hand. Whites, Latinos, Blacks, Asian, all wanted to wish him the best. Leroy would have wanted to join in also. Instead he watched from his window, and thought that if the blade he had sank into Legrand had struck a vital organ, none of that would have been possible. Just what kind of a man had he become that he devalued life as he had? And for what, to be able to claim that he was the shot caller on his tier?

Feeling tired and lonely, seeking relief from his self-loathing, he reached inside a bag he kept under his bunk and pulled out his Philadelphia diary – the account of his search for his mother and the time spent with Tiara. He pressed the pages against his face and closed his eyes. The sight of Tiara drifted into focus. She looked splendid in her tightly fitting cotton dress, the one she had worn the day she had consented to meet him for lunch. He recalled their going for a stroll in a leafy park with winding paths and benches and fountains and how he had treated her to the nicest place he could afford. The stream of memories began to soothe his anguish. But why hadn't he written or tried to contact her? Was he a fool for not trying? Who's to say that she might not get the letter, maybe even reply? And it occurred to him that if that ever happened… why, he might become the happiest man on earth.

It was nearly midnight, just as he was beginning to surrender to the call of Morpheus, when he heard a tap on the wall. It was his neighbor Culebra.

"Dog?" Culebra whispered through the vent. "Leroy?" There was a note of urgency in the voice.

Leroy sat right up. "What's up homey?"

"Got news for you."

"What?" Leroy climbed up on top of the washbasin and leaned against the vent.

"Got a letter from my buddy up in Corcoran. You wanted to find out about Grisholt…"

"Oh yeah. You said some of your people knew something about him. I've been waiting for that."

"He was up there for a few years. He was starting out and he had a mentor and guardian angel…"

"Okay…"

"Guy called Buck Wilson."

"Wilson?" Leroy thought immediately of Joey.

"There was talk Grisholt was involved in some wheeling and dealing with inmates…"

Leroy smiled to himself. The rascal. "They get him for anything?"

"No."

Sneaky Eddie, the man could cover his tracks, thought Leroy. "Is that it?"

"Yeah."

"You know how I've been telling you about sergeant Krause?" said Leroy.

"Yeah?"

"That's who I really want some dirt on. Think your friend can do that for me?"

"He can try. He'll want something for it."

"Sure. Can you call him on the phone? I need it as soon as possible." Leroy glanced at the knuckles in his hands as he held on to the upper bunk for balance.

"I don't have a phone."

"You got rid of the phone?" said Leroy.

"Sold it. I'm getting out in 6 months, remember? I'm not taking any chances."

"You're a smart man."

"No worries. My buddy and I, we've been writing in code for years. We've got it down. I'm going to help him out when I get paroled."

"Don't forget me, either."

"You know I won't."

And Culebra thought to himself that Leroy seemed in great need of the info and, for the sake of speed, he might borrow a phone to make this one last call, this one last favor.

Leroy thought of Grisholt. His old partner in crime was now a free man, out of the prison system for good. Maybe he would get a postcard from him in the future. 'Thinking of you, from Maui, Hawaii, Aloha baby'. Yeah, right, but he sure was going to miss the little income the relationship had afforded. Grisholt brought in the goods and Leroy did the retailing. For half of the price, which was not a bad deal since he could get as much as two hundred bucks from a transaction. On a good month, Grisholt would arrange for two or three drops; not too greedy, just enough; he was smart that way.

"By the way, Venus is waiting for you to pay her," said Culebra.

"I'm good for it. Tell her I'll take care of it tomorrow. Thanks, man."

"Later, dog."

Leroy climbed down from his perch and thought of the earlier conversation with Poncho Sterling and the news of Grisholt's exit. Grisholt must have felt a lot of heat from Krause for him to bolt as he did. Leroy regretted once more that, in his caution, in his loyalty to Grisholt, he had lost a golden opportunity with Krause. He could have turned him in but, in the end, something had stopped him.

But why had Krause, an outside investigator, been brought in on the case? Something didn't smell right. Why was such a big deal being made of an assault on a child molester? Surely Krause was no more enlightened on child molesters than the rest of custody? A piece of the puzzle was missing.

The thought of Legrand returned once more. Had Leroy stabbed him out of envy? He had heard other inmates talk about what the Frenchman had to say when he was congratulated on the news of his daughter. He had said that, even though he was in for a double homicide committed in a moment of intemperance when he was 19 years old, he had tried all his life to be as productive as the system allowed; and because of it he could hold his head high when the moment came to meet his daughter face to face. Those words, which might have seemed preachy, had touched Leroy. They came from a man who had been in prison far longer than he had and who had not given up. So the man had to know something he did not. And it was a very long shot that Leroy would ever see his beloved Tiara but, if he ever did, he would want to feel what Legrand said he felt.

Was it even in the realm of possibilities for a man like him, who had done what he had, to earn some of the self-respect Gardner had talked about? He didn't believe it but the doc seemed to. And maybe the doc, being more worldly, saw something in him that he did not. He had to admit, something did seem to happen in the sessions with Gardner. It felt like a transfer of some kind. Maybe it was his perspective broadening a bit, or a different awareness of himself being stirred from deep within.

Could it be possible then that, with diligence and hard work, he just might evolve to become a better person? It would be a little miracle, wouldn't? A little miracle happening right there in the unit, right there in the middle of the jungle he was forced to call home.

Maybe, just maybe, thought Leroy as he drifted off to sleep, the doc was not full of hot air and knew a thing or two about helping inmates.

46

*P*oncho Sterling didn't get the part of the guard assigned to death row, but he kept auditioning and landed the part of the assassin for hire in an independent film. It was a substantial supporting role involving several scenes with the lead actors. He shared the news with his parents but otherwise kept it to himself. It had to do with his acting confidence; he didn't think he had much - not yet. On the set he felt like an impostor, but he was fooling some people because the director and producers loved his on screen presence and the way he handled himself. They said other things, too, that he was a natural and had an instinctive grasp for the truth, but Poncho did not let it go to his head. He just kept doing everything he was told and never seemed to tire, all the while hanging on to one simple guiding concept, what he called Poncho Sterling's number one rule of acting: pretend that you're not pretending, and mean it. And it was getting the job done.

In the script, he had a fellow assassin, a woman, who was also his wife. They had been married for a while, went to church, and even had two children, boy and a girl, who they took to school and hugged and kissed goodbye before going off to plan and execute their next assignment. As the story went, the whole thing had gone on for years and they were doing well financially. Somehow, in their minds, the couple could put enough distance between these two very different life styles and still manage not to go crazy. To Poncho, however, the whole thing seemed preposterous, but the possibility that the role might get him some recognition kept him at it.

That's when he thought of Jerome C., a lifer who was serving time for murder in Bravo yard and was rumored to have been a hit man.

Jerome was amused that anyone would be interested in his life so when Poncho approached him he gladly consented. Poncho arranged to meet with him in the gym.

Jerome was an old timer: tall, lanky, clean shaven, with shoulder length hair that had turned completely white, a crooked nose and fierce looking eyes. But he also had a quick smile that softened his features and, except for some wrinkles around his eyes, you could say he looked 60. In fact, he was 70.

On his way to meet with Poncho, Jerome heard the barking of the dogs from adjacent A yard's dog training program. It brightened him up. As soon as he was greeted by Poncho, he told him he was an animal lover and wouldn't it be good for the inmates if the dog program in Alpha yard could be extended to Bravo.

"Always loved dogs," said Jerome, "Used to have three, sometimes four. Just got a soft spot for them. The meaner the better, I tame them."

Poncho wondered if Jerome's taming ability had something to do with his fierce eyes, which would let the dog know right away who was boss.

"Why'd you get into it?" asked Poncho.

"The dogs?"

"The crime."

Jerome seemed to drift off in reminiscence and Poncho thought he had noticed a hint of sadness.

"I ask myself that all the time. I grew up in a farm, in Montana, and was up early to help my dad, then school till early afternoon, then back to take care of the pigs and the cows, but as soon as I was done, I'd grab my rifle and go out hunting with my dogs. Same as all the other kids around. No different."

"What'd you hunt?"

"Rabbits, squirrels." Jerome smiled. "You figure those rabbits would've been scared of me the way I was hunting them down but, heck, no, they stayed around. I guess they don't know better. Some days I'd bring in three or four, always made my dad happy."

"Family ate a lot of rabbit."

"Sure did," Jerome chuckled. "I was just my pops and me. When I turned 18 I thought of joining the Army. I might've been good at it.

Maybe even got me some medals, too, since I was a good shot. But I could've come back with PTSD and committed suicide. I hear it's pretty bad if you get it. Main reason I didn't go was I'd got Betty Lou pregnant and her family wasn't letting me go nowhere. But then she fell for another man and took up with him. So I was free to vamoose."

His folksy, lighthearted manner, put the listener at ease.

"Did you murder for hire?"

Jerome looked straight back at Poncho… and he nodded lightly.

"I took off after Betty Lou gave me the kick in the rump. She told me the child wasn't mine. Still, I didn't believe her."

Jerome sat back in his seat and crossed his legs. "I went to Oklahoma, worked the oil fields for a while, saved some money and bought myself a truck. I started to haul goods for a supermarket chain down in Alabama."

"What was that like?"

"Decent money, lousy hours."

Poncho found Jerome likeable and he couldn't help but wonder what on earth had made him stray into the path he'd chosen.

"For a while there I thought of going back, I don't know what for, maybe just to see if the kid with Betty Lou was really not mine… hear what the town gossip was." He shrugged. "I didn't. I headed west, instead, and didn't stop till I hit Vegas. That's where I met Ace."

"Who was Ace?"

"The fellow who put me in touch with the people… the people who gave me the jobs."

Whenever Poncho came across a man guilty of murder, he always asked how long he had been incarcerated, if only to have a sense of whether the person had been out there when his mother had been killed, which had happened 34 years before.

"How long have you been down?"

"Thirty one."

Jerome had been out there.

"I had got a job at a casino, doing security, and on my days off I'd go by this little club, mostly for locals, and I'd talk to the girls and get myself a drink or two. A couple of times some drunk misbehaved and I took care of it. I did it because it was the right thing to do, but it got me Ace's attention. I didn't ask for it, it came to me."

"What was the first job?"

"Collections. Someone owed someone some money. Lots of it. I got it and Ace gave me a fat commission. Tax free. A week later he called me again. Sometimes all it took was a nice chat. Sometimes… a little squeeze. I never looked back."

And there sat Jerome, serving 75 to life, which meant he had another 44 to go, unless he got time off for good behavior. Still, it was unlikely he'd get out before his 100th birthday.

"And then you were asked to kill," said Poncho.

"They wanted me to get rid of the problem. How I did it was up to me." There was no change in Jerome's expression when he said this. It was business. "The money was good and it got better."

"A long run?"

Jerome nodded absently, "Fourteen years. Went back and forth between Nevada and California. Now and then I'd have to travel somewhere else."

"The crime you were sentenced for, where was it committed?"

"Fresno."

Jerome's shoulders had relaxed as he told his story, and was now sitting forward in his chair, arms on his lap.

"I made it back to Montana to see Betty Lou. She seemed happy. She introduced me to the kid. Didn't look anything like me." He smiled. "I was glad for her. She asked me what I was doing. I told her I was working in Personal Security. High profile clients, investors and the like. She was impressed."

"You never married?"

"Almost did. I was seeing a lady I really liked and was thinking about it… when I got caught."

Jerome pressed his lips together and looked off.

Poncho had no idea how much he could get out of him but he was willing to push.

"How many people did you get rid of?"

"Some things I'll take to the grave."

Poncho knew not to expect details of the crimes and would be satisfied with simply getting a sense of the man. That should be enough to help him fill out the character in the script. But then he began to feel uneasy. He was thinking of bringing the session to a close when Jerome began again.

"I had stepped into the underworld…" started Jerome, "… all the people I hit, they were bad players… bad, bad players… people doing bad things to other people… and that's what I kept in mind when I prepared for the hit. Just that."

Some strands of Jerome's long, flowing white hair had fallen forward on his face and he brushed them back with his right hand.

"Do you know I still send money to my father?"

"How old is he?"

"Ninety-five. Still in Montana. Aging well, he tells me. It's a token of my affection." A tinge of sadness crossed Jerome's face.

Poncho wondered what had happened to his mother, since he had not mentioned her.

"I never went back to see him," said Jerome.

"Why?"

"They were bad players, you know? People who were giving a bad name to the neighborhood: drug dealers, loan sharks, extortionists, pornographers, slave traffickers, child molesters, the whole spectrum of evil."

"And you cleaned up the place…" said Poncho.

"I did."

Jerome's expression lit up. "Urban detoxing, I called it," and he chuckled, "I was helping create a place where children could grow up without fear." His eyes twinkled. "A force for good in the world. Too bad it's not recognized."

Some gallows humor was to be expected, after 31 years, thought Poncho, or was the man delusional?

"You still feel that way?" pressed Poncho, curious.

"Absolutely. Nothing has changed for me."

"You would do it again?"

Jerome's eyes narrowed and he paused. "Not with what I know now."

"And what is that?"

Jerome vacillated. "Some things… maybe they had a lot to do with how I behaved… I just didn't know."

Poncho sensed it was a very private moment for Jerome and he let it be. He would let Jerome decide whether to continue or not.

"I've only had a few fights, that's all, at the start, then I got the swing of things and I'm pretty well behaved."

"So I've heard."

"But I belong here. My last crime, not the one I was sentenced... happened in Los Angeles... 32 years ago... or 33... or 34... it gets hazy."

Poncho felt something being sucked out of him.

Jerome gazed at him intently.

"Man or woman?" asked Poncho.

"Does it matter?"

"It does."

"Why? They were evil either way."

Poncho felt his temples begin to throb. "Did you ever kill a woman?"

Jerome drew back, slightly. "When you become evil, it transcends sex," he replied, softly, the fierce eyes brightening. "Man or woman no longer applies. You're just evil."

Poncho needed a straight answer, who was it that was sitting right across from him?

Jerome closed his eyes, the expression now peaceful... and then said gently... "You were close to her...?"

Poncho's face blushed. How dare the son of a bitch. And the words, "I've been looking for the killer of my mother" jumped to the tip of his tongue. But no, he mustn't. He had to hold back. It was too personal. He had thought of this moment a thousand times before but he had never said the words to anyone who could possibly have been the culprit. And no, he would not do it. He would not. Not yet.

Jerome stared at Poncho and then, with great calm, even an air of benevolence, he said, "If she was pushing drugs... I might've killed her."

Poncho let out a gasp. How the hell did he...?

Jerome wasn't daring Poncho, but simply making the statement, and apparently ready to accept whatever the consequences might be. He seemed almost glad that Poncho had taken him there.

Poncho had to remind himself that his mother's autopsy report had shown no drugs in her blood. But had she been pushing? No details had been mentioned. He had nothing to go on. It was all in his head. And then he asked the question he had never asked before. "Where did you kill her?"

Jerome looked intently at Poncho... the fierce eyes now shining... "I don't remember clearly... Newport Beach... Irvine... Santa Monica.... I even had to travel to Seattle. Nice town. Wet. Was she ever in Seattle?"

Who the hell was sitting across from him? How many others had he killed and got away with?

"You're not sure," interrupted Jerome, placidly, "But I will tell you what I know… and if it was me who killed your mother…"

How did he know… he hadn't mentioned her.

"… If it was me who did it… I will surrender to you."

Poncho was fighting to restrain something deep in him, an amorphous rage that threatened to scramble his thoughts and burst.

Then Jerome folded his hands and bowed his head. Without looking up he said, "I will surrender to you… to do what you wish with me. You would be doing me a favor. I have never looked a relative of a victim of mine in the eye. I need to do that… and the circle will be complete."

Poncho felt the tension in him start to ebb and they were quiet. Remembering that Jerome had mentioned his father but not his mother, Poncho asked, "What happened to your mother?"

Jerome raised his head slowly. "She died when I was four… maybe five… my father… he shot her… it was an accident, he told me… he said to say it was an accident… I was four… it happened in the living room… I saw it… and he said to say it was an accident because if I didn't say that… well… who was I going to go live with… who would take care of me… so I said it was an accident."

47

*B*ack in Chino, the Office of Internal Investigations had contacted Buck Wilson to tell him that, in the next week or two, he was expected to appear before sergeant Krause, who would be driving down from Los Angeles County State Prison in Lancaster. Buck had been at home, doing the laundry, when he got the call. Wow, good old sergeant Krause making the drive down just for him. He wondered what kind of accommodations did the State pay for; three star or four star hotel, or maybe just a chintzy motel. The officer on the phone, a woman, had been blunt and to the point. She had not even said hello. But Buck had been on the spot many times before.

Buck thought of Eddie Grisholt. Had his old buddy, feeling pressured from the investigation on the assault, thrown him to the wolves? But what could he have said? They had just talked and Eddie had let him in on his plan to give Legrand a whooping. Grisholt could pin nothing else on him, and no one else could either. During his long career as a guard he had made many mistakes but never done anything illegal. Except for the fighting.

Buck called Grisholt but his phone was disconnected. Hmm. What was going on? He checked with the prison: Grisholt was no longer employed. That was sudden, thought Buck. He would have liked an update on the situation but obviously Grisholt was thinking of saving his own skin, which made him dangerous. Still, unless some high-tech gizmo had been in operation and they had taped the conversations, which he seriously doubted – the State could not even stop the flow of drugs into the prison - they had nothing on him. Anyway, it didn't matter if they had. Buck Wilson had awakened the old brawler in him and he was ready to rumble.

On his own initiative, he had asked permission to speak to an inmate housed in the SN yard. He knew of him because he had been in the ambulance carrying him to the outside hospital the day he was stabbed 18 times by fellow prisoners. While in the ambulance, when Johnny's heart suddenly gave out, Buck had taken turns with the medical technician in giving CPR and they had kept him alive.

Johnny R. was now 37 and serving a 15 year sentence for molesting his stepdaughter, 14 at the time. Buck wanted to hear the man's full story, something he had never done in all his years as a guard.

The captain had asked why he wanted to meet with the prisoner and Buck had replied that he was trying to understand what had gone so wrong with the man's life. The captain looked at him with a wary eye but said nothing else and granted permission.

Buck asked the custody counselor for some details on the case. Johnny had been 28 when the offense had occurred so he had been in prison for the last 9 years.

"I remember you," said Johnny when he stepped into the office where Buck had been waiting.

Buck rose to greet him and asked him to have a seat. It had been 7 or

8 months since the ordeal and now Johnny seemed fully recovered.

"I remember asking you if I was going to live and I heard you say something but I had started to pass out. Then you squeezed my arm. That's all I remember, until I came to, after the surgery. Six hours later, I think. Close call. Thank you for that."

Buck nodded.

"What did you say that day?" asked Johnny.

"Stick around, the Red Sox are headed for the World Series."

Johnny laughed. "I've heard they've made some good trades."

"We'll have to wait. It always looks good on paper."

Johnny had survived injuries to the lung, liver, face and legs but had lost a kidney from a knife going straight through it; three inmates had carried out the attack, each wielding a sharp blade.

"I'm glad you made it," said Buck. And he meant it.

"Thank you." There was a brief pause before Johnny asked, "What's this about?"

"I wanted to know why you molested your daughter."

The bluntness of the request annoyed Johnny. He rose abruptly and made for the door, eager to flee, feeling like he was being attacked again. But then he stopped. Hadn't the man asking the question helped him live?

"I just want to understand," said Buck soothingly.

Johnny looked Buck in the eye. Something about the way Buck had said this touched Johnny. He turned and sat down again.

"No one has said to me they wanted to understand. They all come at me with a smirk in their face, like I'm the worst shit in the world and I don't deserve anything and may someone take me out sooner than later." And Buck thought of his Joey, yes, his Joey, and he felt an ache deep in his heart.

"I'm sorry for what I did," said Johnny, eyes downcast. "She was really pretty, prettier than her mom. She was my stepdaughter, you know, but I had been with them for 4 years, so it was like I was her real dad." Johnny looked up at Buck.

"I just want to understand," repeated Buck.

Johnny had begun to feel anxious, which happened every time the subject came up.

"You must have some reason to make this special trip… you don't even work in this yard."

Buck shook his head slightly. "Just what I told you."

Johnny looked off for a moment. "I still have dreams of being stabbed... like two or three times a week... and I wake up and can't go back to sleep. I wake up sweating." He paused and wiped the beads of sweat from his brow. "Can you get me a single cell? I've been asking for one for a while."

"I can't... but you should ask mental health."

"I try to, but they tell me it's up to custody, and when I ask custody they tell me to ask mental health. No one wants to take responsibility... or they all think they're getting scammed... but I'm telling you, it's for real. The other night I woke up from a nightmare where my attackers were chasing me. I was saying something in the dream and my cellie got scared. He's a good guy but he's afraid that one of these nights, in my confusion, I might attack him."

Johnny leaned forward, a frown on his face. "I still have a few years to go but I don't know if I'm going to make it. Take the clinician I have... he's a piece of work. He comes around at 7 am. He knocks on my door but I'm still asleep, so by the time I get to my feet he's moved on. When I did see him in his office he told me I had a sexual perversion. No kidding! And then he says, 'sexual perversions are not treated in this prison'. Hallelujah! What am I supposed to do, sweat it out?"

Johnny shook his head in disbelief.

"So I asked him, send me somewhere so I can get treatment and he says, 'you don't qualify, you're too high functioning.' What? Is there something wrong with that logic or am I stupid?"

Buck shrugged.

"So I don't bother anymore. See, smart I may be, but I had a problem I didn't realize was a problem, until it was too late."

Buck was skeptical. He thought of answering, 'no, no, you did know you had a problem but chose to ignore it because you thought you could get away with it.' But he was there to try and understand and they had not got to the substance of the problem so it was best to not antagonize Johnny.

"You're not going to take stuff I tell you and spread it around, are you?" Johnny asked challengingly.

"No."

"I knew a guard who did just that," said Johnny, keeping his suspicious eye fixed on Buck. "I don't know you."

"I realize I'm asking a lot," replied Buck gently.

"Whatever got me in here I've had to address on my own, as best as I know how… and maybe I got it licked but maybe I don't," said Johnny. "I'm not the one who's worst off, believe me. There's a poor bastard in the next unit who's been serving a sentence for exposing himself. He goes out, feels the pressure to expose, does it, and sure enough they catch him again. And every time he goes back, the judge gives him a longer sentence. But the poor bastard wouldn't hurt a fly. Never laid a hand on a non-consenting woman. The only thing he's hurt is women's sensibilities. And here's the crazy part about it… he has never got any treatment. Never, as in never. The judges don't get it… and the psychiatrists and psychologists sit around and don't raise their voices. What is it, are they scared or they just don't give a shit?"

Johnny shook his head. "That just ain't right."

He looked down at the table that separated him from Buck, "This same guy, he once told me that a senior supervisor had come to his cell after he had complained about his clinician not treating him, and the senior supervisor had listened for a minute or two, no more, and then sternly wagged his finger at him saying, 'Just don't do it! Don't do it!'" Johnny let out a laugh. "It's so ridiculous. Is that what the taxpayer is getting for his money?"

Johnny had let off some steam and felt himself relax a little. "What do you think?'

"There's a lot of unfairness in the system," said Buck, but as soon as those words came out of his mouth he realized he had never said so. He had thought about it but never said it.

Johnny shifted his weight on the seat and shuffled his feet under the table. A sense of peacefulness had come into his mind and he thought the man sitting across from him maybe really wanted to hear his story. And maybe he would hear it but not that day.

"Listen, I have nothing against you… maybe if I get to know you I'll tell you my story."

Buck nodded. "I understand. I'm glad you spoke from the heart," and he extended his hand to Johnny. They shook hands and Johnny R. stood up to leave. "Call me some other time."

48

That evening Buck told Janice about the session. She sat stock still weighing every word he said and struggling with her disbelief. She had never envisioned that Buck would have it in him to sit down with an inmate who had committed such an act, much less to allow him to vent in his presence. She was surprised at the calm with which he spoke, that not even once had he said anything about having been on the verge of losing control and striking the inmate with his fist. That Buck had been able to do it showed tremendous restraint on his part. Where was that coming from? And what was he leading up to?

They had had dinner, fish and vegetables that Buck had cooked – he was determined to lose the weight and had decided to eat only fish - and were now having low fat yogurt with a sprinkling of raisins for dessert.

"You're going to see him again?" she asked with a trace of annoyance.

"If he wants to."

"What's the point?"

"I want to get closer to him."

She lowered her eyes and pushed back her cup of tea.

"This whole thing has made me review my life," continued Buck. "You know how I didn't get along with my father and then he died suddenly and I never had a relationship with him. Maybe, if I had had one, if I hadn't stuffed my feelings so deep inside of me ... I would've given Joey a chance."

"You certainly have waited long enough," said she, bitingly.

He felt the coldness in her reply but brushed it aside. He was going to stay with the facts. Lifting the dessert spoon in the air, he said, "We've disagreed about the crime... but what's really important here, and I know this from what you tell me about him, is that Joey is doing some serious growing up... and it's about time his dad did some too."

Janice clasped her hands as she rested them on the table. "We've all had to do some growing up."

"I don't know what's going to happen to me when I hear more from this Johnny guy," continued Buck, "Maybe I'll just get up and leave because I can't stand it anymore, send him back to his cell and never see him again... but maybe not. I think I've come to a point where I recognize that all these guys in prison are, first of all, people... very troubled people, warped, twisted and, mind you, some are just beyond repair and can't help themselves... but maybe we can learn from them... because they are people... like you and like me... who've made mistakes... like you and like me."

Janice felt a pang of irritation at the way Buck spoke. Where was all this insight coming from? Had the one interview with the inmate made such a difference? Or had there been a process in motion that she had not perceived.

Buck put down the spoon. "And I'm fully realizing that I have not been a father to Joey... and if I had been more willing to understand... he might not be where he is now."

"So you've decided to become an expert in sexual molestation?" The tone was bitter and Buck didn't understand why. Did she hear what he had said? Weren't they in this together?

"Hardly," he replied, "But I was surprised to see that there was real feeling in Johnny... and I could sense that he wanted to be understood... and the fact that he hadn't been understood had nearly cost him his life."

Buck felt a quiet strength he had not known before. Where were the words coming from? Where they really his? Why had he fought so hard all his life to keep this awareness from surfacing? For the longest time he had rejected Joey, thinking him a mamma's boy, a misfit, a sociopath in the making, but had he, Buck Wilson, not contributed to that development? And there had been that one moment when... in his half sleep... he had pressed his little body against himself and held him there... fleetingly... and yes... he had had an erection... not thinking of the child but of Janice, the Janice who chose to flee with little Margaret and abandon him and Joey. But his own action had been nothing more than a careless mistake. He had never had a sexual thought or feeling for his child and he had pushed him away the instant he had been aware of the contact. But Joey had come back the following morning and put his little back to him... searching for his manhood... and Buck would have none of it and had reacted thoughtlessly - like a brute.

Now, some 17 years later, Buck could allow that all that his 6-year-old child had wanted was contact with his father; and what the child had hungered for was his affection... to fill the void.

In his own grief and confusion, Buck had failed to understand. The moment little Joey had returned to find closeness with him… early the next morning… his little back pushing up against him… searching… yes… 'Fucking little faggot!' he had shouted at little Joey. 'Stay away from me!' And he had smacked the child hard in the back of the head with his big, heavy open hand, and kicking him violently thrown him off the bed with such force that his little body rolled off and slammed against the wall. And the child had stood up to face his father, his expression frozen in a grimace of pain and horror, mouth wide open yet unable to cry, his little hand holding the back of his head.

Yes, Buck now remembered… that he had not gone after his child to console him and ask for his forgiveness. He had never done so.

The next morning, at dawn, little Joey had stabbed him in the back.

Still at the dinner table, eyes closed, Buck reproached himself that what he'd said and done had had a deeply wounding and demeaning impact on a child that was feeling alone and confused. If only he had retained his humanity.

Janice had witnessed Buck's drifting off and had wondered where it had taken him.

Then Buck opened his eyes and looked her directly. "I want to go see Joey."

She let out a deep sigh. So that's where he had traveled, all the way back to a place in the past, wherever that was, where he had confronted his demons. She felt miffed, though, that she had not been invited to the journey.

"We'll have to see about that," she countered defiantly.

Buck bristled. "What?"

"Joey's in therapy and has a lot on his plate. I'll have to tell him you want to see him and he'll consult with his therapist."

"What?" Now Buck had got his dander up. "Since when are you the traffic cop?"

"Since forever," she rejoined. "It's me that's been looking into whether he was alive or not all this time, not you." Janice spoke forcefully and her tone came out angry and bruising. "You may have found a reason to see him, after all these years of being absent as a father, but that doesn't give you the right to barge in on him unannounced." She thrust herself up from the table while her hands held tightly to the edge. She was determined.

Buck saw the fury in her eyes and saw no point in inflaming the matter further. He could visit whenever he wanted to, if he chose to. He didn't need her permission. He needed Joey's. But he was willing to relent. "Okay, then, go ahead and tell him. Tell him that I want to see him. See what he says."

"I will. I'm not trying to keep him from you," said she, softening her tone, "but it's up to him to decide if he wants to… and to choose when… and where." She sat back down again and both were silent.

They stared at their unfinished yogurts.

49

Leroy had thought about Poncho Sterling's request. He still had the audio recording incriminating Tanpuro but had decided not to pursue the matter. However, he wanted to have a chat with the man.

It was early in the morning, shortly after breakfast, when he called for him. Tanpuro was reluctant to go up to Leroy's cell but he went anyway.

Leroy was waiting for him at the cell door.

"What can I do for you?" asked Tanpuro, the tone barely hiding his smoldering rancor.

"Look man, I'm ready to bury the hatchet," said Leroy.

"What's that mean?"

"I got something on you and you know it."

Tanpuro blushed. "You're full of it."

"Listen, dude, you want to hear yourself on the Internet?"

Tanpuro shuddered.

"I'm willing to move on but if you think I'm bluffing and want to call me on it, go right ahead."

Tanpuro had his face pressed right up against the cell door window so he could hear every word. From next door, Culebra was listening in on the conversation.

Tanpuro pulled at the collar of his tee shirt. "Recorded me, didn't you?"

Leroy stared back at him.

"I knew it. I should've ripped that thing out of you that day."

"Well... you think I would've let you put your hands on me?"

Tanpuro swallowed hard. "What do you want?"

"Nothing."

"Ha!" blurted out Tanpuro in disbelief.

"I'm doing a favor for a friend."

"What kind of favor?" asked Tanpuro, distrustfully.

"That's between him and me. But, actually... I do want something from you."

Tanpuro gave a snort. "And what is that?"

"I want you to go over to Zambrano and apologize for what you did."

Tanpuro smirked. "Really?" Contempt dribbled out.

"Simple thing. It will be good for you."

"Let me have the recording."

"Sorry, can't do it because I have other things in there. But I give you my word that I will erase it."

"An inmate's word?"

"Not just any inmate but Leroy Cadenas' word. And be thankful I'm not blowing your career."

Tanpuro didn't have it in him to thank Leroy and left while cursing under his breath. But later that day, before his shift was up, he did go by Zambrano's cell and apologized, or something close, and Leroy saw it from his cell.

It then occurred to Leroy that he had taken a small step toward earning his self-respect. He sat down, picked up paper and pencil, and began to write a letter to his beloved Tiara. He had nothing to lose.

50

*J*anice had met with Joey and informed him of Buck's wish to visit with him. Joey welcomed the idea but he still wanted to run it by Dr Jeffries. Only she knew about his dad. His trusted friend, Legrand, was still in the dark.

"What do you think?" asked Joey as he sat facing Dr Jeffries.

"It's quite a step, isn't it?"

"Yes."

"You think you're ready for it?"

"I believe I am. I am more worried about him, though," said Joey.

"Meaning?"

"I've had the benefit of working with you. He hasn't worked with anyone, not that I know, although my mother says she is impressed by how willing he is to talk about things. She even said that he had met with an inmate serving a sentence for child molestation, just so he could better understand what happened."

"That's remarkable. Of course, there's a wide variety of impairment."

"Where am I, in the spectrum?"

She smiled. "You're working on things."

Joey was in a bright mood. He had always longed for that encounter with his dad and now it was getting closer. "You think I should insist he see a therapist before we meet?"

"No. People arrive at the truth about themselves by different paths. Therapy is one path. Your father, despite his history, is showing an openness that is impressive. He is not only willing to meet you, but he is willing to do so here in prison. Being a veteran, he's likely to run into some people he knows."

"I've always been afraid of that. When they see us together, word will quickly get out, won't it?"

"Most likely."

Joey lowered his eyes for a moment. "I want to see him… but don't want him to deal with that embarrassment."

Dr Jeffries nodded. "One may wonder also… if the knowledge that an officer is your father, will make more likely another attack on you?"

"I'm not worried about that."

She looked out the window for a moment. "All his life he has harbored a prejudice toward child molesters… to the point of abuse…"

Joey frowned when he heard the words.

"…And now he is willing to confront it…" continued Dr Jeffries, but then she noticed Joey's expression and stopped. "What's wrong?"

"Why did you say that?" asked Joey.

"Say what?"

"To the point of abuse?"

Dr Jeffries looked down at her desk. "I misspoke."

"With me it's been the rejection," said Joey, "the not talking, but when you said, 'to the point of abuse,' you meant that my father has been abusive to other inmates. You do not know that."

"You're right… and I apologize… it's my own prejudice speaking," said Dr Jeffries.

He looked down at the ground, the mood pensive.

"But maybe he *has* been abusive…" said Joey… "and if he has… why spare me?"

They looked at each other.

"Could my dad have thought of hurting me?

She arched her brow.

It's a possibility, isn't it?" he pressed.

"A very morbid possibility."

Joey crossed his arms, as if holding himself.

"Prejudice is in all of us…" said Dr Jeffries, "… and when we don't acknowledge it, it blunts our judgment, darkens our minds."

She wanted to keep the possibility of the meeting with his father alive for Joey, and was afraid that, in a fit of anger, he might close a door that had just been opened.

"If I ever learn that he had tried to have me harmed I will never want to see him again," said Joey, bitterly, emphatically. "And I will ask him that question when I see him."

"That is, indeed, an option," she replied calmly.

"An option?" He looked up at her, bewildered.

"He wants to meet you… so it is time to understand… and forgive."

"Forgive? No. I am furious." The muscles in his face tensed and his words came out cutting and harsh, roiling with resentment. "Why didn't I even think about this possibility before?" He glared at Dr Jeffries as if she had gone mad. But she held his gaze and as she did, she challenged him to be patient and to be human. And he allowed, softly, penitently, "I'm not a saint."

"He is trying to reach out to you," she said, "he, whom you know has been a troubled man… and I am asking you to go to that meeting with an open mind… see what he says."

Joey drew back, "I'm not sure I want to do it anymore."

"We don't know if he ever tried to harm you, do we?" said Dr Jeffries, gently.

Joey shook his head.

"Then go to the meeting… I think you're ready."

"I wouldn't be thinking of all of this if you hadn't said what you did about my father being abusive to other inmates. Were you trying to ruin my visit with him?"

"Why would I want to keep you from your father?"

Joey's expression turned contrite, even anxious.

"Like my mother did." And a flash of anger crossed his face. "Why did she want to have me all to herself? She had Margaret."

It occurred to Dr Jeffries that that was the first time Joey had expressed, openly, anger toward his mother.

"She put him down and he let her… and she took me away from him," said Joey.

A guard went by in the hallway and glanced inside.

"I didn't want to be hers only. I hated it." Joey clenched his jaw and gritted his teeth.

"But he didn't fight for me. I'd run away and get into trouble all the time… I wanted him to come looking for me… so he could bring me back home and we could start all over. He never did. He would roar like a lion, throw things and break plates and I'd be really scared… but mom just sat quietly until the storm passed, and then ran all over him."

"She must be very strong…" said Dr Jeffries.

"Like you." The moment he said this he felt his anger start to ebb. "She doesn't look as strong now… but she seemed very strong back then."

Joey looked at Dr Jeffries. "I went to live with Caprice because I felt I was suffocating at home. I owe her a lot. I was so sad after she died. We had just started to have sex."

"You had lived with her for a couple of years...?"

"Yes, but most of the time I just avoided her. She knew something was stopping me... that I wasn't ready. Then it happened... and it was wonderful. We had been having sex for just a few weeks... she was speeding back home in her new red sports car when she crashed."

Joey looked off for a moment.

"When I ran away at 14, my mom told me she was going to call the police. I remember that conversation. And my father took the phone away from her and said, 'No one's calling the police here,' and hung up."

"So he did stand up for you that time."

"Yes... I just remembered that." And Joey's mood brightened. "I want to see him... and get to know him."

Dr Jeffries picked up the pen on her desk.

"Maybe dad's in a journey of self-discovery... like I am," said Joey.

Dr Jeffries thought to herself, 'we all are, aren't we?' And the face of Byron Gardner came to her. She thought of the afternoon at the La Brea Tar Pits... the night together... the birds perched on the bench.

"Are you okay?" asked Joey.

"Why'd you ask?"

"You seem like you went somewhere else just now."

She smiled. "I'm back."

"Thank you for staying with me... and not letting me run off," said Joey.

"You're welcome."

They were quiet for a moment.

"I've been meaning to ask you... is it okay for a man to have an erotic or sexual thought for a child and not be bad?"

"Yes. Thoughts and feelings of any kind are part of what it is to be human and to be free. Nothing should be barred from what we feel and think. But if you find yourself dwelling on erotic and sexual thoughts for a child, you must get help so they can be examined. It is the harmful actions that sometimes come from those unexamined thoughts and feelings that we have agreed to forbid."

Joey leaned forward, arms resting on his thighs, the expression earnest, and looked directly at Dr Jeffries. "I molested Melanie... because I wanted her... and despite all the talk of loving her... I didn't think much of her as a person... and thought I could use her... I didn't think much of myself, either… and while I take full responsibility for my behavior… I think the lack of appropriate relationships with my parents had weakened restraints on my behavior… and I ended up thinking it permissible to have a sexual relationship with a child."

He ran his fingers through his hair and placed his entwined hands behind his neck. He felt relaxed.

"I don't obsess about it. I think about you, instead, but I know you're not available. In fact, you're like a mother to me… or like the mother I wanted to have."

"How so?"

"Someone to accept me, nurture and guide me toward independence and productivity. I'm very sorry I did what I did and hope my actions have not caused Melanie any lasting damage."

Then he turned in the direction of the small vertical window. There it was, that clear blue sky shining through and that freedom always calling to him. He looked back at Dr Jeffries and said, "Guilty as charged."

He glanced at the clock on the wall and knew his time was up. He stood up and crossed to the door, opening it half way, ready to exit, then, looking back said, "Thank you, doctor… thank you for bringing me home."

"You're welcome. You're coming along… but we still have work to do."

Joey smiled mischievously, "That's just you not wanting to let go of me."

"We'll pick it up right there, next time," replied Dr Jeffries.

51

*I*t was a gorgeous Sunday morning in June when Lilly Tambin, Legrand's 30-year-old daughter, drove into the prison parking lot. Word had got out that she was coming and the guards at the entrance were on the lookout. They could not have missed her. Tall, high shouldered, face open and serene, eyes large and intelligent, she had her father written all over her. Dressed in understated elegance - tan slacks, light coral vest that fell to her waist, hair worn short in a streamlined Afro – she strode confidently into the reception area. In the one leather bag she carried she had brought along some magazines and other personal things to share with her father.

She waited till her turn was called - which was not long since she had been one of the first to arrive - complied with all the requirements and was finally instructed on where to go. As she began to walk the stretch of road that led to the visiting area, with no idea what to expect, she could barely contain the excitement at the thought of finally meeting her father. Clutched in her moist hand, she held on to the single photo of Legrand she had ever known: the tall young man, 18, grinning broadly in his cap and gown as he stood just outside his high school, eager to embrace his future.

After the incident that brought him to prison, Lilly's mother had made her decision to cut off all links to him and never visit. Soon after she moved north to Cleveland, Ohio, where she had married and still lived and where Lilly would grow up. Legrand's letters never reached her. He still held on to them, the stamp "Return to Sender" faded but still readable.

Although she had had a good relationship with her stepfather, a Belgian engineer, Lilly had kept a diary of her imagined conversations with Legrand. She wrote about all the things she had wanted to tell him and she made up his answers. She wrote to him when she was in pain, in grief, in joy, and she had patiently created an imaginary bond that was very real to her. She liked reading, and from all the authors she had read she borrowed what would give substance and wisdom to her father's imaginary replies.

Now she was just minutes away from meeting him. How different might he be? Oh, how she had longed for his comfort and advice, how she had yearned for a good night kiss, for a word of praise and encouragement, for his warmth and care.

Walking westward, she went past the gray brown buildings where she imagined her father had spent his life. She saw the slit like windows, the chain link fences with the concertina wire on top. In the distance, a few inmates moving to and fro looked in her direction and she wondered whether one might be her dad.

She arrived in the visiting area and checked in with the guard.

"You're Legrand's daughter?"

"Yes, I am." It pleased her to hear the words. It was the first time.

The guard asked her to step in. The large room was nearly empty. Row upon row of neatly arranged seats and tables stood before her. She sat next to the large windows so she could be close to the sunlight. She had brought a notebook with part of her cherished diary. Should she read passages of it to her dad, or should she wait? First... first what? She just wanted to see him, whomever he had become after all those years.

The wait was not long. Through the door next to the dais at the front of the room, Legrand made his appearance. He and Lilly spotted each other instantly and they smiled triumphantly. Just sighting each other was a victory over the circumstances of life, a conquest over the myriad obstacles that had stood between them. He was stepping towards her, his blue uniform nicely pressed, his face radiant. Oh, how long had she waited. His new set of white sneakers gleamed and squeaked as he neared with determined step, and then she ran, ran towards him, flinging her arms open to embrace him, and he took her in his as tears cascaded down his face. And she smelled his skin and it smelled like she had imagined it, and she held his face and it was hers, and she laughed, laughed with the unbridled joy that 30 years of separation had suddenly come to an end.

They talked and talked. They told each other stories: he spoke of his youth, before and while in prison; he told her about his old cellmate Lenny that now lived in France, in Lyon, and of course, she should meet him at some point. She spoke of her life: she had moved to Paris to teach English but modeling had become her main source of income. She was under contract with an agency and had appeared in several fashion magazines. She showed him, but wait, here was the best part: now he was a grandpa.

"What?"

"He's five, his name is Claude and he's beautiful."

"He stays with you?"

"With both, we take turns, every week."

"What happened?"

"Life." But she was not regretful. "He's a photographer, good dad, good person. It was an amicable parting. But Claude's fine, he's happy. He does well in school and has good friends. I thought I was happy, too, but something was missing, that's when I decided to try and find you." Legrand's eyes moistened. He took her hands in his and held them in a kiss for a long moment. They spoke about everything and anything but she never brought up his crime. Eventually she would hear what dad had to say but now was not the time.

"You don't know what it means for me to finally see you. It's a miracle," said Legrand. They had spent six hours together and they were not ready to part when the officers signaled that the visit was over.

"How long are you going to stay?"

"Another 12 days. I fly to Cleveland tomorrow to see mom but then I'm back. I have some business in LA but I can see you next week."

"Fashion?" he asked tentatively.

"Yes."

Legrand brimmed with pride. His girl had some "business in LA." Wow! He loved the sound of it, the independence and solvency it conveyed. She then touched his face and said softly, "Dad, I'm in position to hire a lawyer for you…"

He lowered his eyes for an instant. "I wouldn't want you to do that… it would be a waste… really… I mean… I was guilty… I don't know how much your mother told you of what happened…"

"Dad… you've done so well in prison… perhaps something can be done. Maybe I can talk to the families of the victims."

"I don't know Lilly. Some laws have changed but they don't affect me."

"Maybe there's a way."

He was deeply touched by her offer. He caressed her face and smiled gratefully. "Maybe there is, my child, maybe there is. We'll talk about it some more next week."

"You can call me in Cleveland. Here's the phone number. I've told mom."

And she gave him a slip of paper.

52

That next day, Monday, Dr Jeffries and Dr Gardner ran into each other in the yard. She was returning from doing a house call, he was going out to do one. She was wearing her wide brimmed floppy hat and sunglasses, both of which were needed since the sun was out in full form. No matter what she put on, though, even as she tried to dress down, she always looked fashionable. Gardner, on the other hand, with his slight paunch and sloping shoulders, had to choose his clothes well to stay in the ballpark. He, too, wore protection against the inclement sun, a large straw hat with a tall crown that had started to fray around the edges. A guard at the gate would kid him and tell him that the hat looked like it had wisdom - the hat, at least.

They stopped when they drew close. She took her shades off to look him straight in the eye, all the while doing a little thing with her lips, like a side pout, that Gardner never could figure out what the hell it meant. All he knew was that it was dangerous.

"I've missed you," she said. And that set his head reeling.

"I've been around." It was his attempt to steady himself, nothing more. Immediately, though, he thought he could have been more creative in his reply and was about to improve on it when she added, "I've been meaning to call you."

"What about?" Okay, now he was finding his footing.

"I'm fighting you and I don't know why."

Now what on earth could he say to that? It was blatant seduction and he was going right along with it. She was clearly in charge.

"Can we meet Saturday?" she said.

"The club?"

"No, I'm taking a break from the music. We can decide later."

"Sure."

"Deal." She slipped her sunglasses back on, smiled again and they went their separate ways. But for the rest of the day Gardner found himself struggling with the thought of letting her back into his life. Or being let into hers, which was more likely the case. He hated the notion of having so little control.

They met in Old Town Pasadena. It had been his suggestion. They got there just before seven and got a window table with a view of Colorado Blvd. Mary Jane didn't bother to look at the menu. The waitress came and she asked her to return in a few minutes. She reached over and covered his hand with hers.

"What do you want from me?" she asked.

Gardner didn't even give it a thought; he just blurted it out, reflexively, shamelessly, as if he had been waiting a lifetime for the question to be asked, "Everything," he said.

"Everything?"

He thought he saw her eyes glisten as she bit her lower lip, jutting her chin ever so slightly.

"Why?"

Why? How could she ask that, wasn't it obvious? Had his candor not spoken for him? In a mood to be bold he pushed on. "Why have you been fighting me?"

"I don't know."

No! That was too easy. Had she truly been struggling with the issue? No, he wouldn't take that for an answer.

"Not good enough," he said to her firmly, and yet with a hint of grief already in his voice as if he were preparing for the knockout punch. "I don't like this on and off thing you're doing. We have a great time together and I adore you and you know it, but somehow you end up backpedaling like if you're searching for something else."

"But I'm always searching, that's part of who I am."

There she was, trying to wiggle out of it again.

"C'mon, now, you know what I'm talking about."

She felt he was shoving her against the wall and she pushed back, "I'm committed to my art, Byron, that's my number one commitment," she said emphatically, all the while keeping her hand on his and adding a squeeze for good measure.

"Well, then, there it is, plain and simple," he said.

"No, it's not plain and simple. I need you, too."

He thought he'd never hear those words dancing out from her lips and he savored the moment. A sense of lightness came over him. But how long would it last? One month? Two? Then again, why the hell was he in need of such certainty?

"Do you need me?" she asked bluntly.

"I do."

Mary Jane looked out the window. Cars were streaming by in the evening dusk and her eyes seemed to fill with longing. Turning to him she said, "I sing better when I think of you… you waiting to embrace me." She smoothed his hand beneath hers. "My last performance… I had you in mind all the way through… and I felt like there was all of me in every phrase, in every note I played… but then it frightened me… frightened me that you could have such influence… that I could need you so much for my art."

Gardner relaxed a little, no longer feeling like he was standing on the edge of an abyss and about to be shoved.

"I know from where you speak, my dear." His words flowed out like caresses, gently surfing the wave of hope that rose in him.

"The more I thought about it the clearer it became I didn't want to give you up," continued Mary Jane, "that it's just fine for me to need you… for me… and for my art… and that the two are separate and one… that they feed each other."

He reached over and ran his fingers through her hair as it fell to her shoulders. She took his hand and kissed it.

"Byron… I realize I'm a work in progress and maybe this is too much to ask but… can we stay in the moment and not make long term plans?"

Ah, the existential challenge, how delightful it sounded, the danger heightening the pleasure. Was it there to shroud her inconstancy? Maybe. But for all he knew he could have a stroke tomorrow. "My beautiful, lovely woman – he spoke assuredly, as if welcoming her into his life – that way of living has always appealed to me."

"Then…?"

The waitress returned, blissfully unaware of the poor timing, "Ready to order?"

Mary Jane, eager that she was to hear Gardner's answer, raised her hand and dismissed her again. "Later, please." The waitress turned to march off, a bit miffed this time.

Gardner leaned forward, folding his arms on the table. "All right, then, here's what I need… sex is important to me… feeling your flesh, squeezing you, biting you…"

"Sush!" she whispered, taking her finger to his lips. "Say no more…

please... save it for later, for when you have me in your arms and you want to devour me and you've gone mad with lust..."

There she was, right in front of him, the woman he'd always wanted. And if it didn't last, he couldn't care less. He wanted her now. If she wanted him to follow her to Alaska the next morning he would have done so - just because. But of course, it would be better if there were a prison nearby because that is where he knew he did his best work, which was to bring hope to people. And there had to be a nightclub close also, so she could sing her tunes and feel creative. And Gardner felt light, even giddy, like if she had swept him off his feet.

"I love the way you talk to me when you make love – she continued - the loose associations, the psychotic ramble, the jumble of thoughts that rushes through your mind... I love it all."

He took her hand in his and peered into her eyes. He spoke slowly. "I want to have sex with you when I want to have sex with you. I don't want to feel like you're putting me on hold."

Mary Jane's lips parted slightly, her breath sweet and alluring. "I'm sorry I've made you feel that way... I'm sorry a thousand times." She put her index finger in her mouth, licked it, reached over and put it in his. He bit it, slowly at first, then "Ouch!" she said, and he relented. But then he took three of her slender fingers into his mouth and started to savor them.

The waitress returned at that very moment and, catching the action, said mischievously,

"Since that is not on the menu I won't charge you for it." She winked at Gardner and went off again.

"You want surrender, don't you?" she asked.

"Completely."

"Will you be mine and mine only for however long it lasts?" she asked.

It was a dream come true and he relished it. Then, smiling, he answered, "I wouldn't want it any other way."

What happened later that night neither of them would ever forget.

53

*B*uck met again with Johnny R. He had arranged to have the same office in the education department of the SN yard and Johnny was waiting outside when he arrived.

"I still think you must have a personal reason to want to know about sexual molestation," said Johnny as soon as Buck had closed the door and they had sat down.

"I've never known a guard to do this."

"I'm doing it because I think there ought to be more of a bridge between inmates and guards," said Buck, "and since you are the guys who are picked on the most, I figured that's where I should begin." Buck half believed what he was saying so he was definitely making some progress, but Johnny was hard to persuade.

"Look, man, I still don't believe you… but I'm going to give you the benefit of the doubt. What do you want to know?"

"Why did you do it?"

"Because I could."

Buck just stared at him. Was he prepared to listen to that?

"But I'm getting ahead of myself," continued Johnny. "I took advantage of her and so I am guilty of grand deceit. Remember those words, please. I met her and her mother at a supermarket and was instantly attracted to the child. I made their acquaintance. Father had long been gone. They were struggling financially and I saw my opportunity. I am an electrician, a heck of a good one, too, and I had money. The child was like a dream, a pleasure just to see her walk. She was 11 and a half when I met her."

Buck thought of the premeditation, the well laid out plan.

"I had not had a real relationship with a woman," said Johnny. "Not because I hadn't tried, I had, but nothing seemed to click. I went through the sex mechanically and had orgasms. I suppose I pleased my partners, I even felt affection, now and then, but something was missing. My heart didn't jump. And I needed that. So I courted the mother because I wanted the daughter." Johnny had not taken his eyes off Buck; he needed to know if he should proceed. Buck nodded his prompt.

"It was a short courtship. I had a home and they moved in with me. All the while I was seeing the girl blossom right in front of me and she sparked that special feeling I had been missing, that I had longed for but never found. She was a smart girl: very bright, very sensuous. I was envious of her, I suppose, she had so much. I didn't try to monopolize her, either. I knew she had her little friends, all age appropriate, and I knew, too, that I had only so much time before she matured and made her choices." Johnny took a deep breath. He placed his folded arms on the edge of the table. For the first time during their session, he took his eyes off Buck.

Buck felt fortunate that he had never been in Johnny's predicament.

"So I treated her like a queen" resumed Johnny, "gave her everything she wanted. I mean, everything. Her mother would rebuke me on occasion but I would give her, too, so that quieted her down. Then, slowly, very slowly... the child and I began to get physical."

Buck winced slightly.

"I started it. Her mom would go out with her friends and the child would stay home. I would ask her to come out to the living room so I could comb her hair. I ran my fingers through it, parting it gently, taking my time, delighting in the smell, while she thumbed through some fashion magazine or graphic novel that I had bought for her and which I had carefully chosen; anything that might stir her senses, anything that might prime her, that might get her ready for me. She didn't object. Instead, she thought it funny and even giggled sometimes. There was a freedom about her that I adored."

Johnny searched again Buck's expression for signs of disapproval. Buck had felt it, but had managed to conceal it, struggling as he was to stay open, to be non-judgmental; he wanted to hear the whole story.

"One day I kissed her on the neck," said Johnny. "She didn't pull back. It was glorious... and I lingered."

Lingered? Buck had been drawn in by the story and now asked himself if he had ever felt sexually attracted to a beautiful, underage girl. And he conceded that he had. But how could he not? Was that not nature blooming, nature demanding, insisting that it be acknowledged? Was he not a man? Was that not nature stating that there stood the power that fused with the other made us whole and released the irresistible force that propelled us forward in our endeavors? Yes, but that power in a child was there to be admired and no more, Buck quickly told himself. Nature unfolding. Nature becoming. Not to be disturbed. Boundaries had been set by society and must be observed. And what about his own daughter, his own Margaret? Had he ever admired her womanly graces? Yes. But he had not lusted after her. He had not been roused by her feminine powers. And he was certain in his conviction that his role was to deliver her to the world unblemished, so she could give herself – unhindered by sexual conflict - to the task of discovering her talents and finding her mate. And Buck felt the immense sense of relief that he had never been burdened with Johnny's obsession. He had his demons, all right, but not those that had cursed Johnny. And he felt pity for him.

"One day, with her mother gone shopping, she sat on my lap, sideways," began again Johnny, "she was wearing shorts. She was on her period that day. I asked her what it was like. She told me. We went into the details, she was very free that way. As she spoke her lips were so close to me. I kissed her on the cheek. She winced slightly. I was throbbing, right under her pretty shorts, and I was sure she could feel me. Then, looking me straight in the eyes, she said, "Should we be doing this?" It startled me, just the sheer common sense in her words. That beautiful child, not even thirteen years old by then, was trying to talk me into reality. She stood up, glanced at my lap. 'I'm going back to my room now.' And she walked off and closed the door behind her."

Buck wondered whether his Joey had gone through anything like that with Caprice. He was fourteen when he had moved in with her. How soon had they had sex? But no, Joey was already a young man at that age and with boys, well, it had to be different. Or was it?

"The next day, I asked her if she wanted me to build her a pool in the backyard, so she could dip in at any time, day or night."

Buck narrowed his eyes in astonishment.

Johnny smiled. "I was willing to do anything. But you know what she said?"

Buck shrugged.

"Why don't you get mommy a car instead?" Johnny chuckled.

It was plain that in the telling of the story, Johnny was reliving every moment of his downward slide, yet Buck sensed, too, that Johnny was asking himself, at every turn, why he had not stopped? Why, indeed, when the girl herself had sounded the alarm.

Johnny had paused and Buck thought he might now be reluctant to go on. Was the telling of the story getting to be more difficult?

"Go on, man," Buck prodded lightly.

Johnny looked off, shaking his head slowly. "She knew she had ignited a passion in me but now she was telling me that she could not be the object of my desire. Just like that. Simple. 'Give me up', she was saying. But I didn't get it. In hindsight, it was all there, 'something is off, Johnny, isn't it? Something is wrong,' she would say, not with words but with her eyes and gestures."

Sensing that the anticipated climax of the story was near at hand and with it the supreme instance of outrageous poor judgment, Buck wondered if he should even hear the end of it. Should he not, instead, tell Johnny to stop? The whole thing had been so inappropriate, one poor choice after the other, from the start.

Johnny was looking at him as Buck came out of his mental aside. "Do you want me to continue?"

The son of a gun could even read his mind, thought Buck, still struggling with his scruples. "Please, proceed," said Buck.

"So I am guilty of grand deceit," resumed Johnny. "I could've walked away and all would have been fine." He appreciated the chance to tell someone what he had gone through but now came the more difficult part and he was hesitant. He put his face in his hands for a moment.

"What happened next?"

"After that time she indulged me now and then… a peck on her cheek… letting me brush up against her… letting me do her toe nails while she was in her bikini… you know, things like that."

Things like that? Buck felt a pang of irritation but managed to hide it. No, he didn't know things like that. Who the hell would want to paint his daughter's toenails while she was in a bikini?

"But she had set her limits. She was a smart kid. I wasn't," said Johnny.

Buck sat back in his chair as he considered the entire grim tale. Nine years had passed since the transgression and, perverse though Johnny had been, there were shades in him of a repenting man.

"In fact, once she even told me, 'I know you don't feel for mom what you feel for me.' It stunned me when she said it; 'But work on the relationship. Just give it time,' she added. I was dumbfounded. Where was she getting all that insight? What was she reading? Who was she talking to?"

"Smart kid," said Buck.

"That was the time to get help, you know? And I missed it."

Buck listened intently.

"I let go for a while, like everything was normal. I even felt a new interest in her mom, emotional and sexual. I was making an effort. But she had turned 14 and had got herself a little friend… a boy… a classmate. I couldn't stand it I was so jealous."

Johnny let out a sigh.

"It was summer and it was hot and she came in from a date…"

Dating at fourteen? Wasn't that a tad early? His Margaret had not dated until fifteen, or was it fourteen? He recalled grumbling about it. But was the girl in the story dating early because she was being sexually stimulated by Johnny? Buck surprised himself with the insight.

"It was around 10 pm," continued Johnny, "I couldn't sleep thinking of her. Her mom was sound asleep at my side. I waited about an hour, went into the living room, saw that she had turned her bedroom light off…"

Buck slid forward to the edge of his seat.

"… I sneaked into her room… she was lying on her back, her pajama top unbuttoned… the bed sheet up to her hips… no more… I knew it was wrong… I was hoping she'd wake up… I tiptoed to her side… knelt beside her… right by her hips… I could see her flat tummy rising and falling with her breathing… I carefully took the sheet and pulled it down… she had her panties on… I got closer… almost touching her…"

Buck held his breath.

"… I just want to smell her… the fragrance… her scent… my heart pounding… I loved her… she was right there in front of me… just under my lips… and I lost it."

"Oh, no…" Buck whispered. "What did you do?"

"I buried my mouth in her pubis."

"What?"

"She shrieked, jumped, whacked me on the side of my head with such force that she knocked me down, sprang from her bed and ran straight into her mother's bedroom."

The two men stared at each other for an instant, Buck astonished.

"I ran after her, begging that she forgive me. I followed her into the bedroom, dropped to my knees in front of them and pleaded that they take pity on me. But it would not do. Sandy – that was her name – was furious and stayed clear of me. Her mom had gone into hysterics, 'How dare you! My God! How dare you!' she kept repeating, and I just crumbled to the ground and lay there. I saw them dress in a hurry and start to leave. They were heading to the police station. 'Please don't do that. I'll move out, you can keep the house, please!' But they left just the same."

Johnny nodded slowly, sadly. "Sexual assault on a minor, that was the charge. By the time they were done and were walking out of the police station, two hours later, I was pulling in to turn myself in."

Buck found himself shaking his head, quietly repeating, "You fool, you fool".

"There was no trial. I pleaded guilty" said Johnny softly, "I got 15 years for it. Served 9, have about 4 to go, maybe less, with good behavior."

Johnny seemed drained. He had slumped back, eyes downcast, the picture of a man defeated. "I gave them everything. The house, the cars, the bank account." Then he looked up at Buck and said, "I know that there are real monsters out there, people that maim and scar for life, but was I one of them? Was I a monster?"

"You did wrong and you knew it," said Buck, calmly and without hesitation. "You knew all along what you were doing."

"That I did. I am guilty. But my question is, was I a monster?"

Buck thought of his Joey and pondered his answer. "You were guilty of assault, Johnny, plain and simple. Premeditated."

"Agreed. I'm not questioning that, I just want you, sir, a human being who had wanted to hear my story, to answer my question, was I a monster?" The words were filled with painful pleading.

"It is not for me to pass judgment..."

"Please, sir, for the grace of God, tell me, was I a monster?"

Still reluctant to answer, Buck finally said, "I don't know... I really don't know."

The two men looked at each other for a moment and then Johnny R. lowered his eyes.

"I'm sorry," said Buck. He then felt the impulse to add that, to him, Johnny didn't appear to be a monster... not now anyway, not now that he had heard the entire story, but the words didn't leave his mouth.

"Thank you," said Johnny softly, "I suppose, then, that that is why I was stabbed 18 times. The court didn't call me a monster but ordinary men have… and that is my real sentence."

Buck didn't know what to say to that and he was quiet for a moment. But Buck recovered. "You didn't deserve that," he said. "No one does." And he thought it a stride forward for him that he meant every word.

Johnny said nothing.

"What happened to the girl, Sandy?" asked Buck.

"She's fine. She's still with the boy she was dating. She is finishing college and wants to be a scientist."

"How do you know this?"

"The mother writes me now and then, sends me an occasional package."

"Did she get help, the girl?" asked Buck.

Johnny chuckled. "If she did, it was to get rid of the guilt of having sent me to prison."

Buck bowed his head, and thought Johnny needed to reflect on his actions or get help from Mental Health.

"Where you molested yourself?" asked Buck.

Johnny narrowed his eyes and looked off for an instant. "No."

Buck thought that the reply had been brusque but it was not his place to inquire further. He felt privileged that Johnny had let him in as far as he had. And Buck thought it unbelievable that, in his 30 years in custody, he had never had the courage to have a heart to heart talk with a child molester.

"Would that change anything?" returned Johnny.

"I don't know… I'm not in mental health."

"Seems like you're trying to get into it," said Johnny with the hint of a smile, the first ever in their session, and Buck had got the impression that Johnny was complimenting him. He smiled back.

"But something must've happened to me…" said Johnny, "something that I've yet to figure out… something to explain my enduring inability to have satisfying intimacy with an adult woman… something other… than simply to say that I'm evil."

54

Culebra got his hands on a cell phone, called up his lifer buddy in Corcoran, and three days later he had something for Leroy. Culebra knocked on the wall. Leroy hopped on the sink and leaned into the vent.

"I got it," said Culebra.

"Okay, great," said Leroy. "What's it say?"

"You read it."

"Oh, all right. Then slide it over."

"It's short. I think this is how a telegram used to read."

"I'm waiting."

A few minutes later Leroy had fished the message from Culebra and was holding it in his hands. It read: "Krause brother – Jennings - died prison. Wilson responsible." That was all; a simple statement. Leroy sat on his bunk, eyes narrowed in concentration, his mind racing. He read and reread the message. 'Wilson responsible...?' That was the second time that guard Wilson was popping up. Then the spark lit up his mind. Could it be...? He folded back the message and slipped it into a little hiding space he had torn on the inside of his sneaker.

Culebra knocked on the wall again. Leroy hopped back up on the sink.

"Is it good?" asked Culebra.

"Damn good," returned Leroy. "Culebra?"

"Yea?"

"How 'bout finding out where guard Wilson works?"

"That shouldn't be hard."

"And how old is he. Thanks, man." Leroy stepped down from the sink and turning to his cell door window scanned the day room below. All was quiet. An earlier message had said that guard Wilson had been a mentor to Eddie Grisholt. But now Krause's brother was dead and Wilson was said to be responsible. Somehow Joey had to fit into all of that. His heart was pounding: he was on to something.

Leroy paced the short length of his cell. He loved having a cell to himself, just so he could pace when he needed. So Krause's brother had been an inmate. Who would've thought? Prickly, prissy sergeant Krause with an inmate for a brother. If guard Wilson were old enough then that would be the link. Why hadn't he thought about it before? Because Joey wasn't getting any protection, that was why. Just that detail had thrown him off the scent. Of course, the Corcoran contact might be full of it but he doubted it.

Leroy got down on the floor and did one hundred push-ups, one after the other. He needed to slow down so he could think clearly. He got up, wiped the sweat off his brow and renewed his pacing. Krause had it in for guard Wilson. He had killed her brother… and if he had done so… why not his own… Leroy stopped cold in the middle of his cell, his eyes staring wildly at nothing, astonished at the thought that had entered his mind. And to think he had almost got Joey. Good old Grisholt had played him. The rascal.

Joey put his arms around himself and rocked, back and forth. It was his meditation. He needed to see Gardner.

Leroy sent an urgent request to see his psychiatrist and two hours later he was sitting across Gardner.

"You've been ignoring me," said Leroy.

"Not deliberately," replied Gardner. They had met only once, and then briefly, since the agreement to begin a course of therapy. "As you may recall, I'd said that I'd have to find the time, since prison, as it now stands, doesn't formally allow me to do therapy. And since we're short of psychiatrists, they keep shuffling me from unit to unit for medication issues. I'm sorry about that."

Leroy told him of the message he'd got via Culebra.

Gardner felt a twinge of discomfort at being pulled into the plot but he reasoned he was there to help his patient, no matter what.

Leroy leaned forward in his seat, hands pressed between his legs. "Just want your opinion."

"If there's any plan to hurt anyone, inmate, guard or staff, I have a duty to warn," said Gardner flatly.

"I would not go there, believe me, doc."

"Okay."

Then Leroy told him what he suspected.

Gardner frowned. "Bizarre, if indeed guard Wilson is his father."

"Grisholt pushed some levers to get me off the hook… you were right about that. The assault was his idea… he started it… but not the shank…

that was me."

Gardner stared glumly at Leroy.

"But now Krause is reopening the case," continued Leroy, "and with Grisholt gone, I'm on the spot."

Gardner listened.

"Krause had expected me to snitch on Grisholt. She made me an offer but I held back."

Gardner felt tempted to ask what the offer had been but resisted.

"My thought now is to go back to Krause and just tell her, 'I know your brother got killed by a guard named Wilson. He's Joey's father.'"

"You don't know that yet."

"I'm pretty sure it's true," said Leroy.

"If it is, she already knows it, so what's the point?" asked Gardner.

"A better offer."

"An offer to do what? Grisholt is gone, isn't he?"

"But Krause is after guard Wilson, and wants revenge. And my testimony may help."

Gardner shook his head, the mood dejected. Leroy kept hiding from the truth... running from it... and now he wanted his approval. Gardner swiveled in his chair... ran his fingers through his white hair... looked at the abstract painting on the wall, the one which an old manic patient had given to him... then turned to face Leroy.

"You stabbed a man, didn't you?"

Leroy nodded.

"Now you're looking for a deal out?"

Leroy felt like Gardner had punched him in the gut.

"Whether Grisholt played you or not, you stabbed Legrand."

Leroy stared back.

"And I have not heard you say, 'stop the investigation... I am guilty.'"

Leroy nodded slowly.

"Why can't you say that?"

Leroy bowed his head.

"Isn't that what you have to do?" pressed Gardner.

And Leroy began to rock slowly. And when he looked up, Gardner saw that his eyes had moistened.

"I will work with you, Leroy..." said Gardner.

And Leroy allowed that... if he did the right thing... maybe he could stop the madness… and maybe one day he could become the man he always wanted to be.

"To fight the good fight…" said Leroy.

"To learn to hold your pain and transform it… and have the courage not to hurt another human being as you do," remarked Gardner.

Leroy peered into Gardner's eyes.

"And it will set me free?"

"Yes."

"Even inside these walls?"

"Yes."

"I want to believe you, doc, I really do."

He was coming around to it, wasn't he? … the notion that a man who found his truth could cut the chains to what tormented his mind, even from behind the walls that imprisoned his body. And Leroy smiled to himself. It was the doc getting to him. The old rascal… and just where the hell had he been all that time?

Leroy turned and looked out the window. The sun was out. The light streamed into the room, splashing it with a golden hue.

55

*I*t was past two in the afternoon, and Joey and Legrand were walking together round the perimeter of Bravo yard. The day was bright and a gentle wind blew in from the west. A group of inmates played basketball, another was immersed in a game of touch football and the rest lollygagged. A short distance ahead of Joey and Legrand, an older convict ambled along trailed by a flock of fluttering pigeons that fed on the pieces of bread he scattered behind.

"Sunday will be our last visit before she goes back to France," said Legrand, his excitement palpable.

Joey put his hand on his shoulder and said, "Pal, it's really amazing the effect her visit has had on you."

Leblanc grinned from ear to ear. "I can't think of anything better that's happened to me in the last 30 years."

"You know how happy I am for you."

"I know."

They walked for another few moments and then Joey said, "LB... I'm having a big visit too."

Legrand turned to Joey, "Your sister?"

"No... my dad's coming to see me."

The news took him by surprise and he stopped. "When did this...?"

"I wasn't sure I'd be able to handle it but I've made up my mind and I'm going ahead with it."

Legrand observed him closely.

"Seeing how much your daughter has done for you helped me decide."

"This is really big," remarked Legrand.

"There is something else I haven't told you..." The two men gazed at each other for a moment. "He's a guard."

Legrand's expression froze. He and Joey had been together about eight months now and he had made it a point not to pry into his business, but he had always wondered about the absent father. Now here he was. Not only was the absent man finally showing up but he was also a guard. But was it the same Wilson he knew? "He's still a guard?"

"Yes"

"Where?"

"In Chino."

In disbelief, Legrand raised his hands to his head and stared at Joey.

"How old is he?"

"About 55 or 56, I'm not sure."

Legrand slid his hands slowly down his face.

"What's the matter?" asked Joey.

Legrand took him by the arm and led him off the perimeter and into the grassy field, Joey growing tense with anticipation. After a short distance, Legrand stopped.

"Did he ever work in Corcoran?"

"Yes."

Legrand closed his eyes for an instant.

"His first name Buck?"

Joey drew in a long breath. He had feared this moment of recognition and had struggled hard to keep clear of it but here it was. "Yes."

Legrand stared at Joey. "Did it ever occur to you I might've known him?"

"It did."

"Why didn't you say anything?"

"I didn't want to hear it," said Joey, "whatever it was you had to say about him. I didn't want to live with it. I think I've been ashamed of him, the way he must be ashamed of me, though for different reasons."

Legrand pressed the palms of his hands together and bowed his head. "I'm sorry, Joey, I didn't mean to reproach you"

"I understand."

"I know your father," said Legrand gently, as he looked at Joey. Joey felt an impulse to flee but held firm. The thought of Dr Jeffries crossed his mind. She would not have wanted him to escape.

"Do you want me to tell you about him?"

"Yes," said Joey.

"Okay. Let's find a spot where we can talk." He glanced about and saw an empty bench near the center of the yard. "Let's go there." They walked without exchanging another word till they came to the bench and sat down, the two men side by side, facing east and casting a shadow. Legrand leaned forward, elbows on knees, his mind deep in thought, while Joey's heart leaped with apprehension.

"I suppose you resemble him in some ways," started Legrand.

"I think I favor more my mom," said Joey, leaning forward also. "What was he like, LB? I'm ready to hear it all."

"You take after him but he was different… I could tell that he was intelligent, but he didn't let it work for him. He did have a temper… and that was his demon." Legrand stared at the ground. As he reminisced a smile formed on his lips.

"Your dad was a heck of a fighter."

"What?" said Joey in surprise.

"You didn't know about the fighting?"

"No. I mean, I remember mom mentioning something about it…"

"Whenever he had an issue with an inmate, if the inmate gave him some lip, he'd challenge him to a fight… that's how it got started. Then it went on from there. He'd fight him in the day room, with everybody looking on, cheering or booing. The guards would lock up the unit, late at night, at around 11 pm or so, and your dad and the inmate would go at it, man to man. It was pretty to see."

"Pretty?"

"Sure. When you're young and filled with energy and you think you're good with your hands, you go for it. There's a time for it. I know it's brutal and you can get badly hurt but there's a beauty to seeing a man fight well with his fists. Like there was a beauty to seeing Ali in the ring or any of the great fighters. If you have the talent, why not? It doesn't last forever. By your mid-thirties you have to stop doing it or else. The short life of an athlete."

"You saw him fight?"

"Many times. People would bet on the match. We had 3 minute-rounds with a referee. Just like a regular boxing match. And each fight would go for 7 rounds. There was one guard who everybody trusted who kept score. As word spread, other inmates who were good boxers, from other units, challenged your dad and he'd take them on. He'd go to their units and have it out. And everybody would bet on it."

"It's wild," said Joey, trying to conjure up an image of his father as a young man.

"Those were the days," continued Legrand, his mood nostalgic. "He won most of his fights, tied a couple and lost one. After the loss, he fought once more and then he retired. He had a great run."

Joey had bowed his head and was quiet. "I never knew any of this. I guess that happens when you don't have a relationship with your father."

"I know what that's like," said Legrand, in a whisper, and he grew quiet as a wave of regret washed over him.

"You got to see your dad in a prison up north, before he died?" said Joey.

"Yes..." said Legrand, "I was at his side when he passed."

Joey stood up and walked off a few paces. Then he turned to face Legrand. "What else, LB?" The hard questions had to be asked, thought Joey.

"I thought he was a fair man. Personally, I never had a problem with him."

"What are you leaving out?" asked Joey, his voice hardening.

Legrand nodded. "Fair as he was... he had the same prejudices that all the other guards had."

"Racial?"

"No, not that."

Joey grimaced. "Go on."

"There was one time when we had one in the unit…"

"One what?"

"A child molester… he had kept quiet about it… somehow your father found out… and he let it be known."

"What?"

"He was a short, skinny guy… didn't know how to fight…"

"What happened?"

"Six weeks later they killed him in the yard."

Joey let out a gasp.

"He had only a year left before he went home."

Joey walked off for a short distance and stopped. He stood there for a few moments, his back to Legrand, his arms wrapped around himself. Legrand rose and went to his side. "Look, Joey… that was 20, 25 years ago. People change. Except for that, he was a fair man."

Joey turned to him, the expression grave, "Except for that?"

"Joey…" Legrand had started to soothe his friend but then stopped. He went back to the bench and sat down.

Joey stood alone for a short while, then slowly returned to the bench.

"I will see him," said Joey, with an air of unmistakable resolve, "He's coming this Sunday… and I will see him."

It occurred now to Legrand that he would likely run into Buck Wilson in the visiting area and there was a story about them, him and Buck Wilson, which had to be mentioned. "Joey… there's something else…"

"What?"

"I fought your dad once."

"What?" Joey was stunned.

"We went the seven rounds, seven hard fought rounds. He knocked me down in the fifth, I knocked him out in the seventh."

Joey smiled faintly as he looked at his friend.

Legrand shrugged. "He was already in his late thirties. I had the advantage of youth."

56

*L*eroy's neighbor, Culebra, had got word from his source up in Corcoran. He was working on it, the Corcoran man had said, but he had hit a wall and there was nothing to add to his previous report. Leroy did not like that: he was not good at waiting. It did not help, either, that he had not heard back from sergeant Krause.

As he mulled over the matter, it occurred to Leroy that having a man to man talk with Joey might clear the air. The idea of it had been tugging at him for a while. It might seem like a leap but there was the undeniable reality that he needed to move on with his life. The folly of buying into the collective prejudice against child molesters was sinking in.

With each passing day, following the attack on Legrand, Leroy had felt worse. He had felt bad before for things he had done, but the sentiment had been fleeting and he could brush it off. What was happening now was different: this ache bore down deep into his soul. It gripped and squeezed something vital because it made him feel anguished and listless. But there was more. The ache came with a fear that wrenched him because it shamed him. It shamed him because it told him that he had got it all wrong.

He looked at his hands: they were strong, big, powerful. But to what good use had he put them? What purpose was he serving in the world? What help had he been to anyone? He was living in a building that had been made by others; he was wearing clothes sewn by others; eating food grown and cooked by others; seeing a doctor who had learned to help others; so just what on earth was he, Leroy Cadenas, contributing to those around him?

He was 28 years old and he had done nothing at all to give to the world he lived in, he had done nothing but react and harm and take. Sure, he had a troubled past, but was it not up to him to fight back? To ask for help? Was it not up to him to do his part and commit to rising above his circumstances? Just why in hell had he not tried harder? He had nearly killed a man, a good man, just so he could have a better reputation on the tier. Just what kind of perverse thinking was that? Why was he not using his mind?

He was sitting on the floor, his back against the cell door, his face in his hands, when the thought of Tiara entered his mind. He had finally written the letter to her. It was a long shot that she would ever get it, but he had told her everything he wanted to tell her. He had told her that he wanted to marry her, even though he knew that would never happen; he had told her that he wanted to have children with her, even though it was a fairy tale; he had said that he wanted to caress her every night till she fell asleep, even though he knew it was impossible; but he had told her anyway.

Leroy had the vague awareness that all those thoughts he was having had something to do with his desire to talk to Joey. Joey, the child molester, sure, but also the man who had a date to leave prison and still had the hope to have all the things that he, Leroy, could never have. And Leroy thought, too, that flawed as he was, he wanted to finally try to move past his anger and bitterness, past his entrenched dysfunction, and reach out to someone who still had a chance to live a life. Why should he, out of spite, out of revenge, stand in the way of life happening for those who had not killed their possibilities?

And then Leroy thought that, in forgiveness, he might find redemption, that in forgiving Joey his mistakes he was helping to give him life. And that simple idea gave Leroy the impression that he was starting on the road to earning his self-respect.

Leroy stood up and knocked on the wall to Culebra's cell. Culebra listened and told him he was losing his mind. But Leroy was adamant: pass along the message and don't question me. And the message was passed along and flew through the tiers. Leroy Cadenas was ready to meet Joey Wilson that same day, right there in the day room, right after chow, in front of all the inmates: just the two of them. But would Joey take him up on the offer?

To Leroy's surprise, Joey sent word back immediately that he was game for the meeting and the expectations went wild. Finally, the long anticipated rematch. Place your bets!

Right at about 7 pm the cell doors were racked open and most of the inmates stepped out. Joey came out of his cell and crossed over to an empty table in the C section of the day room. A moment later, Leroy exited and calmly made his way over to the stairway and down to where Joey waited. They sat opposite each other. The rest of the inmates kept a distance but their eyes were glued to the two men. What would come of the encounter? Anything was possible. Up in the control room the guard stood on alert, rifle cradled in his arms.

Leroy was the first to speak. "Thank you for accepting my invitation."

"I'm always open to talking," replied Joey, tersely.

"I've never done this before… so it might be awkward… but I just wanted to say…" Leroy stopped for an instant, uncertain. Joey gazed at him, warily.

"…I just wanted to say… that I am sorry for what I did."

Joey looked back, unflinching, the expression hard, though a shade puzzled. Leroy's action had taken him by surprise and he had no words for an answer.

Joey had rested his arms on the edge of the table, hands ready to curl into fists to defend himself, but now he relaxed a little. "Why are you doing this?"

Leroy gave a slow shrug. "It's complicated… but I feel I have to."

"You've caused a lot of pain…"

"I know… and I'm sorry."

The doubts that Leroy had had about his initiative were beginning to ebb.

"I think you should apologize to Legrand… you nearly killed him," said Joey.

"You're right. And I will do that… but it was you I wanted to hurt most of all."

Joey stared back. "Why?"

"Because I blamed you…"

"Blamed me for what?"

Leroy leaned forward slightly and said softly, "For what happened to me… a long time ago."

"But what….?" Joey started and then stopped. And looking at Leroy he suddenly understood… and he nodded slowly.

"I don't know what happened in your childhood…" continued Leroy, but Joey raised his hand and signaled for him to stop. There was no need for more.

"We have more in common than we think…" said Joey, and Leroy remembered that once upon a time he had heard Gardner say something similar.

Joey's expression softened ever so slightly. He looked down at the table, then up again at Leroy. If Leroy had been cowardly in ambushing him and Legrand in the middle of the night while armed with a weapon, today he was showing uncommon courage with his self-disclosure. And then Joey extended his hand to Leroy. Leroy reached over and the two men shook hands.

A sigh of disappointment swept across the day room. What happened to the fight? No brain bashing tonight? No coma inducing blows? No gore spilled? No fractured jaws? No entertainment for the gallery?

Then the two men rose to their feet, nodded slightly to each other and Joey turned to go back to his cell as Leroy looked on.

Joey had walked only a few paces when Leroy called to him, "Brother…"

Joey stopped and turned around.

"When you're out there, living your life… spare a thought."

Joey nodded and went back to his cell.

The rest of the inmates, who had been utterly silent during the exchange, now broke out in noisy chatter and took to the tables to play cards, dominoes or saunter about.

Up in the control room, the guard slid his finger off the trigger of his rifle.

Meanwhile, Double X, in section A, resumed mopping the floor by the benches next to the wall mounted TV.

And then Butterfly decided to come out of his cell. It had been a year since he had last done so.

57

Officer Morelos had been perched on the top tier in Section B, leaning against the railing, looking on as the parley between Joey and Leroy had taken place. She had gone by to say hello to Johnson in 225, so she had a unique view of the scene below when she saw Butterfly emerge from his cell in 107 and advance slowly into the day room. Morelos saw also that Double X was out mopping the floor. She remembered that there had been talk that he held a grudge against Butterfly, so she turned on the transmitter she had clipped onto her lapel and spoke to officer Rivers who was at the other end of the day room, speaking with Venus and Chloe.

Rivers excused herself when she heard Morelos' voice on the radio.

"Butter is out," said Morelos, "and so is Double X."

"Got it."

Rivers spotted the big man and began to make her way towards him.

Butterfly walked on to a spot near the center of the day room, close to the podium, and then stopped. Expressions of surprise rippled through as inmates took notice. Butterfly was out and what was he up to?

His head bowed, the 400-pound plus artiste and block philosopher stood quietly as he appeared to gather his thoughts.

"Ladies and gentlemen," he finally boomed as he lifted his massive head. The chatter died down. "I have come out of my cell, after one year, because I was moved by the gesture of Leroy Cadenas to reach out and speak to Joey Wilson."

All eyes were now fixed on him.

"I have no certainty as to what exactly happened when they talked, but I am sure it was an effort at conciliation, a dialogue for peace and understanding. On behalf of all of us, thank you Leroy and thank you Joey."

No one said a word.

"A man who intentionally injures another man, whether in word or deed, is not a free man. He is chained to prejudices and assumptions that do not let him value what freedom is. When childhood is lost, when we miss out on the time to have nurturing relationships, when we miss out on the time to find guidance and get an education, then we fail to acquire the notion of freedom."

"And we come to this hell hole!" cried out Bazooka.

Leroy listened intently from his cell.

"In that sense, others have failed us, those who brought us into this world and society at large. But we can spend the rest of our lives complaining that we have been wronged, forever the victims, or we can stand tall and say loudly, 'I will find my freedom!'"

"Go Butter!" cried out Chloe.

"We need help, yes, indeed, but we must learn to ask for it."

"Get to the point!" shouted Weasel.

"We become our worst enemies when we don't put ourselves on the line and say, 'this is *what* I did and this is *why* I did it'."

"You'll never get out!" said someone from section A.

"But that is exactly what needs to be done because it takes us right to the source of our troubles. And having reached deep within us we can then turn to those who will listen and say to them, 'help me be free! Help me break the shackles to the prejudices and assumptions that led me to injure another human being, in word or in deed. Help me break lose so I can claim my own life…. help me be free!'"

"It ain't gonna happen!" said someone from Section B.

"We need to do our part and say to our doctors and to custody, 'we may need pills but what we need most of all are relationships that inspire, relationships that heal and make us whole, relationships that restore in us a sense of humanity and respect for our own lives and that of others."

"I need my pills!" cried out Paytrell, defiantly, from his cell. "Don't give up your power!"

"Thank you, Paytrell," replied Butterfly.

In the next cell, Legrand and Joey glanced at each other and smiled.

"If you have a serious mental illness you need your pills," continued Butterfly, "but most us do not have a serious mental illness but a serious social illness; most us are broken men that need mending that comes from caring relationships. And we have not learned to ask for that. We have not learned to say, I need relationships that stir in me the thirst for freedom!"

Some men clapped in support.

"What you gonna do when the guard calls you a bitch, or retard or whatever?" shouted New York.

"You say to yourself, this man who is offending me is not a free man. He may wear a uniform and go home at night, but he is not a free man, and he is not because he offends."

"Easier said than done," cried out Casino.

"I didn't say it would be easy. And it cuts both ways. If you are the one to give offense to the guard or anyone else, then you are revealing that you are not a free man, either."

Double X, continuing to swing his mop lazily from side to side, had drawn closer to where Butterfly stood. But Morelos had descended the stairs and was standing nearby, and Rivers was close, too.

"Ladies and gentlemen," resumed Butterfly.

"There's no ladies or gentlemen here, so get real, bro," said Casino.

"I beg your pardon," protested Chloe, "I am a lady!"

"Yes, you are my dear, and a fine one, too," replied Butterfly.

"Woo Woo Woo!" cried out a chorus of inmates.

"You the most beautiful man I've ever known, Butter, and you have a heart like a rainbow, sweetie," said Venus.

"I have talked before about creating a Prison Corps," continued Butterfly, "a civic service that would enlist the progressive youth of our nation to come to prison and help us put out our stories. College grads willing to engage us and deliver our truth to the world; the truth of what conditions brought us here, the truth of cruel sentencing, the truth of the lack of rehabilitation. But it must start with us; we need to be ready to give up that truth. And as our truth is delivered to society then we will have done our part to make prison the open public institution that it ought to be in a free society."

Double X had stopped mopping and now smiled and shook his head as if amused by Butterfly's words. Both Rivers and Morelos had their eyes fixed on him. Sensing their vigilance, Double X glanced at them and the ladies stared back to convey clearly that they were ready for whatever, and if he dared make a move on Butterfly they would make sure he got creamed. Neither of them was new to the business of taking down a problem inmate.

"We have power! We have power! We have power!" a group of men began to chorus.

"Take it to the shower!" replied another and they broke into laughter.

"Don't avoid your truth! Don't escape your freedom!" cried out Paytrell.

"I am a Republican!" shouted an inmate.

"All right, everybody, enough of Butter, let's get back to business," said Weasel.

"Sing!" cried out Chloe.

"Yeah, sing us one, Butter," joined Venus.

"Before I do that, allow me this one last thought…"

"Hurry up, man, my comedy show's coming up," shouted Bazooka.

"…The unconscious is not dead," said Butterfly, "There are unconscious forces in us that keep us punishing ourselves, unconscious forces that may even be keeping us from asking for help. Why on earth do we keep repeating the same self-destructive behavior?"

"Because we're sick!" said one man.

"And unless we seek to understand those unconscious forces we will not be able to unleash our creative powers… we will not be able to see ourselves as brothers… brothers that transcend race… brothers that can act with a common purpose."

"It's easier to hide behind the dope," said Venus.

"And look what it does to us, look what it keeps us doing. It nearly cost me my life, and may still cost me my life. For 300 dollars that I owed, I had my face slashed. Three hundred dollars, ladies and gentlemen."

Double X nodded slowly as Rivers and Morelos kept a wary eye on him.

"I know all of us have an unconscious life that has affected our behavior, and if we have spent our lives avoiding it, what do we have to lose now?"

"Nothing!" cried Leroy from his cell.

"I'm in for murder," continued Butterfly, "Unless a miracle happens, I'm not getting out, but that does not stop me from yearning for a time when I can be a master of myself. It does not stop me from yearning for a time when I can hold my pain and say, proudly, I am free!"

And the men in the day room rose like one man and someone cried out, "Let's fight to be free!" and the rest of the men echoed him, "Let's fight to be free!"

And then Butterfly raised his open hand high up in the air and hung his head. The unit grew quiet.

"Oh, say can you see, by the dawn's early light…"

And all the men stood and placed their right hand over their hearts, but not Double X.

"…What so proudly we hailed at the twilight's last gleaming…" And he sang all the way through to the last phrase… "O'er the land of the freeeee and the home of the brave!"

The men broke into hearty applause.

"Love you, Butter!" cried Chloe and Venus.

Butterfly took a deep bow and sauntered on back to his cell.

"I said I was Republican, damn it!" the partisan fellow shouted again.

Rivers and Morelos walked up to Double X. "Singing not good enough for you?" asked Rivers. Double X grunted something. They then asked him to spread eagle and they patted and frisked him and found no weapon.

"What was that for?" he protested.

"Precautions," said Rivers.

"You guys are paranoid."

"Sure. Just take it in," said Morelos, curtly. And as she saw him return to his cell she could not help but wonder that he, too, had a story to tell.

The next morning, when Butterfly woke up, he found a piece of folded paper under his door. He opened it and read, "Don't be thinking you can hide behind those fancy words. I know how to wait. I got all day. Sooner or later you'll get tired of staying in your cell. And I'll rip out your heart."

"P.S: it's 300, with interest. Fucker."

58

Buck was working second shift when the yard captain summoned him to the program office. The moment he strolled in one of the inmate clerks told him he should wait in the captain's office, someone would be with him shortly. Buck sat down in the seat by the desk. He looked at his shirt and spotted a small stain from the breakfast burrito he'd gulped down as he rushed in to work that morning. It was grease. He knew it wasn't good for him.

He glanced at the walls. The captain had a nicely framed photo of Fenway Park with a little bag of stadium dirt pinned down on the left lower corner of the frame. So he was a Boston Red Sox fan. He didn't know that. He smiled. Then he noticed someone approach and open the door. It was sergeant Krause.

She barely glanced at him when she entered. She went by and crossing to the captain's seat sat down. They looked at each other for a moment, two foes sizing each other up. Memories came hurtling back. The two had met years before. They had exchanged a word or two, nothing memorable, but then their careers had taken sharply different turns. As he took her in, Buck smiled faintly: she had aged well, in fact, she looked more attractive now than when she was younger.

Krause went right to the point. "I intend to file a conspiracy to commit murder charge against you and officer Grisholt."

Buck felt an instant pressure in his chest and a cold clammy sweat quickly enveloped his head and neck. He thought his breathing had stopped. He closed his eyes. He thought he heard his heart skip a beat, maybe two. Where was his breath? Was he feeling dizzy? No, it wasn't that, it was the darkness he was in. He had to open his eyes. He couldn't. A fine tremor had seized his hands and he brought them together to control it. Was he about to faint? No, he was a fighter; he had been on the ropes before. Ah! There… that sweet thought… the fighter in him… he hadn't forgotten, and now his breath was returning. He had to gather his wits. Fast. She was intimidating him, that's what it was. Easy does it, like the fighter in him. He opened his eyes. She was staring at him.

"Do you want me to call medical?" Her words oozed with contempt.

She was cynical too, thought Buck: brusque and brutal. But he had found his footing and he could match her contempt with his own brand of disdain. "I wouldn't give you that pleasure."

"Good," she said bitingly. "Because I have you," she said triumphantly.

"You think you do," replied Buck. "Grisholt won't testify against me if that's what you're thinking."

"Who's talking about Grisholt?"

Buck felt himself squirm but didn't let on. What the hell was she talking about?

"He's not going anywhere, I have him on tape," said Krause.

"What? Who…?" Buck felt his anger rising but he strained hard and checked himself.   She was making up stuff, fishing. She might not have anything at all. He had to calm down. Out of the corner of his eye he saw that an officer was standing outside the door. He was not looking at him but there he was.

"But to return to Grisholt," resumed Krause, "I have him talking to the inmate who tried to stab your son… Grisholt offering payment… and yes… Grisholt talking to you."

Buck was barely able to control himself. He had balled up his fists but now slowly opened his hands. The officer standing outside the office made him feel like he was an inmate and, yes, Krause was baiting him, that's what it was. Grisholt would not testify against him. Not after the talk they'd had. But what else did she have?

"Your son, the child molester…"

And that did it. Buck's emotions gave way. Grimacing in pain, the anger he had been feeling did an abrupt turnaround and Buck now had tears flowing freely down his face. "Please… don't call him that," he said imploringly, "I beg you… please… please don't."

The officer outside looked in. And Krause stared at Buck without pity.

"He's not a child molester… he's not," said Buck between sobs.

"He was convicted of it, wasn't he? He had a full trial," said Krause, unrelenting.

Buck had covered his mouth with his hands. "It's all my fault…" said Buck in anguish, unable to check his outpouring of emotion, "It's all my fault… I wasn't there for him…" And in his desperate desire to atone, Buck didn't measure his words, "Charge me, I'm guilty of his crime, I'm the one."

"You molested him?" Krause said coldly, leaning forward, stabbing him with each word.

"No… not that… I'm guilty of not being a father to him… charge me… that should be an offense."

Krause had him and she pressed on, ruthlessly, "Maybe we can have your son press charges against you… I can look into that."

Buck had started to rock back and forth, rubbing his legs repeatedly. A second officer was now at the door.

"Yes… yes… please…" he pleaded in his despair, "please, ask him to charge me… I deserve it."

"Charge you with attempted murder?"

And Buck stopped. Through his tears he felt a glimmer of peace come to him. He could atone. "Yes… if he wants to… if he wants to… if he wants to… I won't defend myself."

And Krause paused for a moment.

Buck grew quiet. He wiped the tears off his face with his bare hands. He looked down, avoiding Krause's eyes.

"Do you remember a man by the name of Clyde Jennings?"

Buck sat up, and yes, he remembered him, how could he forget Clyde? He could see his face clearly in his mind, "Yes… I do."

"What do you remember?" asked Krause, icily.

"I killed him."

"But you were never charged, were you, Mr Wilson?"

"I was never charged. But it was a fair fight."

"Fair? You fancied yourself a great fighter but you didn't tell any of your victims that you had been a professional boxer, did you, Mr Wilson?"

"They gave as good as they took. They were all strong men," Buck said calmly, his emotions now coming under control.

"If that had happened outside of prison your record of having been a prize fighter would've been used against you, wouldn't it, Mr Wilson?"

Buck nodded.

"But in the prison system, you were not accountable, correct?"

Buck shook his head.

"Why is that, Mr Wilson?"

He shrugged his shoulders.

"You couldn't hack it as a fighter outside so you came to the prison system to beat up on people, correct?"

Buck nodded. There, he could atone some more.

"I looked up an old interview you gave to a reporter in Miami, when you fought the Miami Kid…" said Krause.

"I won that fight," said Buck, sticking out his jaw, a sparkle of pride in his eye. "It was a good fight."

"Please do not interrupt me. When asked why you had become a boxer you replied, 'Because I like to hit people,' isn't that true Mr Wilson?"

Buck pulled himself up. "It wasn't me who said it, it was one of the reporters, I just went along with it, but I told him I boxed because I was good at it." He spoke simply and with conviction. "And that happened after a fight in Caracas, not in Miami."

"But it's a little too late for Clyde Jennings, isn't it?"

Buck nodded.

"What should we charge you with, then, Mr Wilson, you tell me?" pressed Krause.

Buck rubbed his face with one hand, then he looked up at Krause. "I knew he was your brother."

"What?"

"Clyde and I knew each other from San Diego."

Krause sat up in her chair, caught off guard.

"He and I sparred together... and he turned pro about the same time I did."

Krause set her jaw and was clenching her teeth.

"I was a heavyweight and he was middleweight... but when we found each other again, he was an inmate and I was a guard." Buck was beginning to regain his composure. "He had put on weight and he challenged me. The fight itself didn't go long. In the third round, when we clinched, I told him to give it up. He wouldn't. He had money riding on it, he said. I knew it wasn't going to last. I knocked him out in the next round. He didn't get up."

Krause listened intently. Buck stared at her.

"The nurses were called," continued Buck, "On his way out he had the seizures. He had been taking meds for high blood pressure but had stopped them a week before because he thought they might slow him down. That was my last fight.'

Krause's eyes had moistened as she heard Buck's story.

"I am very sorry that happened."

And there was quiet.

Krause slid back in her chair and looked off. She, too, seemed drained. She took a tissue from the desk and dabbed the wetness in her eyes. It was her only brother, her older brother; 15 years her senior; the one with the learning disabilities; the one who was always getting into trouble; the brother she had always yearned to get close to but had not been able. She had known of his brief career as a boxer but did not know he and Buck had met before prison. By the time he died, he had long been estranged from the family so the matter had been dropped. But she had never forgotten.

Krause took a moment to collect herself. She looked down at the ground and was quiet. She shook her head slowly. She sat back and pinched the bridge of her nose as she kept her eyes closed. Then she turned to look at Buck one last time and said, "You can go now."

And he bowed his head and said softly, "Thank you."

59

*T*wo days later, Buck drove up to Lancaster. It was a Sunday. He was going to see his son. It was a pretty day and the mountain pass felt light and fresh. Or maybe it was all him, that he was going through a kind of renewal. He was new to these kinds of psychological transformations and he hadn't yet come up with a better word, but renewal would do. Gone was the oppressive feeling he had borne forever when he thought of Joey and the tension between them.

He thought of the interview with Krause. He had never felt the emotions he felt with her and, at the end of the session, when she said, 'You can go now,' it had been a profound sense of relief.

He still was not exactly sure that Krause was letting him off the hook but he had the distinct impression that the nightmare was over. As far as Grisholt was concerned, he had stopped trying to reach him and, in an act that he saw as a clean, severing stroke, he had erased him from his cell phone.

He had told Janice everything that had transpired with Krause, blow by blow, and she had not flinched. She took it all in and, at the end, had reached over and embraced him. Then he had gone into a secret hiding place he had and took out the old videotape he had saved. He presented it to Janice and said to her, "This was my last fight." It was the tape of his last professional bout, the one where he knocked out the Miami Kid. Janice wept as she watched the tape and then turned to him and said, "Why did you keep this from me, all this time?" He just shrugged. She went to him and held his face in her hands and told him she loved him dearly.

Buck thought of all these things as he kept on driving. He loved the sight of the mountains, the shadows in the crinkled folds of earth, the sloping hills. He patted himself on the back for not having stopped once at a fast food place and just drank water and noshed on the healthy snacks Janice had prepared for him. He thought of the beautiful rainbows he had seen in the afternoons when he worked in Corcoran. There were good memories and not so good ones, but today he was going to see his son.

When he pulled up at the entrance gate, a young guard, part of the new crop, asked to see his papers. It was the visiting papers he had to present, nothing else. He was waved in and he parked near the administration building. He had been in the system so long that, even though he had never worked in Lancaster, odds were that he would be bumping into someone he knew, and that someone would surely ask what he was doing there as a visitor. As it was he didn't have to wait long. He got out of the car and approached the building. Just as he was about to enter, an old acquaintance of his, a sergeant, recognized him on the spot. The sergeant was decked out in a spiffy uniform, complete with the olive green, flat brimmed hat in the style of the Canadian Mounties.

"Buck Wilson?" he said.

"That's me," and Buck extended his hand to him.

"It's been a while, my God."

"It has been." Buck tried to catch the officer's name off his tag to return the courtesy but it was too small for his aging eyes, plus it twisted off a little as the man held up his arm to place it on his shoulder so he couldn't quite get it.

"Ted Gonzalez."

"Oh sure, Ted, I remember."

"How have you been?"

"Fine. Down in Chino, you know."

"Living the dream."

"Ah, yes," returned Buck.

"Last I remember there used to be a lot of dairies down that way."

"It's changed."

"Progress," replied Ted. He sported a thin, carefully trimmed moustache to match the neat attire. The sergeant looked directly at Buck, then asked, "You visiting us... or...?"

"I'm visiting my son. He's an inmate."

Ted cocked his head for a moment, as if pondering what best to say next, then, "I understand. If I can be of any help please do not hesitate. I am on duty today," and he crossed over to the door to the building and opened it for Buck.

"Thank you. Ted," and Buck went in. He sat with the other relatives and waited his turn, just like any other relative would. When his name was up he had to pull off his shoes and his belt and put all his belongings on a box just like any other visitor would. As he did this, another old acquaintance came up to him and extended his hand. Buck looked up and recognized him. The man shook Buck's hand and said he was glad to see him.

Moments later, Buck was walking in the direction of the visiting area. As he did he came up alongside a woman, about his age, that held a young girl, 5 or 6, by the hand.

"Good morning," said Buck.

"Good morning to you," replied the lady.

Without being asked, Buck said, "I'm here to visit my son."

"I'm visiting my son, too," said the lady. "This is his daughter," she said smilingly as she signaled to the young girl. "Say hello, mami." And the small girl obliged, "Hello mister."

"Well, hello," said Buck with a smile.

"What did your son do?" asked the child innocently.

"He…"

"Ay mija, you don't ask those questions," said the lady to the child, in gentle reproach.
And turning to Buck added, apologetically, "I'm sorry. But it doesn't matter, does it? They're still our children."

And the woman's words resonated deeply with Buck. "Yes, mam, you are so right."

Once in the visiting area Buck presented again his papers and was asked to take a seat. The inmate would be told he was there. Buck sat down by the windows, on the other side of the vending machines. He wanted very much to go over and get himself a candy bar or two but was hanging on fiercely to his determination to improve his eating habits.

The wait was short.

Fifteen minutes later Joey stepped into the room. The moment he saw him, Buck rose to his feet. Joey was shorter than Buck and slenderer but both were muscular men. Joey smiled at Buck from across and when he came close he flung his arms open to welcome him. Buck held him close for a long while. It had been years.

"I love you, Joey."

Joey said nothing, but held his father tightly in return. When they pulled apart they looked into each other's eyes, then sat down. Buck had arranged the chairs so they could be face to face.

"How was the trip?"

"It was good. Your mom sends her love."

Buck gazed into Joey's eyes as if in search of a clue for where to start. "You're all grown up, aren't you?" he said, finally.

"I'm working on it, dad."

Buck liked the sound of it. "I came to tell you something, not to ask you for anything."

Joey nodded.

"I came to say that I am sorry for all I did… all the heartache I brought you… all the pain. I am sorry for all of it." Buck felt he was speaking from a very special place inside of him, a new place for him but a strong place. "I am not here to ask for your forgiveness. Time will tell if you are ready to grant me that… and I know that I must wait." Buck shuffled his feet and stared down at the ground. "I suppose that I have started a journey, a journey to understand myself, to learn to accept my emotions… to not bury them… to learn to look them in the eye and see what it is they say about me." Buck stopped again, looked off. A few tables away he saw the woman with the child he had chatted with on his way in. The child was bursting with happiness in anticipation of seeing her father.

"I'm not here to tell you all my mistakes, Joey, there are too many of them. I just want you to know that I have started the journey."

Joey stared at his dad. In a way, he was a stranger to him, a man he had fought with and dreaded but never known. And yet he felt a love for him, and if his father now stood before him confessing to his flaws he, too, had a confession to make.

"Dad… I'm glad you came to see me… and I want you to come back… but I, too, failed. And I, too, have set out on a journey to discover myself."

The little girl jumped out of her seat and ran towards her father as he came through the door. Buck smiled, and as he did he took Joey's hands in his and, leaning over, rested his head on Joey's knees. He didn't say the words but he knew he was begging for forgiveness. Joey ran his hands over his father's head, gently stroking it.

Just then, Legrand's daughter entered the room. She was simply dressed but the grace of her features, the svelte line of her body, attracted everyone's attention. Joey, too, was struck by her presence and gazed at her for a moment. He said to Buck, "Dad… I think that's my cellie's daughter." And Buck looked up and saw her, and he remembered Legrand.

"You know him, don't you?" asked Joey.

"I do."

Five minutes later, Legrand entered the room. He was beaming with pride as he strode directly toward Lilly. They embraced and as they sat down Joey waved at them. Legrand waved back. Then he excused himself from Lilly and walked over to Joey and Buck. Buck rose to greet him. The two men shook hands. They looked at each other for a moment, their memories taking them back to an old battle. Buck was struggling to find the words as Legrand waited, "Legrand," said Buck, finally, "I can't think of anyone who would've been a better cellie to my son. Thank you."

Legrand bowed his head slightly and then returned to Lilly.

In his corner, Legrand feasted his eyes on his beautiful daughter. Lilly was telling him about the lawyer she had found. The lawyer had looked at the transcripts of the trial while she was up in Cleveland, and he had seen that there were points that could be challenged. Yes, Legrand had been under the influence of alcohol and he had been full of anger because of the spat with his girlfriend, Lilly's mom, but when Legrand had run into the three men it had been the men who had challenged him. There had been two witnesses, two young girls, 13 and 14, who had been sitting in their porch when the brawl broke out in the middle of the street. And they had given a statement but their information had not been admitted to the trial. The victims had had a private attorney. Legrand could not afford one. It had been thirty years and Legrand's record in prison was impeccable and it had been his first and only offense. There were possibilities, said Lilly, her face brimming with hope and enthusiasm. Legrand kept gazing at her, so proud to have her in his life. Ever since the first visit they had talked on the phone every day and he had given her all the details he had. Lilly caressed his face and said softly, "Dad, I'm getting you out of here."

Legrand paused. "Lilly… that's not how I remember things… I remember hitting them…"

"You were drunk, dad, the witnesses saw the other guys challenge you."

Legrand shook his head. "I don't remember that…"

"Dad… let's try… if it doesn't work, then…" She held his hands in hers. "But let's try."

"You know," said Legrand, "those guys I killed… they come to me in my dreams… they talk to me… they haven't forgiven me yet… I'm still waiting."

"Dad… let's try, okay?"

"I don't want you to waste your money… my grandson… he needs that."

"Dad, let me worry about that, okay?"

Legrand nodded slowly. "But you know what I would really like?"

"What?"

"If I could just get a furlough…"

"A furlough?"

"Yes. If the judge would just give me a furlough so I could go to Paris for a week and stay with you. I'd come right back."

"Dad, I'm getting you out of here."

60

Mary Jane Jeffries had spent the weekend with Gardner. She had taken the day off from singing at the club and they had driven up the coast, on Pacific Coast Highway, then come back to stroll the Santa Monica Pier, walk up and down Main Street and meander on down to Venice Beach. They were discovering the pleasures of each other's company. It was dusk now and they were sitting at a restaurant in Culver City, near the studios, waiting for the food they'd ordered.

"I've asked you this before, Byron, but you left me in mid air."

"Did I?"

"Yes. What has prison done for you, personally?"

"Ah, that's easy. It's taught me to love."

"That's awfully broad… and, surely, you'd done your share of loving before going to work in the prison."

"True, but what I've learned is different. It's all very personal, of course, and I speak only for myself. All the tragic stories, the lives truncated, the possibilities cut off, remind me of how much our lives rest on a delicate equilibrium, between our fictions and our realities, and how it can shift any day, any moment… even shatter our existences. Loving gives me the strength to keep that balance."

"So the prisoner's story gives you that strength?"

"Yes. The story of love gone wrong."

They were sitting at a table outside and the orange of the setting sun cast a warm, glowing light on Mary Jane's face. He reached over and caressed her lips with the back of his hand. "I have to love to go on, my dear. Love something, love someone, or else I drift without purpose."

She held his hand and kissed it softly.

"And I know it's not forever."

She looked at him with tenderness and she thought they had a chance, at least for a while and not forever.

But he wanted to love like it was forever.

The End

www.ingramcontent.com/pod-product-compliance
Lightning Source LLC
Chambersburg PA
CBHW030433300426
44112CB00009B/973